TIM CHESTER

MATTHEW FOR YOU

thegoodbook COMPANY

Matthew For You

Published by:
The Good Book Company

thegoodbook.com | thegoodbook.co.uk
thegoodbook.com.au | thegoodbook.co.nz

ISBN: 9781784984984

Cover design by Ben Woodcraft | Printed in India | JOB-008023

CONTENTS

SERIES PREFACE

Each volume of the *God's Word For You* series takes you to the heart of a book of the Bible, and applies its truths to your heart.

The central aim of each title is to be:

- Bible centred
- Christ glorifying
- Relevantly applied
- Easily readable

You can use *Matthew For You:*

To read. You can simply read from cover to cover, as a book that explains and explores the themes, encouragements and challenges of this part of Scripture.

To feed. You can work through this book as part of your own personal regular devotions, or use it alongside a sermon or Bible-study series at your church. Each chapter is divided into two (or occasionally three) shorter sections, with questions for reflection at the end of each.

To lead. You can use this as a resource to help you teach God's word to others, both in small-group and whole-church settings. You'll find tricky verses or concepts explained using ordinary language, and helpful themes and illustrations along with suggested applications.

These books are not commentaries. They assume no understanding of the original Bible languages, nor a high level of biblical knowledge. Verse references are marked in **bold** so that you can refer to them easily. Any words that are used rarely or differently in everyday language outside the church are marked in **grey** when they first appear, and are explained in a glossary toward the back. There, you'll also find details of resources you can use alongside this one, in both personal and church life.

Our prayer is that as you read, you'll be struck not by the contents of this book, but by the book it's helping you open up; and that you'll praise not the author of this book, but the One he is pointing you to.

Carl Laferton, Series Editor

Bible translations used:

- NIV: New International Version, 2011 edition (this is the version being quoted unless otherwise stated)
- ESV: English Standard Version

INTRODUCTION TO MATTHEW

Matthew's **Gospel** tells the story of Jesus—Immanuel, God with us, Israel's **Messiah** and the hope of all nations. Whether you're a Jew or a Gentile, this is the story of your Saviour-King. Matthew's Gospel is something of a training manual to show you how you can and should live within this wonderful story.

Jesus Is the Fulfilment of the Scriptures

"Every teacher of the law who has become a disciple in the **kingdom of heaven** is like the owner of a house who brings out of his storeroom new treasures as well as old." So says Jesus in Matthew 13:52. It's a saying only Matthew includes, and it's likely that he saw it as a description of himself. Matthew is a teacher of the law who has become a disciple of Jesus (or a disciple who has become a teacher of the law). And his Gospel brings new treasures out from the storehouse of Scripture. In other words, Matthew shows how Jesus fulfils the Old Testament. In one sense, then, his message is old: the story he tells has been centuries in the making. But in another sense his message is new, for the story has now reached its denouement. Of course the other Gospel-writers also see Jesus as the fulfilment of the Old Testament, but Matthew goes out of his way to spotlight these links. For example, seven times in the opening chapters, he says something along the lines of "This took place to fulfil what the Lord had said through the prophet" before citing a passage from the Old Testament (1:22; 2:5, 15, 17-18, 23; 3:3; 4:13-16).

Matthew's concern to be a teacher of the law is also reflected in the amount of the teaching of Jesus that he includes. Matthew often trims down stories by leaving out details that Mark and Luke cover and instead includes teaching that Mark and Luke leave out.

This focus on teaching is also reflected in the structure of the

* Words in **grey** are defined in the Glossary (page 227).

Gospel. Matthew has a phrase which he uses five times to divide up his Gospel into sections:

- "When Jesus had finished saying these things..." (7:28-29)
- "After Jesus had finished instructing his twelve disciples..." (11:1)
- "When Jesus had finished these parables..." (13:53)
- "When Jesus had finished saying these things..." (19:1)
- "When Jesus had finished saying all these things..." (26:1-2)

These phrases create five blocks of teaching which weave in and out of the story:

Matthew 1 – 2 Beginnings

Matthew 3 – 4 Narrative

Matthew 5 – 7 Teaching #1

"When Jesus had finished saying these things" (7:28-29)

Matthew 8 – 9 Narrative

Matthew 10 Teaching #2

"After Jesus had finished instructing his twelve disciples" (11:1)

Matthew 11 – 12 Narrative

Matthew 13 Teaching #3

"When Jesus had finished these parables" (13:53)

Matthew 14 – 17 Narrative

Matthew 18 Teaching #4

"When Jesus had finished saying these things" (19:1)

Matthew 19 – 23 Narrative

Matthew 24 – 25 Teaching #5

"When Jesus had finished saying all these things" (26:1-2)

Matthew 26 – 28 Climax

The word "law" in the phrase "teacher of the law" was used by Jews to represent the Scriptures as a whole, but it particularly referred to the Torah: the first five books of the Bible (what we sometimes call "the Pentateuch"). So it's been suggested that Matthew designed his Gospel to be a new Torah made up of five "books". We can't be sure of this. Yes, chapter 1 presents the birth of Jesus as a new **Genesis** while chapters 2 – 4 echo the story of the **Exodus**. But it's not possible convincingly to then link each teaching section to the five books in the Pentateuch.

What is clear is that Matthew has a particular concern for the teaching of Jesus and therefore for the training of disciples. It is fitting that the climax of his Gospel is Christ's call to "make disciples of all nations" by "teaching them to obey everything I have commanded you" (28:19-20).

This leads us to a second distinctive feature of Matthew's Gospel...

Jesus Is the Hope of the Nations

It's widely thought that in the first instance Matthew wrote for Jewish believers or maybe Jewish seekers—that maybe one reason for his concern to present Jesus as the fulfilment of the Old Testament.

Yet despite this, Matthew is concerned throughout his Gospel to portray Jesus as the Saviour of all nations. Early in the Gospel the **Gentile** Magi come to worship the infant Jesus, and at the end of the Gospel the **apostles** are sent to disciple the nations (2:1-12; 28:18-20). In between there are stories of Gentiles coming to Jesus; indeed, twice Jesus specifically commends the faith of Gentiles (8:10; 15:28). Jesus fulfils both the promise to **Abraham** that God will bless all nations and the promise to **Isaiah** that a Servant will come in whose name the nations will put their hope (Matthew 1:1; 12:17-21).

Ironically, Mark and Luke may have felt less need to present Jesus as the Saviour of Gentiles because their readers were Gentiles, and so knew this truth first hand! But Matthew encourages his perhaps hesitant **Judean** believers to support the church's global mission. He may even have been countering people like the **Judaizers**, who tried to undermine Paul's **evangelism** among Gentiles (Acts 15:1-2). "Because of this Gospel's familiarity with the Jewish world of its day," concludes Reggie Kidd, "the scholarly consensus is that Matthew is written to a Greek-speaking Jewish Christian community, one that is grappling with Israel's mission to the nations through Jesus the Messiah" (*A Biblical-Theological Introduction to the New Testament,* p. 31).

Jesus Is Immanuel, God with Us

At the beginning of his Gospel, Matthew calls Jesus "Immanuel", "God with us" (1:23). Mark and Luke let the evidence for the divinity of Jesus gradually build. But Matthew is explicit about this claim throughout his Gospel. When Jesus walks on water, for example, only Matthew describes the disciples declaring, "Truly you are the Son of God" (14:33).

Alongside this focus on the divinity of Jesus is a focus on the response of humanity. So Matthew repeatedly describes people worshipping Jesus (2:2, 11; 8:2-3; 9:18, 25; 14:32-33; 15:22, 25, 28; 18:26; 20:20; 28:8-10, 17, which is sometimes translated "knelt before"). The gospel begins and ends with worship (2:2, 11; 28:17).

So Jesus is Immanuel, God with us. That was true during his life on the earth; and it continues to be true, for in the final words of the Gospel, Jesus says, "Surely I am with you always, to the very end of the age" (28:20).

Jesus Is the Head of the Church

Matthew includes more teaching on the church than the other Gospels, including...

- Christ's promise to build his church (16:18).
- the giving of "the keys" to the disciples (v 19; 18:18).
- the need for mercy within his new community (v 12-35).

Only Matthew describes the church as "the light of the world", a community whose distinctive life reveals God to the lost (5:14-16). Indeed, the famous Sermon on the Mount in chapters 5 – 7 can be seen (as we'll see) as a renewed law of God for a renewed people of God. Matthew portrays the embryonic church as a community of "little ones". We only enter the kingdom of heaven if we come like little children, and we're not to despise the lowly and least among us (18:1-10). Jesus is Immanuel, God with us, and sometimes he is with us in "the least of these" (10:40-42; 18:5; 25:45).

Jesus Is Our Saviour and King

I've spotlighted some of the distinctive features of Matthew's presentation of Jesus, by pointing out how his version of the story differs from those of Mark and Luke. But the similarities are far more significant. In common with the other Gospel writers, Matthew presents Jesus as our Saviour and King. His miracles show him to be God's King with the authority to establish God's kingdom and to be God's Saviour with the power to save God's people. Yet, ultimately, Jesus proves to be the King who saves by dying in our place and rising again to give us life.

MATTHEW CHAPTERS 1 AND 2

1. IMMANUEL FULFILS GOD'S WORD

Imagine turning on your television at random to find you're watching the end of a crime drama. The detective has caught the culprit. This is the key point in the story—the moment when everything is revealed. The problem is that you don't really understand what you're seeing because you've only just tuned in. It's like this if you tune in to Jesus with the account of his birth. This is the key moment in the Bible story—the moment that makes everything clear. But if you start at this point, then you're going to struggle to understand what's going on. So Matthew packs his account of the Nativity with references to the Old Testament, to help us catch up with the story so far.

This is why Matthew begins with a **genealogy** (**1:1***). Books are supposed to begin with a bang—something to grab the reader's attention. This does not seem like much of a bang! But Matthew knows what he's doing. This list of names is like the contents page of the Old Testament. For Matthew's Jewish readers, it would have evoked a succession of stories, all of which are about to converge on Mary's child.

Matthew orders this list in a particular way. In case you didn't spot it, he highlights it in **verse 17**: "Thus there were fourteen generations in all from Abraham to David, fourteen from David to the exile to Babylon, and fourteen from the exile to the Messiah". Indeed Matthew only makes the numbers work by leaving a few people out.

---

* All Matthew verse references being looked at in each chapter part are in **bold**.

Seven represents perfection or completion, and three fourteens are six sevens, so perhaps Matthew is wanting to portray Jesus as the seventh seven—the climax and pinnacle of God's purposes. What's clear is that Matthew's groups of fourteen focus on three key moments:

1. Abraham: the father of the nation (**v 2**)
2. David: Israel's greatest king (**v 6**)
3. Babylon: the time when the Jews went into exile (**v 12**)

As we look at Mary's child the question is: who is he? These three moments answer that question.

1. Abraham: from Curse to Blessing

God had promised Abraham, "I will make you into a great nation, and I will bless you ... and all peoples on earth will be blessed through you" (Genesis 12:2-3). Blessing here doesn't simply mean good things. It has a specific meaning in the context of Genesis: the reversal of the curse. When humanity rejected God, we became enemies of God, our relationships with one another became strained, and we were exiled from **Eden** (Genesis 3). Even the land was cursed, becoming prone to famine and disasters. But in Genesis 12 God promised that through Abraham's offspring, the curse would be reversed. Our relationship with God would be restored, human relationships would be mended, and the earth would be made new.

The message of Matthew's genealogy is that this promise has passed down the generations until we meet Mary and her child. Jesus is the true son of Abraham: the one who reverses the curse, bringing blessing to all nations. How is Jesus going to bring this blessing? By bearing the curse: "Christ redeemed us from the curse of the law by becoming a curse for us ... He redeemed us in order that the blessing given to Abraham might come to the Gentiles through Christ Jesus" (Galatians 3:13-14).

2. David: from Slavery to Freedom

The curse came because we rebelled against God's rule. God's rule was one of peace, provision and protection. But Satan portrayed God as a tyrant, and humanity believed that lie. Yet, instead of finding freedom, they became enslaved to sin and self. Scale that up to neighbourhoods and nations, and you find conflict and prejudice. Our world is in chaos.

God had every reason to write us off. But instead he made a promise to David, Israel's greatest king, that one of his descendants would set God's people free—free to enjoy life under God's rule (2 Samuel 7:11-16). There was a glimpse of this in the reigns of David and his son Solomon. But, by the time Matthew wrote, things had gone horribly wrong. Instead of restoring God's reign, successive kings led people further from God. So the Davidic dynasty no longer reigned over Israel, which instead suffered under Roman occupation. But the prophets had promised a new King David, who would restore God's life-giving rule.

The message of Matthew's genealogy is that this promised descendant of David is Mary's child. Israelite kings were anointed with oil, so the promised king was known as "the anointed One". The Greek word for this is "Christ", and the **Hebrew** word is "Messiah". So Matthew begins, "This is the genealogy of Jesus the Messiah the son of David" (Matthew **1:1**) and he ends his genealogy with "Jesus who is called the Messiah" (**v 16**). Jesus is God's promised King, coming to set not only Israel but humanity free.

3. Babylon: from Exile to Home

The history of ancient Israel ended in disaster: exile in Babylon. The prophets made it clear that God himself had exiled his people in judgment against their sin. In time, Ezra and Nehemiah led the people back to the land, but they still weren't free (Nehemiah 9:36-37). The underlying issues of human sin and divine judgment had not been addressed.

This is why Matthew's genealogy bypasses the Exodus, even though the Exodus was one of the key moments in Israel's history. The Exodus rescued God's people from slavery, but the Exile had taken them back into slavery. The Exodus provided the pattern for liberation, but the story has left us needing another exodus—a bigger exodus that will free God's people not simply from slavery in Egypt but from slavery to sin. The Exile in Babylon was a picture of humanity's plight. We're all exiles from Eden, and we're all estranged from God. That's why we're so restless. Our hearts are hardwired for God, and yet it's as if we'll head in any direction except back to God, looking for fulfilment in our careers, homes, families or entertainment.

The message of Matthew's genealogy is that the end of exile is lying in the manger. Jesus is the one who will lead us home. He not only shows us the way back to God; he himself is "the way" (John 14:6).

A Way Home for Sinners from All Nations

Jesus is the way home not just for Jews but for people from all nations. Interspersed among the fathers who populate Matthew's genealogy are four Gentile mothers (Matthew **1:3, 5, 6**). Tamar and Rahab were **Canaanites**, Ruth was a Moabite and Bathsheba is called "Uriah's wife" to spotlight her connection to a Hittite (see Genesis 38; Joshua 2; Ruth 1 – 4; 2 Samuel 11). Woven into a genealogy designed to establish Jesus' Jewish credentials are four Gentile women—a picture of the way Jesus will weave all nations into the story of God's people.

Moreover, three of these women come with question marks hanging over their morality. Tamar disguised herself as a prostitute to sleep with her father-in-law, forcing him to do right by her deceased husband (Genesis 38). Rahab was the Canaanite prostitute who hid two Israelite spies (Joshua 2). Bathsheba was involved in an act of adultery, though her culpability is unclear (2 Samuel 11). Perhaps we're meant to see Mary as a fifth woman whose morals were questioned, but who proves integral to God's purposes (Matthew **1:16**). These names break Matthew's pattern of "[was] the father of" to spotlight the fact that

Jesus came to save Jews and Gentiles, men and women, sinners and sinned-against. "If the Lord Jesus was not ashamed to be born of a woman whose pedigree contained such names as those we have read today," said the 19th-century bishop J.C. Ryle, "we need not think that he will be ashamed to call us **brethren**, and to give us eternal life" (*Expository Thoughts on the Gospels*, p. 4). It's a truth Matthew is about to reinforce as he explains the naming of Jesus.

They Will Call Him Immanuel

The story is familiar. Mary conceives a child "through the Holy Spirit", even though she's still a virgin (**v 18**). Through the Holy Spirit, the eternal Son of God took on a human nature as that human nature was formed in the womb of Mary. Though Mary is unmarried, she is betrothed—in a binding commitment to marriage. Joseph, her husband-to-be, initially assumes she's been unfaithful. Matthew presents Joseph as a model of someone who takes the law seriously but applies it with compassion—in this case, by planning to divorce Mary quietly rather than publicly shaming her (**v 19**). But Joseph lacks the full facts, and so an angel appears to reassure him that this baby has been conceived by the Spirit of God (**v 20**). As a result, Joseph takes Mary as his wife (**v 24-25**) The word "birth" in **verse 18** is literally "genesis". The same word is used in **verse 1** (translated "genealogy" in the NIV), so the Gospel literally begins "[the] book of genesis". The Old Testament is about to be fulfilled and replayed. Just as the first Adam was given life through the Spirit of God (Genesis 2:7), so Jesus, the second Adam, is given human existence through the Spirit in the genesis of a new humanity.

To spotlight the meaning of these events, Matthew includes two acts of naming. First, the angel says, "You are to give him the name Jesus, because he will save his people from their sins" (Matthew **1:21**). "Jesus" is the Greek equivalent of "Joshua", which means "The LORD saves". This baby is going to deal with the problem of human sin and divine judgment.

Second, Matthew comments, "All this took place to fulfil what the Lord had said through the prophet: 'The virgin will conceive and give birth to a son, and they will call him Immanuel' (which means 'God with us')" (**v 22-23**). God himself is coming to save his people from sin.

Matthew follows his genealogy with four stories surrounding the birth of Jesus, each of which contains a quote from the Old Testament. The birth of Jesus is the fulfilment of the Scriptures (**1:22-23**; 2:15, 17-18, 23; see also 2:5-6; 3:3; 4:14-16; 8:17; 12:17-21; 13:13-15, 35; 21:4-5; 26:56; and Blomberg in *Commentary on the New Testament Use of the Old Testament*, p. 3-11). **1:23** is a quote from Isaiah 7. In Isaiah's day, Ahaz was the king of **Judah**. He was the descendant of David on the throne of David, just as God had promised. But he wasn't like his father David. He led the people into **idolatry**, even sacrificing his children. So the kings of Syria and the northern kingdom of Israel formed an alliance against him, and Ahaz was terrified (Isaiah 7:1-2). The house of David—the means through which God had promised to restore his reign—was in mortal danger. Isaiah promised divine deliverance if Ahaz would entrust himself to God (v 3-9). God even offered to give Ahaz a sign (v 10). But Ahaz refused (v 11), opting instead for an alliance with Assyria (the rising superpower of the day).

So God gave Ahaz a sign that Ahaz was not looking for: "The virgin will conceive and give birth to a son, and will call him Immanuel" (v 14). Ahaz thought he could do without God; but it was God who didn't need Ahaz. For God could bring the reign of David's sons to an end (as he did when Judah was exiled in Babylon) and then start afresh by raising up a new king from a virgin. In the meantime, Assyria would turn on Judah with devastating consequences (v 15-25).

The first fulfilment of the promised child may have been Isaiah's own son, Maher-Shalal-Hash-Baz, whose name means "quick to the plunder, swift to the **spoil**" (Isaiah 8:1-3). Immanuel would be in this judgment (v 8). But Immanuel also offered hope-beyond-judgment for his people (v 10). When Isaiah spoke with King Ahaz, he took his son Shear-Jashub, whose name means "a **remnant** will return" (7:3). God's king would be deposed and his people would be lost, but a new king would arise and a remnant would return (9:6; 10:20-23).

The word "virgin" in Isaiah 7:14 means "a sexually inexperienced woman". It was usually used to describe a virgin, but not always. R.T. France concludes, "It does not explicitly mean 'virgin', but it suggests something other than a normal childbirth within marriage" (*The Gospel of Matthew*, p. 55). So, it could describe Maher-Shalal-Hash-Baz's mother, but Matthew recognises that its ultimate fulfilment is in the virgin Mary (Matthew **1:18**).

This is why Matthew draws together two lines of promise from Isaiah 7. First, God will raise up a new king from a virgin: a king who will trust God and restore God's rule. Second, God himself will come as Immanuel to save his people from their sins. These two trajectories converge on Mary's child. God himself has come in the person of his Son. In his humanity Jesus is the descendant of David; in his divinity he is Immanuel, God with us.

We should find confidence in the promises of God.

Notice that for Matthew, "fulfilment" can involve any of the following:

- a prediction coming true
- a pattern being repeated in a bigger or better way ("filled full")
- an event, person or ritual from ancient Israel being seen as a picture of Jesus (what theologians call "typology")

God has written into Israel's history numerous pointers to Jesus.

How should we respond? By doing what Ahaz should have done: "Be careful, keep calm and don't be afraid" (Isaiah 7:4). Ahaz should have found confidence in the promises of God. He should have trusted the promise of a Saviour. And so should we.

- We live in a cursed world with broken relationships. We need to trust God's promise of blessing. Otherwise we may despair and live for the fleeting treasures of this world.
- We live in a rebellious world in which people mock God and disregard his reign. We need to trust God's promise that Christ will be triumphant and his people will be vindicated. Otherwise we may despair and start to align ourselves with the rebellious majority.
- We live in a restless world in which people are exiled from God. We need to trust God's promise that Christ will lead us away from the slavery of sin to home in glory. Otherwise we may despair and give up the struggle against sin in our lives.

Think about the struggles you're facing and pray, "My Jesus, Saviour, save me from sin and self today. My Immanuel, God with us, be with me today."

Questions for reflection

1. How does thinking of Jesus as the fulfilment of the promises to Abraham and David, and as the end of the exile, cause you to appreciate him more?
2. Jesus' family line includes four women who were either outsiders or had "question marks hanging over their morality". What difference does that make to the way you reflect on your own past or to your view of yourself?
3. How would you sum up what it means for Jesus to be the promised "Immanuel" sign?

PART TWO

Out of Bethlehem Will Come a Ruler

Matthew embeds his second Old Testament quotation in the story of the Magi (probably Persian astrologers). The Magi have followed a special star to find a special king (Matthew **2:1-2**; Numbers 24:17). They arrival disturbs the Jerusalem elites (Matthew **2:3**), presumably because talk of another king is a threat to their cosy arrangement with the Roman occupiers. **Herod ("the Great")** asks the religious leaders where the promised Messiah is to be born (**v 4**) and they answer by quoting prophecy from Micah 5:2-4 (Matthew **2:5-6**). Those who know most about the Messiah are those who welcome him least! Meanwhile, now informed by the Scriptures, the Magi find Jesus and worship him (**v 9-11**). The Magi's knowledge has caused them to seek Jesus, but they need the Scriptures to locate him. Finally the Magi are warned in a dream not to pass on their "intel" to Herod (**v 12**) since Herod's intentions are not what they seem (**v 7-8**).

The prophet Micah (whom Matthew quotes) condemns the injustice of God's people and says judgment is inevitable (Micah 3:9-12). But then his tone changes. He speaks in effusive language about the continuing purposes of God and the certainty of his promises. God's people will one day attract people from every nation to God (4:1-5). From little Bethlehem will come a great king (5:2) who will shepherd God's people like David, Israel's original shepherd-king (5:4; see 2 Samuel 5:2). This is Jesus, says Matthew (Matthew **2:5-6**). Jesus will create a community which will attract and include people from all nations.

Out of Egypt I Have Called My Son

An angel warns Joseph to take Jesus to Egypt to escape the murderous intent of Herod (**v 13**). So Jesus begins his life as a refugee (**v 14-15**). He's learning what it is to be truly human with all its dangers, so that he can sympathise with us in our weakness (Hebrews 4:15; 5:8-10).

This, says Matthew, fulfils the words of Hosea 11:1. Hosea 11 begins by looking back to the way God led Israel out of Egypt through the Exodus (v 1-4). Tragically, as Hosea was speaking, the Israelites were heading back into foreign hands because of their determination to turn from God (v 5-7). Yet God in his love could not give up on his people, and so he promised to bring them home once again (v 8-11). The odd thing is that Matthew quotes from Hosea when Jesus escapes to Egypt (in Matthew **2:15**) rather than when Jesus returns from Egypt (in **verse 21**). This is because faithless Israel has become the latest manifestation of "Egypt", with a king massacring children just as Pharaoh once did (**v 16**; see Exodus 1). Once, Israel "my son" escaped from Egypt (Exodus 4:22-23); now, Jesus the Son escapes from "Egypt" into Egypt.

The nation of Israel has failed to live as a faithful son of God. But Jesus is a new Israel, the true person/people of God. Like Israel, Jesus comes out of Egypt. But unlike Israel, Jesus is a faithful son of God. God has not given up on his people; he's sent Jesus, the true Son, to be faithful on our behalf and to lead us home.

Weeping and Great Mourning

When Herod realises the Magi are not going to pinpoint the location of Jesus, he opts for indiscriminate killing—a brutal massacre of all male infants in Bethlehem (Matthew **2:16**). This, says Matthew, fulfils Jeremiah 31:15 (Matthew **2:17-18**). Jeremiah was describing the deportation into exile of the children of Rachel. Rachel was one of Jacob's wives, and Jacob's children made up the twelve tribes of Israel; so "Rachel" represents the mother of the nation weeping for her lost children.

The massacre in Bethlehem is the latest in a long sequence of attempts to wipe out God's people, starting with Pharaoh in Exodus 1 and including Haman in the book of Esther. So it is that Rachel's lament is heard again in Jesus' day, just as it had been heard in Jeremiah's. That continues today when regimes try to eradicate the church.

They are all attempts by Satan to thwart God's purposes by slaughtering those through whom the promises will be fulfilled. If Satan and Herod can murder Jesus, then the story of salvation will come to a premature end.

But God's purposes are not derailed, and they will soon reach their climax at **Calvary**. In Jeremiah 31:16 the Lord responds to Rachel's tears by saying, "Restrain your voice from weeping ... They will return from the land of the enemy." Her tears have been heard by God, and God has sent Jesus to bring an end to the exile.

He Would Be Called a Nazarene

After Herod's death, Joseph brings the family back from Egypt (Matthew **2:19-21**) and settles in the northern backwater of Nazareth, well away from the gaze of the authorities (**v 22-23**). "So was fulfilled what was said through the prophets," says **verse 23**, "that he would be called a Nazarene". There's no specific prophecy that speaks of the coming Messiah as a Nazarene, and Matthew's use of "prophets" (plural) suggests he's summing up a prophetic theme rather than referring to a specific text. It seems Matthew is using "Nazarene" as a derogatory slang term for someone coming from an insignificant place like Nazareth in Galilee. (This is how Nathanael refers to Nazareth in John 1:46.) This fulfils passages like Psalm 22:6-8 and Isaiah 53:2, which speak of Jesus being despised (both Psalm 22 and Isaiah 53 were often applied to Jesus by early Christians). The ultimate sign of the King in Matthew's Gospel will be the sign of the cross—the climactic moment when Jesus is despised and rejected (Matthew 27:39-44). If you serve in an out-of-the-way place or with marginal people, you may not make a name for yourself, but you are following in the steps of your Lord.

Put all this together and we can see that Matthew has high hopes for Mary's child!

- Jesus is Immanuel, God with us, coming to save God's people (**1:23**).

- Jesus is the Shepherd-King, drawing the nations to God (**2:6**).
- Jesus is God's true Son, remaining faithful when tested (**v 15**).
- Jesus is the one who brings hope in the midst of tears (**v 18**).
- Jesus is the despised one who will one day receive the worship of the nations (**v 23**).

A Child for All Nations: the Magi Revisited

Matthew's Gospel is widely thought to have been written in the first place for Jewish readers. Yet Matthew is also interested in how salvation goes beyond Judaism to the world. The climax of the Gospel will be the Great Commission to go to the nations with the message of the gospel (28:18-20). And right from the start we see a concern for global mission.

- Matthew presents Jesus as the fulfilment of the promise to Abraham that Abraham's family will bless all nations (Genesis 12:3; Matthew 1:2).
- Matthew weaves mothers from all nations into the story of God's family (v 3, 5, 6).
- Jesus will create a community which attracts people from all nations (Micah 4:1-5; Matthew **2:6**).

This is exemplified in the story of the Magi. Matthew begins and ends their story with references to worship (**v 2, 11**). In addition, the gifts of the Magi echo the story of the queen of Sheba bringing gifts to King Solomon (1 Kings 10:10) and Isaiah's promise of tribute from the nations (Isaiah 60:1-10; see also Psalm 72:10-11), including "gold and frankincense" (Isaiah 60:6, ESV).

Mark only uses the word "worship" twice, and one of those references describes the soldiers mocking Jesus. Luke also only uses it twice: once when Satan tempts Jesus and once after the resurrection. But it's one of Matthew's favourite words, sometimes translated "knelt" in our English translations (Matthew **2:2, 11**; 4:10; 8:2-3; 9:18, 25; 14:32-33; 15:22, 25, 28; 18:26; 20:20; 28:8-10, 17). Repeatedly Jesus receives worship from people. It starts with the Magi here and continues throughout the story.

Here, though, is the problem. In Matthew 4, when Satan offers Jesus the kingdoms of the world if Jesus will worship Satan, Jesus replies, "It is written: 'Worship the Lord your God, and serve him only'" (4:10). It's the same word. Matthew deliberately creates a conflict in our minds: Jesus repeatedly received worship, and yet Jesus said only God should be worshipped. The clear implication is that Jesus thought he was God. Under normal circumstances, we might assume this means Jesus was crazy. But Jesus didn't receive worship under normal circumstances:

> Jesus repeatedly received worship, and yet Jesus said only God should be worshipped. The implication is clear.

- Jesus received worship when cleansing sinners (8:2-3). You became spiritually unclean if you touched a leper, but Jesus made the leper clean.
- Jesus received worship when controlling the waves (14:30-33). The Old Testament says only God can control storms (Psalm 89:8-9). Even with 21st-century technology, human beings can't control the weather. Jesus can.
- Jesus received worship after conquering death (Matthew 28:8-10). Jesus is the very source of life, so not even death can hold him.

Remember, too, that Matthew had spent three years living in close proximity to Jesus. Despite this, or perhaps because of it, Matthew wasn't embarrassed to describe person after person worshipping Jesus as God. Both the actions of Jesus and the reactions of people prove that Jesus is God. God is infinite, unchanging, self-sustaining, eternal, invisible. He's not just a bigger version of us; he's utterly different. Yet there was a moment in history when he lay in a manger. If that's true, then the only sensible response is to join the Magi in worshipping Jesus.

The Gospel begins with the Magi worshipping Jesus and ends with the disciples worshipping Jesus.

There are two things about the Magi that make them unique in the Nativity story. First, they're the only people in the story who are Gentiles (**2:1**). Second, they're the only people in the story who worship Jesus. Matthew's Gospel begins with the Magi worshipping Jesus, and it ends with the disciples worshipping Jesus (28:17). Everything is enclosed by this double call to worship Jesus. The story ends with the disciples being sent to call all the nations to worship Jesus (28:19). John Piper comments:

> "Mission exists because worship doesn't ... Worship, therefore, is the fuel and goal of missions. It's the goal of missions because in missions we simply aim to bring the nations into the white hot enjoyment of God's glory. The goal of missions is the gladness of the peoples in the greatness of God. But worship is also the fuel of missions. Passion for God in worship precedes the offer of God in preaching. You can't commend what you don't cherish." (John Piper, *Let the Nations Be Glad! The Supremacy of God in Missions*, p. 17)

One other person in the Nativity story talks about worshipping Jesus: King Herod (**2:8**). But in fact Herod sees Jesus as a rival to be extinguished. Herod, of course, is the bad guy in the Nativity story—the one who massacres children. But there's something of Herod in all of us. Like Herod, by nature we see Immanuel as a rival and are "disturbed" by the thought we might have to submit to his rule (**v 3**). Today, therefore, the challenge comes to us: are we going to follow the example of Herod, seeing Jesus as a rival to eradicate from our lives? Or are we going to follow the example of the Magi, seeing Jesus as Immanuel and worshipping him with our lives?

Questions for reflection

1. What is striking about the way that Jesus accepts worship throughout Matthew's Gospel?
2. "Mission exists because worship doesn't" (John Piper). How does this challenge and/or motivate you today?
3. In what way would you be most likely to see Jesus as a "rival" to your desire to rule yourself? What is it about Jesus that would be helpful to remind yourself of when you're tempted to think like this?

MATTHEW CHAPTERS 3 AND 4

2. IMMANUEL RENEWS GOD'S PEOPLE

Jesus Comes to Liberate God's People

Matthew introduces a new character in chapter 3: John the Baptist. John declares, "Repent, for the kingdom of heaven has come near" (Matthew **3:2**). This implies that God's kingdom is in the process of arriving (because, as we'll see, God's messianic King is arriving). Then, in **verse 3**, we're told of "a voice of one calling in the wilderness" (echoing "in the wilderness" in **verse 1**). This time it's not Matthew who speaks but the prophet Isaiah. Matthew's quote from Isaiah 40:3 points to the significance of John's arrival. In chapter 40 of Isaiah, the prophet promises an end to exile through a new exodus. "Comfort, comfort my people," says God (v 1). Matthew's point is this: this comfort is on its way.

Often today a British town will spruce up its civic spaces in preparation for a royal visit. The voice in the wilderness calls for a major civil-engineering project to prepare for the coming of God—the construction of "a highway for our God" (Isaiah 40:3). Except God's coming is not a courtesy call—he's coming to liberate his people. So it was that 70 years after their exile into Babylon, God's people were able to return to Judea under Ezra and Nehemiah. But, as we saw in chapter 1, the exile in Babylon was a picture of humanity's alienation from God. Now God is coming in the person of his Son to liberate his people from this deeper, darker exile. And John is his herald. John has run on ahead, as it were, to let the world know that God is on his way. For the coming of Jesus is the coming of God since Jesus is "Immanuel", "God with us" (Matthew 1:23).

A camel-hair coat and a leather belt, locusts and wild honey (**3:4**): suddenly Matthew is interested in what someone's wearing and eating. That's not just because this is quite a look! It's because it would have reminded Matthew's readers of the prophet Elijah, who was recognised by his hair coat and leather belt (2 Kings 1:8). Elijah was taken up to heaven without dying, so the expectation arose that he would return to announce the coming of the Lord (2 Kings 2:1, 11; Malachi 4:5). Matthew spotlights John's appearance to portray him as Elijah returned. This is also the clothing and diet of wilderness life; John is spotlighting the ongoing exile of Israel.

How do you prepare for the coming of God? Not with road building—that was just an image. John's call to his hearers—and Matthew's call to his readers—is to repent (Matthew **3:2**) and to express that repentance in **baptism** (**v 5-6**). God's coming will mean liberation for his people and judgment for his enemies. But we've all become enemies of God, and so we need to change sides.

Jesus Comes to Purge God's People

In **verse 7** the Pharisees and Sadducees come to see what all the fuss is about. They were two rival groupings within 1st-century Judaism. John doesn't hesitate to condemn them, for reasons that will become clear as Matthew's Gospel unfolds (**v 7-8**). Here, John's focus is on their presumption. "We have Abraham as our father," they say (**v 9**). God had promised to make Abraham's family a great nation in a great land (Genesis 12:2, 7), and so the religious leaders assume that their ethnicity means their future is secure. But John says God can "out of these stones ... raise up children for Abraham" (Matthew **3:9**). God can fulfil his promise to Abraham with or without the religious leaders (just as God could fulfil his promise to David with or without King Ahaz, as we saw in 1:23).

3:10 reiterates this message. John imagines a lumberjack positioning his axe at the bottom of a tree trunk as he prepares to take his first cut. It's an image from Isaiah 10:24-25, 33-34, where God is about to cut down Assyria. Now that axe is poised over Israel. But Isaiah continues: "A shoot will come up from the stump of Jesse; from his roots a Branch will bear fruit" (Isaiah 11:1). Jesse was the father of King David, who ruled centuries before Isaiah lived—so this shoot is a new King David, emerging from the carnage of God's judgment. God can create a new people, with a new king, out of judgment. In the garden of God Jesus is, as it were, going to cut out the trees (the people) who don't produce good fruit (the good works that flow from true faith). God is going to **purge** his people and redefine the children of Abraham (Galatians 3:6-9).

God can create a new people, with a new king, out of judgment.

This idea continues in Matthew **3:11-12** as John contrasts his baptism with the baptism of Jesus. Matthew spotlights lots of verbal similarities between the messages of John and of Jesus (**v 2**, and 4:17; **3:7**, and 12:34 and 23:33; **3:10**, and 7:19, 12:33 and 21:43; **3:9**, and 8:11-12; **3:11-12**, and 13:30, 40-42). But John himself emphasises the discontinuities. John was a great prophet (11:11), but the great John pointed to one who is even greater (**3:11**). John's baptism with water was merely an outward sign; Jesus will effect the reality to which John's baptism pointed. We often contrast the outward cleansing of John's baptism with the inner cleansing of Jesus' work; Jesus cleanses our heart through the work of the Spirit, washing away our guilt and reorienting our desires. That's implicit here in the reference to baptism "with the Holy Spirit". But Matthew's focus is on another type of cleansing or baptism: Jesus will purge God's people with fire. In Mark's account, John says Jesus will baptise with the Spirit, but Matthew and Luke both add "and fire". Jesus will judge unfruitful people just as farmers burn unfruitful trees or chaff (**v 10, 12**). Harvested wheat was first threshed to separate the wheat from its inedible outer case (the "chaff"). Then a winnowing fork was used to throw the wheat and chaff into the air so the lighter chaff would blow away. John says Jesus is coming to winnow God's people.

Pruning. Purging. Winnowing. The coming of Jesus would divide 1st-century Judaism. The Pharisees and Sadducees represent those who reject Jesus, thereby confirming that they are deserving of judgment. But what happened to 1st-century Judaism is now happening today throughout the world as the gospel is proclaimed. The message of Jesus divides humanity. Since Jesus is Immanuel, God with us, to reject Jesus is to reject God, and those who reject God will be rejected by God. One day Jesus will return, with axe and winnowing fork in hand, as it were, to enact this judgment. How can we prepare for this coming? In the same way that they did in the 1st century: "confessing their sins, they were baptised" (**v 6**). And then we are to "produce fruit in keeping with repentance" (**v 8**).

Jesus Comes to Lead God's People Home

In **verse 13** there's a strange twist in Matthew's story. John has just said that Jesus is a greater person with a greater baptism. But then Jesus comes to be baptised by John! The incongruity of this is not lost on John, who tries to dissuade Jesus (**v 13-14**). But Jesus says, "It is proper for us to do this to fulfil all righteousness" (**v 15**). In **Paul**'s writings, "righteousness" means the right standing with God that Jesus shares with his people. But in Matthew's Gospel, fulfilling righteousness means obeying God's will. By being baptised, Jesus is obeying God's will. But John's baptism is a sign of repentance linked to the confession of sin (**v 2, 6**), and Jesus doesn't need to repent, nor does he have any sins to confess. So why must Jesus be baptised, and how does doing so obey God's will?

To answer these questions we need to go back into the prophecy of Isaiah. Isaiah promised a suffering servant who would redeem God's people by bearing their sin in their place: "He was pierced for our transgressions, he was crushed for our iniquities ... and was numbered with the transgressors" (Isaiah 53:5, 12). By being baptised, Jesus identifies with his sinful people and so accepts the role of the suffering servant to which God has called him. Jesus fulfils righteousness by signalling his willingness to obey God's will, which for him will mean suffering for his people. This resolution is affirmed as Jesus rises from the water. The "suffering servant" is first introduced in Isaiah 42:1 with these words: "Here is my servant, whom I uphold, my chosen one in whom I delight; I will put my Spirit on him, and he will bring justice to the nations". So it is that as Jesus rises from the water, the Spirit descends "on him", and the voice of the Father echoes Isaiah's word (Matthew **3:16-17**).

The words of the Father also echo 2 Samuel 7:14 and Psalm 2:7, which speak of God adopting King David's son as his son. In addition, when David was anointed as king, the Spirit descended on him (1 Samuel 16:13). Now Jesus is anointed and empowered by the Spirit to be God's King (as Isaiah 11:1-4 had promised). There's also an allusion to Isaac, Abraham's son and the inheritor of the promises to Abraham, who was described by God to Abraham as the one "whom you love" (Genesis 22:2). Jesus, too, is the beloved Son. But Jesus will not be spared in the way Isaac was in Genesis 22, because Jesus is the true sacrifice for sin. "Jesus is Abraham's son not only because of genealogical descent but also because he embodies the fulfilment figuratively foreshadowed by Isaac" (Hays, *Echoes of Scripture in the Gospels*, p. 140). Matthew has stacked up the Old Testament allusions to show that Jesus is the beloved divine Son, the suffering servant, the anointed King and the true Isaac, all rolled into one. Additionally, "the Trinity is here conveyed to us plainly and without leaving room for doubt or hesitation," comments the 4th-century bishop and theologian Augustine of Hippo. "The Father is in the Voice, the Son in the Man, the Holy Spirit in the Dove" (Sermon 2.1 in *The Nicene and Post-Nicene Fathers: First Series*, Volume 6, p. 259).

At first sight, the phrase "he went up out of the water" in Matthew **3:16** seems redundant. What else was going to happen after a baptism?! So why does Matthew highlight this? First, water in the Bible story often represents judgment. Noah's flood is the prime example. Genesis 7:11 says, "The floodgates of the heavens were opened". Now heaven is again opened, and Jesus passes through water. This baptism in water is a sign: the real baptism Jesus must endure is to be immersed in divine judgment on the cross (Mark 10:38). But Jesus will emerge from judgment in triumph.

Second, Matthew twice tells us that this took place in the River Jordan (Matthew **3:6, 13**). That's because, many centuries before, God's people had passed through the Jordan to enter the promised land (Joshua 3 – 4). Baptism was a rite Gentiles underwent to become Jews. It was as if they were catching up— passing through the Jordan as the Jewish people had collectively already done in the days of Joshua. So John's baptism was a recognition that God's people had become like Gentile sinners, who now needed to become God's people all over again. Now Jesus passes through water to lead his people into a new creation (to which the promised land was a pointer).

Questions for reflection

1. "The message of Jesus divides humanity" (p. 32). How does this set your expectations for what you'll see as you live and speak as his follower?
2. What does "fruit in keeping with repentance" look like in your own life? What "fruit" would you like to ask God to grow more in you, by his Spirit?
3. In what ways is Jesus fulfilling Old Testament prophecies in his baptism? In what ways is he greater than the Old Testament figures who prefigure him?

PART TWO

Do you like exams? Of course not. No one does. So much is at stake. Fail and you don't get a job or you're not allowed to drive or you can't go to university. What if there was an exam to see if you could be part of God's people? In Matthew 4 just such an examination takes place! What's more, we all pass with flying colours—in and through Jesus.

Jesus Comes to Pass the Test for God's People

Just as Israel was led by the pillars of cloud and fire to be tested in the wilderness (Deuteronomy 8:6), so Jesus is led by the Spirit to be tested in the wilderness (Matthew **4:1-2**). Just as Israel was in the wilderness for 40 years, so Jesus is there for 40 days. Just as Israel was tested because they lacked food (Exodus 15:25; 16:4), so Jesus is tested when he's hungry from fasting (Matthew **4:2**). Just as Israel was tested as a son (Deuteronomy 8:5; see also Exodus 4:22), so Jesus is tested to see if he is the true Son (Matthew 3:17). Jesus responds to each test with a quote from Deuteronomy—a book written during the time Israel was in the wilderness.

This story also takes us back to an earlier test. Like Adam, Jesus is tested by Satan. Adam was the representative of humanity, and his failure became our failure. Jesus is the representative of a new humanity, and his faithfulness becomes the faithfulness of all who are in him by faith (Romans 5:12-21). Jesus is rerunning the stories of Adam and Israel. Twice it seemed that God's plan for humanity had been derailed by human sin—but God was actually preparing us to see the true glory of Jesus. Jesus rewrites our story, but this time he writes a different ending. Israel failed to be a faithful "son" of God, "but pointed to the 'Son' who would never fail" (D.A. Carson, *The Expositor's Bible Commentary*, p. 112).

Test #1

At his baptism, Jesus fulfilled all righteousness by accepting the role of the suffering servant. To fulfil that role, Jesus had laid down his privileges as God's Son (Philippians 2:6). Satan's first temptation is an invitation to take up those privileges again and so bypass the task of suffering for his people (Matthew **4:3**). So this is not so much a temptation to prove he's God's Son as to use his rights as God's Son to avoid the suffering he must undergo as the representative of God's people. Indeed, it's a temptation that will be repeated at the cross, when the crowd cry, "Come down from the cross, *if you are the Son of God*" (27:40. emphasis added)—the same words as those used here in **4:3**. In effect Satan says, *You're the Son of God; so you don't have to suffer like this.* In one sense that's true: Jesus does have the rights of the divine Son. But Jesus has laid down those rights to obey his Father and save his people. When Israel was hungry in the wilderness, the nation became a grumbling "son" who didn't trust their Father (Exodus 16:1-3; Deuteronomy 8:2-3). Jesus remains a trusting Son who's nourished by God's word (John 4:34). Adam sinned by eating because he doubted God's word; Jesus obeyed by abstaining because God's word sustained him (Matthew **4:4**).

Test #2

Second, Satan invites Jesus to prove his divine sonship by throwing himself off the temple with a view to God sending angels to rescue him (**v 5-6**). But Jesus doesn't need to prove his sonship. He's heard it declared by the Father, and he's happy to trust his Father's word (3:17). Again, this is an invitation to use his rights as God's Son to avoid suffering. Again, this temptation will return during the **passion** of Jesus. When Jesus is arrested, one of his companions draws his sword, but Jesus tells him to put it away:"Do you think I cannot call on my Father, and he will at once put at my disposal more than twelve legions of angels? But how then would the Scriptures be fulfilled that say it must happen in this way?" (26:53-54). The "angel option" is always there. But it would be opting out of the task God has given Jesus—the task of being the servant who suffers for his people. So Jesus responds with a quote from Deuteronomy 6:16: "Do not put the Lord your God to the test" (Matthew **4:7**). Satan has taken a divine promise and twisted it into a divine test. Again, it takes us back to Israel in wilderness, where the Israelites failed the test by testing God—in effect putting him on trial (Exodus 17:1-7; see *Exodus For You*, p. 126-129). The result of repeating this failure would be exile, warned Deuteronomy 6:13-19, a warning that became a reality when Israel was exiled in Babylon. Now Jesus passes the test by not testing God, paving the way for Jesus to be the one who *ends* the exile.

Test #3

The first two temptations were subtle: Jesus was invited to use rights he genuinely had but to bypass the task God had given him. The third time round the temptation is clear: "Would Jesus be God's Messiah by following the path of suffering, even to death on a cross? Or would Jesus be Satan's Messiah by simply bowing down to him, and not having to die on a cross?" (Mark Jones, *Knowing Jesus*, p. 112). Jesus dismisses Satan and chooses to serve God, even though that means accepting the cross (Matthew **4:10-11**). Again Jesus quotes from Moses' review of Israel's history in the wilderness to show he is doing what Israel should have done (Deuteronomy 6:13).

Three times Jesus rejects the option to take a shortcut to glory. He could have arrived at his destination without suffering, but he would have arrived without a people. Only by dying in our place can he secure our place alongside him in his glory. For now, Satan leaves him (Matthew **4:11**). But, as we've seen, these temptations will return as Jesus approaches the cross. Having *rejected* the help of angels to bypass the task God has given him, Jesus now *receives* help from angels to sustain him *in* that task. It's a reminder that God sometimes uses angels to protect and provide for his people (Hebrews 1:14). In 1 Kings

19:4-8 angels sustain Elijah for a 40-day period, a precursor that suggests that Jesus is a true prophet of God.

There are lessons for us here as we face temptation. Like Jesus, we're to see ourselves as children of God and so trust in his fatherly care. Like Jesus, we're to extinguish the flaming arrows of Satan's temptations and lies by countering them with the promises of God's word (Ephesians 6:16). But first and foremost, we're to see ourselves not so much as "like Jesus" as "in Jesus". I'm not simply left trying harder to be *like* Christ. I can rest assured that I've already passed the test *in* Christ. I'm already an obedient child of God because Jesus has obeyed on my behalf. If I'm baptised into Christ, then God's verdict on Christ at his baptism becomes God's declaration to me: *You are my son, my daughter, whom I love; with you I am well pleased* (adapting Matthew 3:17).

If I'm baptised into Christ, then God's verdict on Christ becomes God's declaration to me.

Jesus Comes to Light Up the World

When John the Baptist is imprisoned, Jesus withdraws to Galilee (**4:12**). Perhaps Jesus wants to avoid John's fate—though he continues to preach a message like John's (3:2; **4:17**). Matthew suggests another reason for this move (**v 13-16**): Jesus went to Galilee to fulfil the prophecy of Isaiah 9:1-2. Centuries before, when the northern empire of Assyria had conquered Israel, the darkness of the Assyrian invasion had fallen first on the northern tribes of Zebulun and Naphtali. But Isaiah had promised that they would be the first to see the light when God came to liberate his people. Matthew says that that's now happening, through the ministry of Jesus. A new day or era is coming. That day will fully arrive only at the end of history. But already the first rays of dawn have appeared over Galilee. Meanwhile the religious elites in Jerusalem remain in darkness.

Matthew extends the quote from Isaiah 9 to include allusions to Isaiah 42:7-9 and 60:1. (Matthew loves to let Bible passages interpret one another through this kind of blending.) In this case "we should hear in Matthew **4:16**," says Richard Hays, "a complex harmonic fusion of *three* passages from Isaiah that associate the image of a rising light with the theme of revelation to the Gentiles" (*Echoes of Scripture in the Gospels*, p. 178). Israel had failed to be a light to the nations. But Jesus is a light that will reach across the globe. It has spread from out Galilee, and today it's reached your door.

The life of Jesus offered a glimpse of God's coming new world. **Verse 23** speaks of Jesus "proclaiming the good news ... and healing every disease". Matthew's language points to the comprehensive scope of God's coming renewal: "every disease," "all over", "various diseases", "severe pain", "the demon-possessed", "large crowds" (**v 24-25**). Through word and deed, Jesus lights up the world with "the good news of the kingdom". We respond first by seeing ourselves among the crowds that come to him for help. Then second, we join Jesus in bringing light to the world in word and deed (as we'll see in 5:14-16).

Jesus Comes to Gather God's People

We see this pattern of coming to Jesus and then being sent from Jesus to invite others to come to him in the next stories. Jesus calls Peter and Andrew, and then James and John, to follow him. Then he promises that they in turn will call other people to follow him (**4:18-20**). They're to leave their role as fishermen to fish for people (**v 19**).

Here we meet a recurring characteristic of Matthew's: he pares stories down to their essential point. In Luke's account of this story, Simon Peter has had a frustrating night when Jesus tells him to try to catch fish once more. The result is a miraculous haul of fish, and Peter has to call for help. Peter is so overwhelmed by this display of power that he tells Jesus to "go away" (Luke 5:8). All this Matthew ignores and instead zones in on the key thing for his readers (including us): "Come, follow me ... and I will send you out to fish for people" (Matthew **4:19**). You might want to ask yourself: What is Jesus asking me to leave behind? And what might it look like for me to fish for people?

Verse 23 is repeated in 9:35 to create two bookends to Matthew 5 – 9. **4:24-25** is a kind of preview: we're going to see Jesus *proclaiming* good news in chapters 5 – 7 and *demonstrating* that good news in miraculous healings in chapters 8 – 9.

John the Baptist has arrived to announce the coming of God. Jesus is coming to end the exile and lead us home to God. Jesus represents the true people of God, passing the test which Adam and Israel failed. And now Jesus begins to call people to be his people, for Jesus is forming a new humanity in readiness of the new day that is dawning. That call has come to you—and now it's your turn to pass it on.

Questions for reflection

1. How does it make you feel to remember that God the Father's verdict on his Son is now, by faith, God the Father's verdict on *you*?
2. In what ways are you struggling to resist temptation? What have you learned from Jesus' example in the wilderness?
3. "The life of Jesus offered a glimpse of God's coming new world" (p. 39). How does reflecting on this truth excite and/or comfort you?

MATTHEW CHAPTER 5

3. THE RENEWED LIFE: PART 1

Christians generally ask two questions of the Sermon on the Mount in Matthew 5 – 7:

1. Is it practical? Or is it designed for a future era or to make people realise their need of Christ?
2. Does it offer a personal or a social **ethic**, or both? Should I, for example, renounce violence in my personal interactions? Should I also become a pacifist?

Wrestling with these questions has given rise to a number of ways of reading the Sermon:

- A "dispensational" reading: the Sermon tells us how to live in a coming age but isn't an ethic for the present.
- An "existential" reading: the Sermon isn't a code of conduct but a summons to decide whether to follow Jesus or not.
- A "Lutheran" reading: the Sermon presents an impossible ethic that drives us to Christ.
- A "liberal" reading: the Sermon is a recipe for the advance of civilisation.

I want to suggest that the Sermon is primarily an ethic for the new people of God. It describes how human beings can flourish as they live in the world as part of Christ's kingdom, in **communion** with God. Alongside this, it critiques self-righteousness or superficial righteousness, in which a person's actions are merely for outward show. These purposes reflect the two audiences for the Sermon: "his disciples" are told how to live as followers of Jesus while "the crowds" are challenged to repent of self-righteousness (**v 1-2**). But these two purposes intersect because Jesus repeatedly says, *Don't be self-righteous like this... instead, be like this...*

An Announcement of Liberation

Different Jewish groups responded in different ways to Roman rule. The Sadducees collaborated with the Romans. The Pharisees thought their religious purity would pave the way for the purification of the land. The Zealots were violent revolutionaries—the terrorists of their day. The Essenes withdrew into isolation until the tide turned. As we've seen, Matthew 1 – 4 presents Jesus as the liberator who will end the exile through a new exodus and lead God's people home. The longed-for liberation is happening—though not in the way most Jews have been expecting. This theme of liberation continues in the Beatitudes:

- Jesus announces the restoration of God's rule (**5:3**).
- Jesus announces the comfort Isaiah promised when the exile ended (**v 4**; see Isaiah 40:1-3).
- Jesus says his people will inherit the land as Psalm 37:11 promised (Matthew **5:5**).
- To thirst for righteousness is to long for God to put things right (**v 6**).
- Jesus says his community will be "sons of God" (**v 9**, ESV), which is what Israel was first called during the exodus (Exodus 4:22-23).
- Jesus promises his kingdom to those who suffer in his name (Matthew **5:10-12**).

But Jesus is speaking of something much bigger than the political liberation of 1st-century Judea. He has come to liberate his people from sin and death, and lead us home to God. Jesus has come to end the curse of Genesis 3 and establish a kingdom of blessing (**v 3-12**). Psalm 37:11 promises the land to the meek, but Jesus expands this to encompass the earth (Matthew **5:5**). This liberation is political in the sense that it will end injustice and establish a new government. But this political dimension will only take place when Christ returns in triumph. **Verses 4-9** all point to the future ("they will..."). In the meantime, the followers of Jesus are not to be violent revolutionaries but "peacemakers" (**v 9**) who "turn ... the other cheek" and "love [their] enemies" (v 38-48).

An Invitation to the Broken

The first hearers of the Sermon wouldn't have found an announcement of liberation shocking (even though they hadn't grasped the scale of Jesus' liberation). What would have shocked them was who gets to be part of this coming kingdom. It's not the Sadducees or Pharisees, for "blessed are the poor in spirit" (**v 3**). It's not the Zealots, for "blessed are the merciful" and "the peacemakers" (**v 7, 9**, 38-48). It's not the Essenes because, rather than being "hidden", these people are "the light of the world" (**v 14**).

Instead it's "the poor in spirit", or broken people, to whom the kingdom is given. This is how Jesus begins in **verse 3**, and it sets the tone for the whole Sermon. Because the poor had nowhere to turn but to God, in the Old Testament poverty became a picture of spiritual dependency. Jesus comforts those who mourn their sin (**v 4**). He bequeaths the earth not to the grasping but to "the meek" (**v 5**). He gives righteousness to those who long for righteousness (**v 6**). He reveals himself not to the outwardly religious but to "the pure in heart" (**v 8**). The weight given to the final blessing in **verses 11-12** and the switch to the second person ("you") suggest that the poverty and mourning of **verses 3-9** may be the result of being persecuted as followers of Jesus.

In summary, Jesus gives his kingdom to people who feel their brokenness. Broken people receive his kingdom as a gift, and broken people let the giftedness of the kingdom shape their attitude to others.

The Devil's Beatitudes

- Believe in yourself because you're great as you are! (The opposite of v 3.)
- Don't take life too seriously and shrug it off when you make mistakes (v 4).
- Always look after No. 1 and don't let anyone put you down (v 5).
- Avoid campaigns and causes—they're not worth the effort (v 6).
- Demand your rights because you're worth it! (v 7).
- You'll be okay as long as you tick the right boxes (v 8).
- Don't get involved in other people's fights—let them sort it out themselves (v 9).
- Learn to compromise, chill out and join the party! (v 10-12).

Do any of these sound familiar?

A Way to Flourish

So Christ's liberation is already beginning among his people: "for theirs is the kingdom of God" (present tense, **v 3**). Already the future kingdom is taking shape among God's people. The Sermon therefore describes life under Christ's kingship—the good life we're called to embrace.

Based on the Old Testament use of the corresponding Hebrew word, Jonathan Pennington suggests "blessed" is a misleading translation of the Sermon's opening word. "Blessed" implies something

God has done for us, whereas Jesus is describing how we are to live (albeit in communion with God and within his kingdom). A beatitude, Jonathan Pennington says, "is a pronouncement, based on observation, that a certain way of being in the world produces human flourishing and felicity" (*The Sermon on the Mount and Human Flourishing*, p. 42). The Greek word translated "blessed" carries the sense of "happy". Pennington translates the opening beatitude, "Flourishing are the poor in spirit because the kingdom of heaven is theirs" (p. 143). Jesus is a new Solomon, dispensing wisdom so we can flourish and embodying that wisdom in himself.

So the Beatitudes are not the entrance requirements of Christ's kingdom, nor rewards for good behaviour. They're descriptions of how we can live a good life under Christ's kingship—both individually and communally, both now and more fully when Christ returns. The second half of each Beatitude explains why this is the best way to live even when this life is accompanied by sorrow and suffering, as Pennington explains:

> "The reason Jesus can boldly claim that the poor in spirit are truly flourishing is because, despite appearances, these lowly ones are actually possessors and citizens of God's heavenly kingdom." (p. 156)

A Community of Light

Jesus describes his followers in **verse 13** as "the salt of the earth". Throwing salt was used in the Old Testament to confirm an agreement—the equivalent of us shaking hands or signing a contract today. So salt was added to sacrifices as a sign of covenant commitment (Leviticus 2:13). Numbers speaks of "an everlasting covenant of salt before the LORD for both you and your offspring" (Numbers 18:19). Salt without flavour is therefore a picture of an unfaithful community (= old covenant Israel). It's good only to be "thrown out" (= exiled) and "trampled underfoot" (= conquered by enemy armies). So when

Jesus calls his disciples "the salt of the earth", he's saying they are God's new covenant community.

As his disciples flourish under Christ's rule, they become "the light of the world" and "a town built on a hill" that "cannot be hidden" (Matthew **5:14**). It's as if the community of Jesus is an enclave in enemy territory—the one place on earth where God's coming kingdom can be seen. Their lifestyle has missional power. Israel was called to be a town on "the highest of the mountains" to which "all nations will stream" as they display "the light of the LORD" (Isaiah 2:1-5). But instead of attracting the nations to the ways of God, the Israelites were attracted to the ways of the nations. Jesus came as the true light of the world (Isaiah 42:6; 49:6; John 8:12). And now he calls us to be a town on a hill and the light of the world. Instead of following the culture, the church is to offer a distinctive witness. In practice this looks like doing "good deeds" that point people to God (Matthew **5:16**).

The community of Jesus is an enclave in enemy territory—the one place on earth where God's coming kingdom can be seen.

The challenge in **verses 14-16** is to "let your light shine before others". It would be madness to buy a new lamp, plug it in and then put it under a bucket. Lamps are meant to shine, so you put them where their light can be seen. Jesus has formed us as a community of light and placed us where we can be seen—in our homes, workplaces and neighbourhoods.

Jesus and the Old Testament

The Sermon draws on Old Testament wisdom and reflects certain aspects of Greek "virtue ethics" (in which a good life is not simply about what you do but who you are). But Jesus sets these traditions in the context of the coming of his kingdom. Just as Moses received the old covenant law on a mountain, so Jesus gives a new law in the Sermon on the Mount (compare **verses 1-2** with Exodus 19:3, and Matthew 8:1—at the end of the Sermon—with Exodus 34:29). Yet Moses never said as Jesus does, "But *I* tell you..." Moses was only God's spokesman whereas Jesus speaks as the Law-giver—the God of **Sinai** come down to lead his people.

So how does the Law of Jesus relate to the Law of Moses? Does it "abolish the Law [of Moses] and the Prophets"? No, says Jesus in Matthew **5:17-18**. "I have not come to abolish them but to fulfil them."

Notice first that Jesus doesn't abolish the Old Testament. He continues, "For truly I tell you, until heaven and earth disappear, not the smallest letter, not the least stroke of a pen, will by any means disappear from the Law until everything is accomplished". It's literally "not an iota, not a dot" (**v 17-18**, ESV). An iota is the smallest letter in the Greek alphabet. (Jesus may have originally said *yod*, the smallest Hebrew letter.) The word translated "dot" means a horn or hook. It's the equivalent of a "serif": the little hooks at the ends of letters in fonts like Times New Roman. So Jesus is saying that absolutely nothing should be removed from the Old Testament. It's all part of God's revelation, and it should all be read with a corresponding seriousness (**v 19**).

But Jesus does "fulfil" the Old Testament. The options are *not* between "abolish" and "keep-in-the-same-way", but between "abolish" and "fulfil". This is reflected in the repeated formula: "You have heard it said... but I tell you..." (e.g. v 21-22). "Christ makes it clear that he is not contradicting the law, but neither is he preserving it unchanged" (Craig Blomberg, *Matthew*, p. 103).

The question is: what does this fulfilment involve? Some people suggest that Jesus abolished the ceremonial law but confirmed the moral law. The problem with this is that Jesus never made this distinction, and it's countered by **verse 18**. Other people suggest that

Jesus expanded the law to include heart attitudes as well as external behaviour. The problem with this is that while heart attitudes are a big theme in the Sermon, they were also important in the Old Testament (the first and last commandments, for example, concern heart attitudes—Exodus 20:3, 17).

"The best interpretation of these difficult verses," comments Don Carson, "says that Jesus fulfils the Law and the Prophets in that they point to him, and he is their fulfilment" (*The Expositor's Bible Commentary*, Volume 8, p. 143). The Old Testament continues to be authoritative and relevant, but now it must be read in the light of the coming of Jesus (Luke 24:25-27, 44-47; John 5:39). Carson adds, "The manner of the prophetic foreshadowing varies" (p. 144). So…

- sometimes Jesus fulfils the Old Testament by completing what it promised or being what it pictured. We no longer sacrifice animals because Jesus is the sacrifice to which they pointed. The law is not thereby abolished as if it was wrong. Instead, it's fulfilled because it's achieved its goal of pointing to Jesus.

- sometimes Jesus fulfils the Old Testament by affirming what it taught or deepening its meaning. So when Jesus says, "You have heard it said… but I tell you…" he doesn't *cancel* the original command; he *expounds* (and sometimes extends) its true meaning.

A New Ethic for a New People

Let's come back to our opening questions. First, is the Sermon practical? Or is it designed for a future era or to make us realise our need of Christ? The answer is: yes, the Sermon is practical. In one sense it does belong to a future era, but that future has broken into the present through Jesus. It's also true that unbelievers will find it impossible to obey and so, yes, they ought then to realise their need of Jesus. But primarily this is an ethic for Christ's new community, living in the light of his coming and empowered by his Spirit. "The standards of the

Sermon," says John Stott, "are attainable all right, but only by those who have experienced the **new birth**" (*The Message of the Sermon on the Mount*, p. 29).

Second, does it offer a personal or social ethic? The answer is that the Sermon is to be lived by the Christian community. So it's neither an individual ethic to be practiced in isolation nor an ethic for society as a whole. "The duties and functions of the state," says Stott, "are quite different from those of the individual" or someone acting in their capacity of as an officer of state (p. 111). The Sermon is about how the church conducts itself in the old age while it witnesses to the coming of the new age. The state (and Christians acting on behalf of the state) may rightly use the sword (violence) to prevent evil, but the Christian community should never try to grow or defend itself through coercion (see Romans 12:17 – 13:7).

Questions for reflection

1. Has your view of the Sermon on the Mount changed in any way as a result of reading this section? How?
2. Are you in danger of falling for any of the "devil's beatitudes"? What would it look like for you to live out Jesus' beatitudes instead?
3. How can you—individually and as part of your church—make sure that the light shines before others this week?

PART TWO

Imagine a community in which people resort to violence to settle disputes; people readily shout abuse at one another and rain down curses; people get mad when another car driver cuts them up or the call centre cuts them off (Matthew **5:21-22**). Imagine a community in which it's common to find someone who is distraught because their partner has been unfaithful; husbands boast of their fidelity, but secretly watch porn (**v 27-28**); and children blame themselves for their parents' divorce (**v 31**). Imagine a community in which people say one thing but do another; people have to swear on their mother's grave because no-one trusts anyone; and you're always suspicious of people's motives (**v 33**). Imagine a community in which people stab you in the back when they get the chance; where people always demand their rights and disagreements escalate into feuds (**v 38, 43**).

I suspect you don't have to work too hard to imagine this. This probably describes your community. It's not always like this. But this is where you live.

Now imagine another community —a different kind of community. In this community people get angry, but they don't let it escalate. They take the initiative and seek to be reconciled (**v 23-26**). In this community people are prone to lust, but they prevent it escalating (**v 27-32**). In this community people don't have to swear they're telling the truth because they have a reputation for honesty and people trust one another (**v 34-37**). In this community people get wronged, but instead of feuds escalating, people repay those wrongs with a blessing (**v 39-42**). They do good to people—even when those people have let them down (**v 44**).

A community like that would be attractive. People would want to live in that kind of place (v 14-16).

This is the "city on a hill" to which Jesus is calling his liberated people (v 14). This is life in the kingdom of God.

God's people are to treat God's Old Testament law fulfilled in Jesus with the utmost seriousness (v 19). Indeed Jesus says, "I tell you that unless your righteousness surpasses that of the Pharisees and the teachers of the law, you will certainly not enter the kingdom of heaven" (**v 20**). This would have shocked his hearers because they thought the Pharisees were the epitome of righteousness. So Jesus seems to be saying that we've got to be better than the best. But in the Sermon, Jesus exposes the Pharisees as "hypocrites" (6:2, 5, 16; 7:5, 21-23). Their righteousness is simply for show. It's skin deep; it doesn't come from the heart.

Pharisaical righteousness is simply for show. It's skin-deep; it doesn't come from the heart.

But one of the ways Jesus fulfils the law is by doing something the prophets had promised God would do: Jesus writes God's law *on our hearts* (Jeremiah 31:31-34). He puts his Spirit in his people so that we *want* to obey God because we *love* God (Ezekiel 36:25-27). We surpass the righteousness of the Pharisees not by making an even greater effort than they did. Quite the opposite—we begin where the Sermon begins: by admitting we're "poor in spirit" (Matthew 5:3). As recipients of God's grace, we're able to obey from the heart. We won't always be faultless, but we can live this life enough to be a light in our neighbourhoods. John Stott says:

> "Here is [Christ's] picture of God's alternative society. These are the standards, the values and the priorities of the kingdom of God ... Only when the Christian community lives by Christ's manifesto will the world be attracted and God be glorified."
>
> (*The Message of the Sermon on the Mount*, p. 222)

Jesus makes this new life very practical. For each topic:

- Jesus presents the command of the law: the traditional version of righteousness.

- Jesus shows how this is fulfilled in the heart: how the law is written on the heart.
- Jesus presents a practical step: a way to take the initiative to break the cycles of escalating conflict or lust or distrust or greed.

(For more on this approach see Glen Stassen, *Living the Sermon on the Mount*.)

Breaking the Cycle of Escalating Violence

The *traditional command* is "You shall not murder" (**v 21**). That's pretty straightforward. But Jesus immediately moves on to the *heart fulfilment*: Don't be angry in your hearts (**v 22-23**). Jesus says murder is just the symptom. The real disease is selfish anger in our hearts. And that can take many forms. Sometimes it takes the form of violence or even murder. Sometimes it's verbal abuse ("You fool!"). Sometimes it's the silent treatment—giving someone the cold shoulder. Sometimes it's being two-faced—polite in someone's presence but gossiping behind their back. What does the Law of Jesus look like? Not just don't murder but don't be angry. Jesus not only addresses the symptoms; he wants to heal the disease.

Violence escalates. You see it in children. *She said, he said, she grabbed, he snatched, she hit, he pushed…* and so it goes on. You see it on the sports pitch: an aggressive challenge, an exchange of words, a push, a shove, others join in and a melée forms. You see it in gangland feuds, where every act of revenge makes things worse. The same dynamic goes on in the staff room, in the officers' mess, on the building site and even sometimes within the church community. Left unchecked, bitterness grows. It takes hold of your heart and then your life and then your family or church. James 3:5-6 says an angry word is a like a spark that can set a forest ablaze.

So Jesus gives a *practical step* we can all take: take the initiative to settle matters quickly (Matthew **5:23-26**). We may not be presenting offerings on altars or being sued in court, but we all face situations in which we can settle matters quickly. Don't quietly nurse your resentment. Don't make a virtue of your angry silence. Take the initiative. Get it sorted. Swallow your pride. Don't huff about your status. The health of your family and the witness of your church depend on you not leaving it to others. Get it sorted before it escalates and you end up in court.

Breaking the Cycle of Escalating Lust

The *traditional command* is "You shall not commit adultery" (**v 27**). Again Jesus moves on to the *heart fulfilment*: do not lust in your hearts (v 28). Adultery is the symptom. The cause is lust—that's the real issue. That's where sin begins: in the heart.

What's the *practical step* to tackle this issue at its root? Take the initiative to *avoid temptation*: "If your right eye causes you to stumble, gouge it out and throw it away" (**v 29-30**). Jesus doesn't expect us to take this literally, otherwise most men would be blind! So what *does* he mean? It's the same message as with violence: don't let it *escalate*. Lust can so easily escalate—a lingering look leads to an "innocent" flirtation which leads to a little touch which leads to adultery which leads to divorce. An indulged fantasy leads to porn, porn leads to more porn, soft-core leads to hard-core. So cut off temptation at the source. End the cycle of lust. When you feel that lust in your heart, say "No". "Behave as if you had actually plucked out your eyes" (Stott, p. 88). Turn away. Switch off. Block it. Make yourself accountable. Do whatever it takes to stop appreciation turning into lust turning into adultery turning into divorce (see 19:3-12). Stott says:

> "To obey this command of Jesus will involve for many of us a certain 'maiming'. We shall have to eliminate from our lives certain things which (though some may be innocent in themselves) either are, or could easily become, sources of temptation … We may have to become culturally 'maimed' in order to preserve our purity of mind."
>
> (*The Message of the Sermon on the Mount*, p. 91)

Don't assume it can't happen to you. Better people than you have succumbed to lust and wrecked their marriages and their ministries. King David was a courageous warrior who took on giants, a great leader whose men followed him through thick and thin, a psalmist with a deep relationship with God. Yet he was brought down by his lust. He let his eye wander and didn't say, "No" to temptation. As a result, he committed adultery and then murder (2 Samuel 11 – 12). He wreaked havoc in his family: three of his sons died as a result of that lingering look (2 Samuel 12:10-14; see 12:18; 13:28-29; 18:14). If you're struggling with porn, take the initiative to sort it out by telling your pastor. Lust puts you on a road that leads to hell (Matthew **5:30**). Get off that road before it's too late.

Breaking the Cycle of Escalating Suspicion

The *traditional command* is "Do not break your oath". The underlying issue is dishonesty. The Pharisees said that a vow made in God's name was binding but not a vow made "by heaven". Jesus says everything is under God's authority, so this is ridiculous reasoning that reveals a dishonest heart. The *heart fulfilment* is a commitment to honesty (**v 34-36**), and we break the cycle of escalating suspicion by the *practical step* of earning a reputation for honesty (**v 37**). Some have taken this as an absolute prohibition of swearing an oath (in court, for example). But God himself sometimes swears an oath and so may we. But God doesn't do this to distinguish his honest declarations from his dishonest ones! He does it to reassure our doubting hearts (Hebrews 6:17; Genesis 22:15-17).

Breaking the Cycle of Escalating Revenge

The *traditional command* is "Eye for eye, and tooth for tooth" (Matthew **5:38**). It was a command to not retaliate more than you were wronged. The original aim was to limit reprisals (Exodus 21:24; Leviticus 24:20; Deuteronomy 19:21). But it's is all too easy for one party to repay a wrong with interest and then for the other party to over-react so that the conflict escalates. That's because the underlying issue is a lust for revenge and pride in our hearts. The *heart fulfilment* in the law of Jesus is to "love your enemies and pray for those persecute you" (Matthew **5:44**). One *practical step* is to take the initiative to repay with a blessing (**v 39-42**). Another is to pray for our enemies (**v 44**).

If a right-handed person slaps your right cheek, they've used the back of their right hand—it's not a harmful blow but it is an insulting one. So **verse 39** is not talking about someone who's in the process of attacking you—you can defend yourself from harm. But if someone insults you, then break the cycle of revenge by applying the "eye for eye" law (in this case "cheek for cheek") in a subversive way by accepting the retaliation that they deserve. Opt to be insulted twice rather than escalate matters.

Exodus 22:26 outlawed taking a coat as a legal pledge. But if someone seizes your shirt instead, you should let them have your coat rather than escalate the conflict (Matthew **5:40**). Plus, your resulting nakedness (since people only wore two layers and many had only one set of clothes) might expose their exploitation.

> Jesus is telling us not to withhold help from someone as an act of revenge.

Roman soldiers had a right to force citizens of occupied lands to carry their load for one mile, but only for one mile. Instead of plotting revenge (like the Zealots), Christians are to seek to bless such people (**v 41**). "Give to the one who asks you, and do not turn away from the one who wants to borrow from you" is not a universal prescription (**v 42**). That would quickly overwhelm us. The context is revenge. It's telling us not to withhold help from someone as an act of revenge. By loving our enemies, we break the cycle of escalating revenge (**v 43-44**; Leviticus 19:18). By taking the initiative, we behave not as passive victims but as active agents of the kingdom of God. This is not weakness. Quite the opposite—the verses "depict the strong man whose control of himself and love for others are so powerful that he rejects absolutely every conceivable form of retaliation" (Stott, *The Message of the Sermon on the Mount*, p. 107). To which we might add: a man like Jesus.

Jonathan Pennington adds, "The practical outworking of these principles—even these specific illustrations of cheek turning, coat giving, and mile walking—requires localized wisdom" (p. 197). In other words, we need to work out practical steps that are appropriate to our context as we seek to fulfil the law from the heart. That may or may not involve literally refusing to swear an oath or turning the other cheek. What matters is that we're taking steps to avoid conflict, lust, dishonesty and revenge.

Imagine a God of Love—and Imagine His People

Jesus isn't simply giving us a new ethic; he is also giving us a new motivation. As the chapter goes on, the focus becomes more and more on doing what God does. "Love your enemies and pray for those who persecute you," says Jesus in Matthew **5:44-45**, "*that you may be children of your Father in heaven*" (emphasis added). We're to love our enemies because our Father in heaven loved us when we were his enemies. In this way we begin to live like the children of God that we have become through our connection to Jesus the Son. We turn our anger into reconciliation because God turned his anger into reconciliation. We take the initiative because God took the initiative with us. We gouge out our eyes to avoid hell because the body of Jesus experienced hell on the cross. Jesus was slapped and had his clothes taken from him (26:67; 27:35; Isaiah 50:4-7).

The climax of the chapter is "Be perfect, therefore, as your heavenly Father is perfect" (Matthew **5:48**; Leviticus 19:2). "Perfect" here doesn't mean "moral perfection but wholehearted orientation toward

God" (Pennington, *The Sermon on the Mount and Human Flourishing*, p. 78). It's the idea of wholeness or integration. We're not to be two-faced or double-minded. Even though we continue to fail, we're to be wholehearted in our commitment to God's will, just as God is wholehearted in his commitment to holiness (in his case, unfailingly so). Unlike the hypocrites, who do the right thing simply to win the praise of others (Matthew 6:2, 5, 16; 7:5; 15:7; 22:18; 23:13-29), our outward actions are to mirror our inner desires.

In the darkness of a world in which anger, lust, mistrust and hatred often escalate out of control, we are "the light of the world" (5:14). Martyn Lloyd-Jones puts it well:

> "The glory of the gospel is that when the Church is absolutely different from the world, she invariably attracts it. It is then that the world is made to listen to her message, though it may hate it at first."
>
> (*Studies in the Sermon on the Mount*, Volume 1, p. 37)

Questions for reflection

1. How have you been challenged to change in your heart attitude as you've thought about this part of the Sermon on the Mount?
2. Is there anyone you know whom you need to encourage, or challenge, or confess to?
3. "Jesus isn't simply giving us a new ethic; he is also giving us a new motivation" (p. 56). What is that motivation, and how does that help you to put into action your answers to the two questions above this one?

4. THE RENEWED LIFE: PART 2

"Our Father in heaven," begins the Lord's Prayer (**6:9**). It's a line that not only shapes the prayer but all the teaching in Matthew 6. Jesus is telling us how to live on earth as his community of light (5:14), and his two guiding principles are these:

1. View God as your Father.
2. View heaven as your home.

Five times Jesus speaks of "your Father in heaven" or "your heavenly Father" (**6:1, 9, 14, 26, 32**; see also 7:11, 21), and he refers to "heaven" two more times (**6:10, 20**) and "Father" seven more times (**v 4, 6, 8, 15, 18**).

Seeking the Reward of Your Heavenly Father

A new building is named after a wealthy benefactor. On holiday with believing friends, you spend more time in personal prayer than usual. A businessperson is photographed handing over a donation. Someone posts a quote about the value of fasting on social media. At the church prayer meeting, you pray for the first time this week. It's all too easy for us to "practise [our] righteousness in front of others", as Jesus puts it in **verse 1**. (Remember that, while in Paul's letters "righteousness" means a right standing before God which we receive in Christ, for Matthew "righteousness" means obeying God—though the Sermon's critique of self-righteousness does prepare for Paul's teaching on God-given righteousness.) If you perform to impress other people, warns Jesus, "you will have no reward from your Father in heaven". We normally think of a "hypocrite" as someone who says one thing and does another—but the hypocrite in the Sermon is someone who does the right thing for the wrong reason.

> In the Sermon on the Mount, a hypocrite is someone who does the right thing for the wrong reason.

Jesus gives three case studies: giving (**v 2-4**), prayer (**v 5-8**) and fasting (**v 16-18**). These are all good things to do; Jesus introduces each with the word "when" (**v 2, 5, 16**), which suggests that he assumes these are practices his people will adopt. But each time he gives us a choice: we can impress other people or we can be rewarded by God. Either way we get a reward. Three times Jesus says of those who are trying to impress others, "Truly I tell you, they have received their reward in full" (**v 2, 5, 16**). The key words are "in full". They do get a reward—people will be impressed by them. But that's all they get—this is their "*full*" reward. In other words, they don't get anything from God.

The counter-proposal of Jesus is to give, pray and fast in "secret" (**v 3-4, 6, 18**). Christ's community of love committed to serving the world should and will be seen (5:16), but that's a far cry from doing our religious devotion in an ostentatious way. We don't need to take this so literally that we end up being furtive. You can't contribute to a church prayer meeting in secret! But this is a good test of our motives. What we can do unseen, we should do unseen. No one but the treasurer needs to know about our giving. We can pick a day to fast when we're not due to share a meal with others. Leading public prayer is different from private prayer because we're praying on behalf of everyone there; nevertheless *who we are* before others in the prayer meeting should be who we are on our own before God in our room (**6:6**). The key thing is that we're looking to our heavenly Father rather than looking to gauge the reaction of people on earth. Jesus says your Father "is unseen"; so we are godlike when we (in terms of our righteousness) are unseen.

Jesus extends his prayer case study in **verses 7-8** to warn against trying to impress God. If you think of God as a reluctant deity, then you'll try to win him over through your long prayers or elaborate rituals or personal sacrifices. But Jesus is inviting us to share his father-child relationship with God. When he begins the Lord's Prayer "Our Father", he means *My Father and your Father—the Father we share, now that you're connected to me*. The relationship Jesus has with God the Father is now the relationship you have with God the Father. The **Reformer** John Calvin says that Christ, "while he is the true Son, has of himself been given us as a brother that what he has of his own by nature may become ours by benefit of adoption" (*Institutes*, 3.20.36). And if we see God as a generous Father, then our prayers can be short and sweet. We don't need to nag God as if he's reluctant nor inform him as if he's ignorant (**v 8**). No, God is "our Father". If he doesn't give us what we ask for, it's not because he can't be bothered. It's because, in his wisdom and love, he knows better than we do what we need. Think of the confidence with which a child approaches a loving father. Prayer is not something we achieve—it's a child asking their father for help. Charles Spurgeon says, "Our prayers are little broken things … But our Father, he will hear us" (*The Treasury of the Bible: The New Testament*, Marshall, Morgan & Scott, Volume 1, p. 82).

Reflecting the Life of Your Heavenly Home

Jesus has just warned against long prayers designed to manipulate God (**v 7**). Having invited us to see God as a gracious Father who cares for his children, Jesus now gives us a short prayer, which is nevertheless a big prayer:

- *Our Father in heaven.* Jesus is God's Son by nature, and we are now God's children by grace, sharing the same access to God that Jesus enjoys.

- *Hallowed be your name.* "Hallowed" means "holy". It's a prayer that God's holiness might be acknowledged: that your life or your church will glorify him.
- *Your kingdom come.* God's kingdom is growing as the "seed" of his word is proclaimed and people submit to his rule in faith, until one day his kingdom is established in glory (13:18-23, 31-32). So this prayer encompasses requests that people would be saved, that we ourselves would submit wholeheartedly to God, and that Christ would come again.
- *Your will be done.* In the Garden of Gethsemane, as he contemplates the agonies of the cross, Jesus prays this prayer: "Your will be done" (26:42). We make genuine requests to God in prayer, which, in his sovereignty, he uses to accomplish his purposes. But one function of prayer is to accept as God's will what we cannot change, recognising that God uses suffering to glorify his name and sanctify our hearts.
- *Give us today our daily bread.* Jesus invites us to bring our daily needs to God so we can be free from worry and so serve God's kingdom—a theme he expands in **6:25-34**.
- *Forgive us our debts.* By "debts" Jesus means our sins—the obligations of love and obedience that we've failed to give to God. Christians have already been forgiven for our past, present and future sins. But confession restores our relational connection with God and resets our obedience.
- *Lead us not into temptation.* "Temptation" covers both being enticed by sin and tried by adversity. "The prayer is more that we may overcome temptation than that we may avoid it" (Stott, *The Message of the Sermon on the Mount*, p. 150). It's a prayer to keep following Jesus, even when we find life hard.

(Adapted from chapter 8 of Tim Chester, *Life with Jesus*.)

These are the priorities which should shape the prayers of every Christian every day. I encourage you to use the Lord's Prayer as a framework for your prayers, saying a line at a time and then elaborating that line in ways that are specific to you and your church.

The first three lines all have four words in the original Greek in the same pattern, along the lines of "honoured be the name of you; come the kingdom of you; happen the will of you." Then, after the middle line ("Give us today our daily bread"), there are three more lines with a similar pattern (each with six words). Seeing this pattern spotlights the two added descriptions that break the pattern:

- "on earth as in heaven" (**v 10**)
- "as we also have forgiven our debtors" (**v 12**)

Both are about connecting earth and heaven. We're to obey on earth in the way that obedience is done in heaven. And we're to forgive on earth as forgiveness is done in heaven—an idea Jesus elaborates in **verses 14-15** and 18:21-35. It's not that we earn God's forgiveness by being forgiving: the direction of travel is from heaven to earth. But our conduct on earth must match the life of our heavenly home. If we refuse to do this, or if that's a direction we refuse to work towards, then we prove ourselves not to be children of the merciful Father (**6:15**).

Valuing the Treasure of Your Heavenly Home

In **verses 19-24** Jesus invites us to choose between treasure on earth and treasure in heaven—just as he invited us to choose between reward from people and reward from God in **verses 1-18**. In **verse 10** we were connecting heaven and earth; now we are contrasting them. There is real treasure to be had on earth (just as there was a full reward from people in **verses 2, 5 and 16**). But earthly treasure is vulnerable and transitory, while heavenly treasure endures (**v 19-20**). Go to a thrift store or your city dump and you'll see this truth before your eyes. We plan, labour, sacrifice and save to buy "stuff" that doesn't truly satisfy and never really lasts. Even in the best-case scenario, you still can't take it with you.

But Jesus isn't simply concerned to spare us from futility. His concern is our hearts. "For where your treasure is, there your heart will be also" (**v 21**). He's not simply saying we try to get the things we desire. The movement is in the opposite direction: what we own shapes what we desire. Wealth is not neutral—it exerts a pull on our affections and can control our lives. That's why Jesus says, "You cannot serve both God and Money" (**v 24**). Money forms a connection for good or ill. Buy a new sofa, for instance, and you become cautious about guests sitting on it, and that then shapes the way you offer hospitality. But give money to missionaries and you become invested in their work, praying and supporting them with more enthusiasm. Giving is a liberating act. It loosens our ties to wealth and replaces them with ties to people.

Verses 22-23 might appear to be a digression, but Jesus is saying that what you look at shapes what you value. Spend time watching adverts, scrolling through social media, leafing through glossy magazines and watching lifestyle programmes on TV and you'll want the lifestyle they portray. Don't, then, be surprised if you feel dissatisfied or find giving difficult. But spend your time looking at the glory of Christ and you'll end up with a very different set of priorities.

What should you do if you realise your priority is storing up treasure on earth? First, think of heaven as your home. Second, pray, "Hallowed be your name" (**v 9**). By doing so, you set your eyes on the treasure of heaven, which is the glory of God seen in the face of Jesus Christ.

Trusting the Care of Your Heavenly Father

Wealth can not only make us greedy, it can also make us anxious. Either way, wealth is in control. So Jesus continues, "Therefore..." Since we serve a heavenly Father, we should not, and need not, worry about earthly things (**v 25**). We can entrust ourselves to our Father's care. And the evidence of his care is all around us. Jesus argues from the lesser to the greater: God cares for birds and clothes flowers (**v 26-31**); *how much more* will he care for his children who are "much more valuable than they" (**v 30, 26**)?!

Again Jesus warns us not to live like **pagans**. In **verse 7** the pagans are *talking* too much, and in **verse 32** they are *doing* too much—all because they don't have a "heavenly Father" who "knows [what you] need". If we're overworking, it may be because we're not valuing the treasure of our heavenly home (so we're working hard to accumulate earthly treasure), or it may be because we're not trusting the care of our heavenly Father (so we're working hard to secure our future). It's this anxiety that drives the overconsumption that risks threatening the planet; we overspend because we fear missing out, and we overwork because we fear for the future. Trusting our Father's care frees us to prioritise his kingdom rather than our possessions (**v 33**). It allows us to "seek ... righteousness", including the "righteousness" of giving to the needy (**v 1-2**). There's also a futility to worry; it doesn't achieve anything (**v 27**), and you can never keep on top of it (**v 34**). Jesus is not calling us to a lesser life. He's calling us to live without fear as we enjoy our Father's generosity and share with those in need.

In prayer, God's business becomes your concern, and your concerns become his business.

What should you do if you're worrying about your needs rather than seeking God's kingdom? How can you switch focus? First, you need to think of God as a Father who knows what you need. Second, you can pray, "Your kingdom come" and "Give us this day our daily bread" (**v 10-11**). By doing so, you are handing over your worries to your heavenly Father. His business becomes your concern, and your concerns become his business.

Questions for reflection

1. Are there any priorities of the Lord's Prayer that you'd like to make a more regular or prominent part of your own prayers?
2. "Wealth is not neutral—it exerts a pull on our affections and can control our lives" (p. 64). Do you see this effect in your own life in any way?
3. What are you worrying about at the moment? How might Jesus' words about worry reshape your thinking and your praying?

PART TWO

In Matthew 7 we return to the hypocrites we met in 6:2, 5 and 16 (**7:5**). In chapter 6, the hypocrites boosted their sense of self-worth by impressing other people. In chapter 7, they boost their self-worth by putting other people down. They view righteousness as a ladder we climb to reach God, and, as long as they're higher than most people, they can feel happy with their progress. Every Pharisee needs a sinner—someone they can look down on from above. **Secular** people do this self-righteous superiority—it's not only religious people. **Liberals** may feel superior towards people with views they regard as unenlightened or out of date. Self-made people may feel superior towards people who live in poverty. But Jesus says the blessed ones—those who are righteous before God—are the poor in the spirit who mourn their sin and thirst for a righteousness they feel they lack (5:3-6).

Care as Children With a Gracious Father

Don't judge other people, says Jesus, *or whatever criteria you use to judge others will be used against you* (**7:1-2**). This is an echo of 6:14-15, where, if you find a reason not to forgive, then that reason will be used against you. Here's the logic:

1. To judge someone is to say that they've not made the grade.
2. To say they've not made the grade is to say that a grade exists which people must meet.
3. To say there's a grade is to say that you yourself must meet that grade to be accepted.
4. Being measured by God's standards leaves us all under judgment.

The good news is that Jesus has met the grade, or passed the test, on our behalf (as we saw in 4:1-11). So being righteous or right with God becomes a gift God gives through faith in Christ. But to reintroduce a measure or standard that must be met is to reject God's gift.

In **7:3-5** the self-righteousness of the hypocrite is dressed up as pastoral concern. *Let me help you make the grade,* the hypocrite says. *Let me give you some rules so you can be an acceptable Christian.* Jesus is not banning pastoral care or **church discipline**. We should help one another grow more like Christ, and sometimes that requires discernment (which is a form of judgement). **Verse 5** acknowledges that this can be appropriate. The problem here is that "speck-removal" is being performed by a hypocrite. Sometimes the plank in the hypocrite's eye is a worse offence, which they fail to acknowledge—but more often it's their self-righteousness. Even if they improve a person's outward conformity, they make matters worse because they reintroduce the idea of needing to make the grade. Those who follow their lead may look like good people, but in fact they're mini-Pharisees.

If you don't pastor people out of a strong sense of God's grace—both his grace to you and his grace to those you're helping—then you will leave them feeling condemned, and there is no condemnation to those who are in Christ Jesus (Romans 8:1). So self-righteous people make bad pastors. At best they create **legalists** in their own image; at worst they leave people crushed and condemned. We all have faults and struggles (specks), but the big fault (the plank) is to be self-righteous and think you're superior. So we need to care for one another as children with a gracious Father. Yes, we exhort people to live like Jesus. But first and foremost, we reassure believers that they're accepted in Jesus.

The call not to give what is sacred to dogs or throw pearls before pigs in Matthew **7:6** is probably a warning not to waste time arguing with the religious hypocrites of **verses 1-5**, who have no real interest in the message of Jesus (see 10:14; 15:14; Acts 13:44-47; 18:5-6). Functionally they are like Gentile "dogs" and "pigs" (dogs were not a popular animal; pigs were unclean). All they want to do is to show you how wrong you are ("tear you to pieces") so they can feel good about themselves. Alternatively, Peter Leithart sees Matthew **7:6** as a call not to seek the patronage of Gentile powers (who will eventually turn on us), but to entrust the church and its mission to God (**v 7-8**).

Pray as Children With a Generous Father

In 6:5 the hypocrites prayed to be seen by others and received their reward in full (namely. being seen by others). What they didn't receive was a hearing from God. But in **7:7-11** that's exactly what Jesus promises to those who see God as their Father. God will give when we ask (**v 7-8**).

A large stone could look a little like a loaf of bread, and a snake might look like a fish. So it's conceivable that a cruel father could use them to trick a gullible son, laughing as his son tries to bite into a stone or as he recoils when his fish turns out to be a snake. It's conceivable. But even sinful fathers "know how to give good gifts to [their] children" (**v 11**). Jesus argues from the lesser to the greater (as he did in 6:26, 30). If evil fathers give good gifts, "how much more will your Father in heaven give good gifts to those who ask him" (**7:11**). God may not always give us precisely what we ask. Blomberg says:

> "'It' in verse 7 is somewhat misleading. The word does not refer to any particular thing requested but forms part of a divine passive construction that means *ask and God will give you [what he deems best].*" (*Matthew*, p. 130)

Verse 11 speaks of God giving "good gifts", and we don't always ask for what is good. So God always answers our prayers in accordance with his love and wisdom (**v 7-8**).

It's Time to Choose

Verse 12 echoes the language of 5:17. The Beatitudes introduce the Sermon; then the main body is enclosed by these two references to the Law and Prophets, which Jesus has come "to fulfil" (v 17). Our "measure" or "rule" (**7:2**) is simply the rule of love (**v 12**). Then, from **verse 13** onwards, Jesus brings the Sermon on the Mount to an end with a series of choices we must make as we respond. "The teaching of the Sermon on the Mount is not meant to be admired but to be obeyed" (France, 1985, p.146).

We might suppose that the choice is between a good life and a bad life. But when you look back over the Sermon, that's not what you see. The alternative life that Jesus rejects is an apparently good life lived for the wrong reasons. He rejects the "righteousness of the Pharisees" (5:20). They think they're being righteous for God, but really they're doing it for themselves (**7:21-23**)—"to be honoured by others" or to manipulate God (6:1-8). Their righteousness doesn't come from the heart (5:21-48). So the options Jesus presents are between self-reliance and reliance on God, a good life lived for the wrong reasons and a good life that arises from God's grace. The Sermon doesn't begin, "Blessed are the good people" or "Blessed are the successful people". It begins, "Blessed are the poor in spirit" (5:3).

Two Roads into the Future

The demands of a rigorous self-righteous life might seem like a narrow path which few take. But that's not what Jesus says. Jesus says they are a wide gate onto a broad road (**7:13**). That's because they are about self-accomplishment. We make holiness manageable by reducing it to a set of rules and then pride ourselves on making the grade. In contrast, the road of faith has a narrow gate. That's not because it's beyond the capacity of people—quite the opposite. It's because it requires us to admit that we're poor in spirit (5:3). God's grace humbles us, and people don't want to be humbled. Christ's law is "do to others what you would have them do to you" (**7:12**). Viewed as a standard of righteousness, that crushes us because no one except Jesus has loved as they should. But viewed from the perspective of grace, it becomes a delightful way to live together in Christ's community.

Two Types of Prophet

False teachers look innocent enough at first (like "sheep" in Christ's flock), but eventually their true colours are exposed (they're "ferocious wolves", **v 15**). In early spring, one tree may look much like another.

But at harvest time, it's clear which is which from their fruit (**v 16-18**). Then bad trees can be rooted out and destroyed (**v 19**). False teaching often starts as a rationale for selfish or proud behaviour, and therefore then it produces selfish or proud behaviour. So twice Jesus says, "By their fruit you will recognise them" (**v 16, 20**).

This warning against false prophets can be applied to all forms of false teaching. "Truth matters," says Stott: "For it is God's truth and it builds up God's church, whereas error is devilish and destructive" (*The Message of the Sermon on the Mount*, p. 203). But in the context of the Sermon, the false teaching particularly in view is that of self-righteous **legalism**. It looks impressive to begin with because we see people giving, praying and fasting (6:2, 5, 16). But its long-term fruit reveals the bad roots of this teaching. When self-righteous people do well, they're full of pride because their acceptability is their achievement; and when they fail, they're left crushed.

Two Types of Disciple

These verses have brought fear to many sensitive souls who worry whether they're truly saved. But we need to read them in the light of Christ's denouncement of self-righteousness. The people who don't enter the kingdom of heaven are the self-righteous people, who think they've done enough to earn their way in (**7:21-23**). Meanwhile, those who feel they lack any righteousness in themselves and so come to Jesus in faith—the poor in spirit who thirst for righteousness—are those who, Jesus says, are blessed (5:3, 6).

Two Foundations for Life

The Sermon ends with a choice between two foundations. Jesus tells the story of a wise man whose house withstood the storm because he built it on rock (**7:24-25**). In contrast, a foolish man built his house on sand. When the storms came, "it fell with a great crash" (**v 26-27**). The wise man, says Jesus, represents "everyone who hears these words of mine and puts them into practice" (**v 24**). First, we need to listen to Jesus (and, by implication, reject the teaching of the false prophets in **verses 15-20**). Second, we need to put his words into practice. The message of Jesus in the Bible is to be the foundation for our life. Only this foundation will enable us to stand firm in the storms of life and in the final storm of death.

Again, this warning can be applied to God's word in general. Trusting any alternative is like building on sand. But, in the context of the Sermon, the choice is more specifically between building your life on the shaky foundation of self-righteousness and the firm foundation of trust in Christ. There is no neutrality—no middle way. You're either with Jesus or against him, coming to him in faith or trusting your own righteousness, submitting to his lordship or opposing his kingdom.

When Jesus finished, the crowds were "amazed" because "he taught as one who had authority, and not as their teachers of the law" (**v 28-29**). As we saw in the Introduction, Matthew repeats the phrase "when Jesus had finished saying these things" five times in his Gospel (**v 28**). It creates five blocks of teaching, possibly mirroring the five books of Moses in the Torah (the Pentateuch). The teaching of Jesus is not a rehash of other people's ideas. Jesus speaks as the new Moses, the Law-Giver, the God of Sinai, come down to be Immanuel, God with us. And this teaching is his liberating law for his liberated people.

Questions for reflection

1. How would you explain to someone what Jesus means (and doesn't mean) by "Do not judge"?
2. What are you making sure you build on rock, not sand?
3. Reflecting on the Sermon on the Mount as a whole, what's the one big thing you want to remember about it and/or change because of it?

5. THE AUTHORITY OF THE MESSIAH

Matthew closes off the previous section of teaching with his usual formula: "When Jesus had finished saying these things" (7:28; see also 11:1; 13:53; 19:1; 26:1). It's an echo of Genesis 2:2: "By the seventh day God had finished the work he had been doing". God created the world through his word. Now Jesus is recreating the world through his words. Chapters 8 – 9 give us a glimpse of this new world. It's a world of cleansing, welcome, healing, freedom, calm and life. It's a world in which the threats of illness, evil, natural disaster and even death meet their match in God's Saviour-King. Chapters 8 – 9 present what Matt Searles calls "a fully-orbed picture of the restorative reign of God" (*Matthew: One Greater than Solomon*, p. 15).

There are ten miracle stories in these chapters—nine stories in three groups (numbered 1.1 to 3.3 below), with one story containing two miracles (9:18-26). Matthew may intend us to see them as ten life-giving wonders to match the ten deadly plagues that liberated God's people from slavery in Egypt. In Numbers 14:22, Israel is said to have tested God ten times in the wilderness (possibly a rejection of God's revelation in each of the ten plagues). But here Jesus is faithful on ten occasions as the beginning of a new people of God.

As is often the case, Matthew's versions of these stories are usually shorter than those in Mark's and Luke's Gospels. Matthew pares each story down to its essential point, sometimes adding an extra saying to drive home its significance.

1.1 - The Leper: A Welcome for Outsiders

What strikes us first about the story of the man with leprosy is the power of Jesus to heal. "Immediately he was cleansed of his leprosy" (**8:3**), "as a testimony to them" (**v 4**)—that is, a testimony of Christ's healing power. But the man's question is equally striking. You might expect him to ask, *Will you cleanse me if you can?* But the man doesn't doubt the *ability* of Jesus. What he doubts is the *willingness* of Jesus: "Lord, if you are willing, you can make me clean" (**v 2**). The reason is that this man is not just ill; according to the Law of Moses, he's unclean. The stipulations alluded to in **verse 4** are a reminder of this. So this man and Jesus should have kept well away from each other. But instead Jesus says, "I am willing" and *touches* the man. As the next story demonstrates, Jesus doesn't have be near someone to heal them. But here he touches the man with leprosy not simply to heal him but to include him. It was a touch that should have made Jesus ceremonially unclean but instead made the man clean. In the kingdom of Jesus, outsiders are welcomed in. Today Jesus looks on you with compassion and says, "I am willing" (**v 3**).

1.2 - The Centurion's Servant: A Welcome for the Nations

The power of Jesus is on display again in the healing of the centurion's servant. Jesus offers to go to the centurion's house, but the centurion recognises the authority of Jesus (**v 9**). Just as the centurion's men must obey his commands, so the natural world must obey the commands of its Commander-in-Chief. The centurion is part of a chain of command that reaches up to the emperor; Jesus is part of a chain of command that reaches up to his Father.

Matthew leaves out key elements that appear in Luke's account of this story (Luke 7:1-10) and instead focuses on the centurion as an example of Gentile faith. He includes a saying that Luke locates elsewhere: "I say to you that many will come from the east and the west, and will take their places at the feast with Abraham, Isaac and Jacob in the kingdom of heaven" (Matthew **8:11**; Luke 13:28-29). It echoes Old Testament promises that God would gather exiled Jews, except here Gentiles are being included (Psalm 107:2-3; Isaiah 43:5-7). The kingdom of Jesus is not just for the physical descendants of Abraham; indeed, unbelieving Jews will be left outside (Matthew **8:12**). The centurion is a sign that the kingdom includes people from every nation. In Mark 6:6 Jesus is "amazed" at the "lack of faith" in his home town; here he is "amazed" at a foreigner's faith—a faith that surpasses anything he has so far encountered in Israel (Matthew **8:10**). Matthew is trailing the climax of his Gospel: the call to go to the nations (28:18-20). Among the nations, we can expect to find "great faith".

If you're a Gentile, then here you are in the story of Jesus. We, too, can join the feast—just like the centurion and his servant. The centurion recognises that he's unworthy and therefore without any claim on Jesus (**8:8**)—but the kingdom of Jesus is a kingdom of grace.

1.3 - Healing Many: A Welcome for All

The leper was healed "immediately" (**v 3**). The centurion's servant was healed "at that moment" (**v 13**). Now Peter's mother-in-law begins "to wait on him" without any need for recuperation (**v 15**). The authority of Jesus is complete in the sense that his word fully accomplishes what he commands (**v 16**)—and his authority is complete in its coverage, for he healed "all who were ill".

Then Matthew adds a word of explanation: "This was to fulfil what was spoken through the prophet Isaiah: 'He took up our infirmities and bore our diseases'" (**v 17**). It reinforces Matthew's concern to portray Jesus as the one who fulfils the Old Testament. It's a quote from Isaiah 53, where Isaiah promises that the servant of the Lord will **justify** many by bearing their sins in their place. Jesus can heal not simply because he has power but also because he will lay down his power at the cross.

Sickness is a symptom of humanity's sin. It's not that a particular sickness is caused by a particular sin (as Jesus himself makes clear in

John 9). But, as a result of humanity's fall, the world is under a curse that includes sickness and disasters. So sickness can only be ultimately addressed by dealing with its underlying cause: sin. As Jesus is addressing sickness in Capernaum, Matthew uses the quote from Isaiah to suggest that Jesus will deal with sin at Calvary. A touch cleanses a man with leprosy but makes Jesus unclean. A touch restores Peter's mother-in-law but infects Jesus. Jesus is taking up our infirmities. Searles writes, "Jesus is the one who brings this restorative reign of God, but he will do it through being 'pierced for our transgressions ... crushed for our iniquities' (Isaiah 53:5)" (*Matthew: One Greater than Solomon*, p. 15).

Counting the Cost: A Welcome That Demands Complete Allegiance

A welcome for outsiders, for Gentiles, for all—this is the glorious grace of the kingdom of Jesus. But Jesus then reminds us that following him can be costly.

It seems that Jesus wants to get away from the crowd (Matthew **8:18**). Perhaps Jesus senses that people want his blessing but not Jesus himself. They want to marvel at his authority over sickness, but they don't want to accept his authority over their own lives.

"Teacher, I will follow you wherever you go," says a teacher of the law (**v 19**). Maybe it's a declaration of loyalty, or maybe the man is saying that Jesus can't shake him off so easily. Either way, he's reminded of what following Jesus involves. Jesus isn't on the road to a palace. In fact, Jesus has no home at all to which he is heading (**v 20**). To follow Jesus doesn't guarantee earthly blessings. Indeed, we're to live as exiles on earth because our home is in heaven (Hebrews 11:13-16).

Another potential follower asks if he might delay following Jesus until he's buried his father (Matthew **8:21**). It's possible that the man's father hasn't yet died and he wants to postpone following Jesus until he's free from family duties. But it's more likely that Jesus is responding to the man's ambivalence with an exaggerated declaration: "Let the [spiritually] dead bury their own [physically] dead" (**v 22**). Jesus isn't literally banning participation in funerals any more than he expected us literally to gouge out our eyes in 5:29. His aim is to claim our allegiance, even over family obligations (10:34-37).

Are there ways in which you're putting off following Jesus or evading aspects of obedience? You can't pick and choose the teaching of Jesus. His call is all or nothing.

2.1 - Calming the Storm: Authority over the Natural World

The next three miracles demonstrate the complete authority of Jesus over (1) the natural world, (2) the spiritual world, and (3) sin (**8:23 – 9:8**). Having introduced the theme of discipleship in **8:18-22**, Matthew, in recording these miracles, also describes how people react to the authority of Jesus (a less prominent feature in the three miracles in verses 1-17). Matthew is asking us to consider how we're going to respond to Jesus.

First, with a word Jesus commands a storm, "and it was completely calm" (**v 26**). Matthew uses the word "rebuke". I can rebuke my children because I have authority over them. But if I tried to rebuke a stranger, I would be considered a ranting madman. That Jesus rebukes the storm is a sign of his authority as God's King; that the storm obeys only reinforces this.

The story ends with the disciples asking, "What kind of man is this?" (**v 27**). It's the question Matthew poses to us. What do *you* make of Jesus? Who do you think he is? It's a question that will be answered in 16:16, but along the way Matthew is giving us plenty of clues. Here he (uniquely) records the disciples crying out, "Save us!" (10:25). Jesus can save people from a storm—but Matthew wants us to wonder whether Jesus can save us from more than this. Is he in fact God's promised Saviour, the one who will save his people from sin, judgment and death? According to the Old Testament, it's only God who stills the waves (Psalm 89:8-13; 107:23-30). Yet that's precisely what Jesus has just done. Matthew leaves the obvious implication unspoken (though that will change in Matthew 14:33).

Jesus declares, "You of little faith, why are you so afraid?" (**8:26**). Mark and Luke include this statement *after* the storm has been stilled, but Matthew places it in the *midst* of the storm. The choice is between fear and faith. "I will follow you," declared the teacher of the law in **verse 19**. Now the disciples have "followed" Jesus, and following him is proving to be a stormy ride (**v 23**). Fear is a natural response to threat, but it easily spirals out of control. Its antidote is faith in the care of Jesus. The phrase translated "furious storm" in **verse 24** is literally "great earthquake". It's the phrase used by Matthew at the resurrection when Jesus awakes from the sleep of death to declare, "Do not be afraid" (28:2, 10). When our world begins to shake, our hope is in the one who has conquered death. Only in Matthew's Gospel is this statement directed to "you of little faith" (**8:26**). It's an echo of 6:30-31, where the way God clothes the flowers reminds us that we don't need to worry about what we'll eat or wear. The way Jesus stills the storm reminds us that we don't need to fear the storms of life.

Fear is a natural response to threat. Its antidote is faith in the care of Jesus.

2.2 - The Demon-Possessed Men: Authority over the Spiritual World

In their Gospels, Mark and Luke focus on only one violent demon-possessed man in the Gadarenes (Mark 5:1-20; Luke 8:26-39). But, as he does elsewhere, Matthew tells the story of *two* men (Matthew **8:28**; see also 9:27-31; 20:29-34). In other respects, though, Matthew pares down this story to focus on the complete authority of Jesus over the spiritual realm. Both the physical and spiritual worlds were created through Jesus and are subject to his power. The interaction with the herd of pigs highlights this; the demons can only act with his permission. It's too much for the townsfolk: "They preferred pigs to persons, swine to the Saviour" (Carson, p. 219). So they beg Jesus to leave just as the demons begged Jesus to be allowed to leave ("begged" and "pleaded" in **8:31** and **34** of the NIV translation are the same word in the original Greek). These people are Gentiles. Just as being Jewish doesn't guarantee inclusion (**v 12**), neither does being Gentile. What counts is faith (**v 10, 13, 26**).

One detail Matthew adds is the phrase "before the appointed time" in **verse 29**. It hints at a future, final judgment for Satan and his demons. The verse speaks of "torture", and the same word (translated "tormented" in the NIV) is used of Satan's ultimate fate in Revelation 20:10. Again Matthew is inviting us to see this incident from the life of Jesus as a foretaste of God's coming salvation. God is going to recreate the world, and in this new creation the forces of nature will no longer be a threat (the stormy sea of Matthew **8:24** will be no more, according to Revelation 21:1), and evil spirits will have been defeated. This future is previewed by Jesus in the stilling of the storm and the liberation of the demon-possessed men. The miracles of Jesus are the promise of a world-made-new for all who turn to him in faith.

The people who are dying can rule the dying world (Matthew **8:22**). Jesus invites us to be part of his kingdom of life—the new age that's already dawning in his ministry. Indeed, this chapter fizzes with life. Touching someone with leprosy made you unclean in the same way that touching a corpse did, but the touch of Jesus restores life. Peter's mother-in-law "got up"—the word used for Christ's resurrection in 28:6-7; and she rose from "lying in bed"—a biblical image of death (**8:14-15**; see 9:24). The two demon-possessed men are liberated from life in "the tombs" (**8:28**). The chapter starts with a man who "knelt before him and said, 'Lord" (**v 2**; see also 9:18; 15:25). The word "knelt" is the word translated "worship" in 28:17. It's the response Matthew wants us to make as we see our life-giving Saviour-King.

Questions for reflection

1. Which of the ways in which Jesus performs an act of recreation with his words in this section most resonates with you? Why is that, do you think?
2. "Are there ways in which you're putting off following Jesus or evading aspects of obedience? You can't pick and choose the teaching of Jesus. His call is all or nothing" (p. 77). How do you answer this challenge?
3. What storms of life are you currently facing, and what difference does it make to know that Jesus is taking care of you in and through them?

PART TWO

2.3 - A Paralysed Man: Authority to Forgive

Perhaps you can remember this story from Sunday school, with all the drama of pieces of ceiling falling on Jesus until there's a hole large enough to lower the paralysed man through. Except that Matthew leaves all this out. As he so often does, he focuses in on what really matters: "The Son of Man has authority on earth to forgive sins" (**9:6**).

Jesus has referred to himself as "the Son of Man" already in 8:20. At one level it's a colloquial way of referring to a human being—the son of a human being is a human being. It's with this sense that God repeatedly addresses the prophet Ezekiel as "son of man" (Ezekiel 2:1, among many other places). But "son of man" has another, bigger Old Testament echo. Daniel records a dream in which "one like a son of man" is given everlasting authority by God over all nations (Daniel 7:13-14). So when Jesus describes himself as "the Son of Man" (as he often does in the Gospels), he's making a big claim for those with ears to hear it. He's claiming to be the one whose kingdom will supersede all other kingdoms.

Today, as we read about the healing of the paralysed man, we're shocked that Jesus ignores the man's obvious physical need and instead speaks to his spiritual need (Matthew **9:2**). "Empty stomachs don't have ears," we tell one another. But Jesus thinks escaping eternal judgment is more important than escaping a lifetime of physical pain.

Yet this is not what shocks those in the room (**v 3**). Forgiving sin is God's **prerogative**. So for Jesus to declare the man forgiven is to act as God—and that's blasphemy: unless, of course, Jesus really is Immanuel, God with us. Matthew tells us that Jesus knew their thoughts (**v 4**), and so he demonstrated his authority over sin by demonstrating his authority over sickness, which is a physical manifestation of sin's impact on humanity (**v 5**). He tells the paralysed man to get up, and the man gets up (**v 6-7**). "Get up" is the same word Matthew uses to describe Jesus rising from the dead (28:6). The ultimate proof of Christ's authority to forgive will be his own resurrection. The crowd exemplifies how we should respond: we should praise God for giving this authority to Jesus (**9:8**).

Calling Matthew: A Kingdom of Grace

Here the human author of the Gospel enters his own story (**v 9**): Matthew tells his own story as part of Christ's story. (Mark and Luke call him "Levi", but it seems to be the same person.) Not that Matthew is claiming a leading part or a glamorous role. His appearance is for the purpose of spotlighting the grace of God in Christ.

There's a lesson here for our own witness. Telling the story of how Jesus has saved us and changed us is a powerful way of sharing the gospel. The key thing is to ensure that the spotlight falls on Jesus and his grace. We need to ensure that our story nestles within Christ's story. Think about how you could tell Christ's story by telling your story—and to whom.

Matthew is a tax collector—which means he's a collaborator with the Roman army. Gentiles have occupied God's land, and Matthew is funding their cause, and that makes him a traitor to the nation and an enemy of God. But when Jesus says, "Follow me", Matthew immediately leaves his old way of life behind. Matthew gives us no clue to his state of mind and no indication of his reasons for following Jesus, but, as the 20th-century pastor and martyr Dietrich Bonhoeffer describes...

> "It is Jesus who calls, and because it is Jesus, Levi follows at once. This encounter is a testimony to the absolute, direct, and unaccountable authority of Jesus."
>
> (*The Cost of Discipleship*, p. 61-62)

Matthew then throws a party for Jesus and invites his friends, including "many tax collectors and sinners" (**v 10**). The religious leaders are outraged (**v 11**): how can Jesus eat with such obviously sinful people?

Jesus' response is to say that welcoming sinners is central to his mission: "I have not come to call the righteous, but sinners" (**v 13**). It would be crazy for a doctor to refuse to treat the sick because she disapproved of sickness! Physically ill people need a doctor, and spiritually ill people need Jesus (**v 12**). The reason why Pharisees don't come to Jesus is not because they're genuinely "righteous" but because they won't acknowledge their need.

Matthew includes a quote from Hosea 6:6 (which Mark and Luke leave out): "But go and learn what this means: 'I desire mercy, not sacrifice'" (Matthew **9:13**). "Go and learn" was a **rabbinic** formula, which Jesus co-opts in an ironic fashion, since the Pharisees prided themselves on their knowledge of Scripture. In Hosea 6, God lamented the fact that his people's love had disappeared "like the morning mist". They performed their religious duties (offering sacrifices), but the love they professed was empty. What God really wants are people who show mercy to others because they've *received* mercy from God. Tax collectors are like a litmus test of our hearts. Today it might be addicts or **prodigals**. Are you delighted when a notorious sinner receives God's blessing? Or are you shocked that they should so easily be forgiven?

> There's a place for both feasting and fasting in the Christian life.

This meal at Matthew's house is a powerful embodiment of the mission of Jesus. Jesus is eating with God's enemies because they're welcome in his kingdom. The fact is that, having rebelled against God, we've all become enemies of God (Colossians 1:21-22). Yet anyone can be reconciled to God through faith in Christ. This is the amazing grace of God. Our meals, too, can be part of the mission of Jesus as we embody God's grace in the welcome we extend to those in need. Like Matthew, we can invite people to meet Jesus around the table.

Questioned About Fasting: A Kingdom of Joy

The questioning of Jesus continues. This time the disciples of John the Baptist ask Jesus why his disciples don't fast (Matthew **9:14**). Fasting was a sign of repentance, and John had called people to repent in readiness for the coming of the Lord (3:1-3). So, by not fasting, it seems, the disciples of Jesus either don't believe the Lord is coming or don't think they need to repent. But Jesus gives a third option: the Lord has already come! A wedding party can't really get going until the bridegroom arrives (**9:15**). But once the bridegroom comes, it's time to celebrate and feast (**v 10**). The picture of a bridegroom was a particularly appropriate image for John's disciples, since John had presented himself as the "best man" who was awaiting Jesus the true Bridegroom (John 3:29; see also Isaiah 54:5-6; 62:4-5; Hosea 2:16-20). In the next story, a woman touches the hem of Jesus' cloak: an act which functions as a marriage request in Ruth 3:9 (Ezekiel 16:8). Jesus is the husband who has come to woo his bride and offer her protection (Ephesians 5:25-33).

But Jesus then adds, "The time will come when the bridegroom will be taken from them; then they will fast" (Matthew **9:15**). This may be a reference to the time between his death and resurrection, but it's more likely to refer to the time between his **ascension** and return. Now there's a place for both feasting in the Christian life (especially at the **Lord's Supper**), because Jesus has come, *and* fasting, because Jesus is yet to return.

The key point in these stories is that God is doing something new in history. Though God's kingdom hasn't yet come in glory, it has come secretly in grace (as we'll see in Matthew 13). The new age has begun because Jesus has come. Jesus illustrates this point with two mini-parables: you can't patch an old garment with new cloth, and you can't fill old wineskins with new wine (**9:16-17**). In both cases, two things are incompatible. In the same way, the coming of God's kingdom is not compatible with the status quo. The new thing that God is doing in Christ is going to burst apart the religion of the temple, along with every other religion and ideology. Becoming a Christian doesn't mean making a few adjustments to your old way of life; it creates a whole new way of living. As Paul will say in 2 Corinthians 5:17, "If anyone is in Christ, the new creation has come: the old has gone, the new is here!"

3.1 - A Sick Woman and a Dead Girl: A Kingdom of Life

Under the Law of Moses, menstruating women were temporarily unclean, and to touch a menstruating woman was to become unclean (Leviticus 15:25-33). It was a picture of the polluting effects of sin and the need to exclude anything tainted by sin from among God's people. But the woman in this story has been bleeding continuously for twelve years (Matthew **9:20**). That means she's been socially excluded for twelve years. She embodies the exile of Israel, experiencing a kind of living death. Alongside her, Matthew places the story of a girl who is literally dead (**v 18-19**). Any return to life for her seems laughable (**v 23-24**).

But everything changes with Jesus. His touch imparts cleansing to the woman, liberating her from the living death of her exclusion (**v 21-22**). And his touch raises the girl from death, just as one might raise a sleeper from their bed (**v 24-25**). The kingdom of Jesus is a kingdom of life. More than that, it's a kingdom of life in the face of sin and death. This is why Jesus can say to the paralysed man and the bleeding woman, and you, "Take heart, son ... Take heart, daughter" (**v 2, 22**).

3.2, 3 - The Blind and Mute: A Kingdom of Light

Jesus meets two blind men, and again he heals them with a touch. As with the bleeding woman (**v 22**), Jesus highlights the need for faith, first by asking if they believe (**v 28**) and then by declaring, "According to your faith let it be done to you" (**v 29**).

For these two men, light has come, both physically and spiritually. They're the first people in the Gospel to recognise Jesus as the "Son of David" (**v 27**; see 1:1). But light has not come for the Pharisees. When Jesus heals a man who is a demon-possessed and mute (**9:32-33**), the Pharisees declare Jesus to be in league with Satan (**v 34**). In them darkness still reigns, blinding them to the light of Christ's kingdom. The words "according to your faith let it be done to you" are still ringing in our ears (**v 29**), but they take on a darker meaning when people lack faith.

Jesus warns the men who were previously blind not to tell anyone what's happened to them (**v 30**). Unsurprisingly, perhaps, they do the very opposite and the news spreads throughout the region (**v 26, 31**). Why does Jesus give this apparently unrealistic command here, as he did in 8:4? The answer is that Jesus doesn't want people to acclaim him as God's Messiah until they realise he's the Messiah who must suffer and die for his people. (This may also be why in **9:28** Jesus heals them indoors, away from the crowds.) Then and now, people want someone who can cure their sicknesses, increase their wealth and liberate them from oppression. But Jesus has a bigger agenda: to forgive sin and grant eternal life by dying in place of his people (**v 2, 25**). There can be no true preaching of Jesus that does not include the message of the cross.

Workers for the Harvest

Verse 35 echoes 4:23. In between these literary markers, Matthew has given us a snapshot of Jesus' ministry in Galilee. This ministry, says **9:36**, has been driven by Christ's compassion. He sees people as "harassed and helpless, like sheep without a shepherd". It's an allusion to Ezekiel 34, where the corruption of Israel's leaders left God's people scattered and vulnerable. In Ezekiel, God promised both that he himself would shepherd his people and that he would send a new King David. Matthew wants us to see Jesus both as God shepherding his people and as the new David. Jesus is your Shepherd-King.

But Jesus also adds that "the harvest is plentiful but the workers are few. Ask the Lord of the harvest, therefore, to send out workers into his harvest field" (Matthew **9:37-38**). Matthew has been describing the mission of Jesus, and Jesus now shares the task of mission with us, his people. The encouragement is that, if we "sow" by proclaiming the gospel, God will use our words to produce a harvest. The challenge is that what limits this harvest is a lack of willing workers. The answer is a call to prayer. How will you respond to that call to pray today?

It's worth pausing to see who is welcoming the coming of the kingdom of Jesus. A Roman centurion and his servant; a fisherman's mother-in-law; two demon-possessed men from an area with unclean pigs; a tax-collector and his friends; an unclean woman; a dead girl; the blind and the mute. This bore no relation to the guestlist of the religious leaders! Outsiders and outcasts, enemies and strangers, notorious sinners, the troubled and broken, the sick and unclean. This is divine grace in action. Who's on your guestlist?

Questions for reflection

1. Again, reflect on which of the ways in which Jesus performs an act of recreation with his words in this section most resonates with you, and why.
2. With whom could you share your story in a way that shares Christ's story this week?
3. How could you maintain a pattern of both feasting and fasting in your life?

6. THE AUTHORITY OF THE MESSIANIC PEOPLE

Matthew 9 ends with Jesus looking on the crowds with compassion and inviting his disciples to pray for more workers (9:36-38). In chapter 10 he **commissions** the Twelve to be those workers.

The Beginning of a Renewed Nation

Jesus has been "healing every disease and illness" (9:35). Now he gives his disciples "authority to drive out impure spirits and to heal every disease and illness" (**10:1**). Their message is to be his message (**v 7**; 4:17). In other words, the disciples are to continue and expand the mission of Jesus. They're to pass on what they've received, because the blessing of Jesus is not divided when shared—it is multiplied (**10:8**).

Jesus gives his disciples his authority (**v 1**). In his ministry on earth Jesus gave us a foretaste of his coming kingdom. A world without mourning, crying or pain (Revelation 21:4) is anticipated in feeding the hungry, healing the sick, raising the dead and casting out demons. Jesus reigning on earth gives us a picture of Jesus reigning in eternity. We now have that foretaste. So, while miracles can and do happen today, it shouldn't worry us if we don't see miracles on the same scale today as in Jesus' day.

Matthew chooses this moment to list the twelve disciples (Matthew **10:2-4**). The number is significant. The nation of Israel was made up of twelve tribes, the descendants of the twelve sons of Jacob (or

"Israel", as God renamed him in Genesis 32:28). So, by appointing twelve apostles, Jesus is signalling the beginning of a renewed Israel. As we saw in Matthew 3 – 5, Jesus is forming a renewed people based not on ethnicity but on faith in him.

Mission to the Old Nation

What then of the existing people of Israel? The answer is that Jesus now sends the Twelve "to the lost sheep of Israel" (Matthew **10:6**)—"the sheep without a shepherd" of 9:36. They're to be gathered into the renewed Israel centred on Jesus.

This is a chapter with lessons for contemporary mission. But not everything here applies today because this missionary campaign belonged to a specific moment in the story of salvation. As Jesus prepares to head to Jerusalem, he's giving Israel as a nation an opportunity to acknowledge him as their national Messiah. This explains the strange instructions Jesus gives to his disciples.

- *The disciples are to go only to towns in Israel (**10:6-8**).* Why are Gentiles excluded, especially when Jesus himself has already healed the servant of a Gentile centurion and visited a Gentile region (8:13, 28)? The answer is that the time for Gentile mission will come (28:18-20), but for now Israel is the priority.
- *The disciples are not to take spare money or clothes (**10:9-10**).* That's because this mission campaign is a short-term project. Events will accelerate to a climax in Jerusalem. This mission has a use-by date.
- *The disciples are not to stay where they're not immediately welcome (**v 11-14**).* Today missionaries often take time to get to know a new culture, build relationships and gain credibility. All this takes time—but time is running out for this mission because in a few months Jesus will enter Jerusalem as Israel's King, and people will have to decide where they stand. So there's no time for the patient work of relationship-building. If people show no

interest, then the disciples are to move on (**v 11-13**). Pious Jews re-entering Israel from Gentile territory might shake off the dust of their feet to symbolically rid themselves of the pollution of pagan nations. To do so *within* Israel was to denounce a town as godless (**v 14**). **Verse 15** spotlights what's at stake: those who reject Jesus will suffer a fate worse than that of Sodom and Gomorrah (Genesis 19)—a point Jesus expands in Matthew 11:20-24.

All this will change on the **day of Pentecost**. Then mission moves into a different mode. The Jewish people remain a priority: in the book of Acts, mission starts in Jerusalem and Judea, and when Paul goes to a new city, he starts in the synagogue. But the mission of the church soon spills out to the Gentiles. And now missionaries are in it for the long haul. Indeed, in Luke 22:35-36 Jesus himself rescinds the instructions in Matthew **10:5-15** (Luke 9:1-6; 10:1-12). So this section of Matthew is not a blueprint for mission today. Nevertheless, it does remind us that the church has grown out of the Old Testament people of God. Gentile believers have been **grafted** into a tree with roots stretching back to Abraham (Romans 11:11-24). These verses also remind us that, like Jesus, we should be concerned for the salvation of Jewish people.

Be Braced for Rejection

Matthew **10:11-13** implies that the disciples have a reasonable prospect of a warm welcome in some locations. But **verses 13-15** suggest this will not always be the case, and the prospect of rejection comes to the fore in the remainder of the chapter. The disciples may have authority over spirits and sickness (**v 1**), but this doesn't make them immune to suffering.

When mission goes badly, it's easy to assume the problem is with us, and it's good to ask whether we've been insensitive or arrogant. But more often our message is rejected through no fault of our own. Jesus prepares his disciples for opposition so that when it comes, they're not alarmed or disturbed. The disciples will be "like sheep among wolves" (**v 16**); that is, they'll encounter people who are intent on their harm. We're to be wise to people's underhand ways ("be as shrewd as snakes"), but we're not to adopt those underhand ways ourselves (be "as innocent as doves").

> We're to be wise to people's underhand ways but we're not to adopt those underhand ways.

While **verses 17-20** apply to the temporary mission to ethnic Israel upon which the disciples are about to embark, they seem to look beyond this to the ongoing mission of the church. There's no indication that the Twelve were brought before "governors and kings" at this stage, and they've been explicitly told to avoid "Gentiles" (**v 18**). The key point is that we can expect the Holy Spirit to speak through us (**v 20**). This is true of all evangelism: "We are therefore Christ's ambassadors, as though God were making his appeal through us" (2 Corinthians 5:20). But it's particularly helpful to remember this when we're defending our faith in a hostile context (Matthew **10:19-20**). Jesus describes the Holy Spirit as "the Spirit of your Father" (**v 20**). It's a lovely reminder that believers are part of the divine family, with God as our Father and Jesus as our brother. But, as Jesus says in **verses 21-22**, this new identity often brings conflict with our biological families.

Verse 23 again reminds us that the mission of the Twelve here is a short-term campaign. "When you are persecuted in one place, flee to another" is another variation on **verses 11-14**. Then Jesus says, "You will not finish going through the towns of Israel before the Son of Man comes". He's talking about his coming to Jerusalem as Israel's King (21:1-11). This is the moment when Israel as a nation must decide what they will do with their King. That decision will set in motion a chain of events ending with the destruction of the temple in AD 70. People's rejection of the disciples reflects a deeper rejection of Jesus (**10:24-25**).

Do Not Be Afraid

So far it's not been the most motivational missionary call! The disciples are being invited to a life of rejection, flogging, arrest, betrayal, hatred and persecution. But **verses 26-31** begin and end with the words, "Do not be afraid". Why not?

1. *Because the message will be heard (**v 26-27**).* These verses could refer to the exposure of conspiracies against God's people, but similar language is used in Mark 4:21-23 and Luke 8:16-17, where it's linked to the image of Christians as lamps shining in the darkness (which Matthew uses in 5:15). In Matthew's version, what Jesus speaks in private is what the disciples will declare publicly. In Luke's version what the disciples speak in private (perhaps for fear of persecution) will become well-known. In both cases the point is that, despite all opposition, the message of Jesus will spread. No matter what the world throws at the church, our mission will succeed.

2. *Because we're in God's care, now and for ever (**10:28-31**).* The worst thing people can do to us is to take our lives. But for Christians, death is the gateway to eternal life. While **verse 28** is not saying that the soul is more important than the body, it is saying that eternal life is more important than our present temporary lives. So don't fear those who can destroy your physical bodies (merely taking away this temporary life); instead fear the one who can destroy your spiritual self (taking away eternal life)—except you don't need to fear this one because he's "your Father" (**v 29**). In 6:26, the birds taught us that God cares for his world and even more so for his children. Now Jesus applies the same truth in the midst of persecution. If you're facing hostility for your faith, this is Christ's promise: *You will not fall to the ground outside your Father's care* (**10:29**). The hostility may not go away, and it could even end in death. But God is in every detail (**v 30**), you are a precious to him (**v 31**), and he will bring you safely home to glory.

Sharing the Mission of Jesus

What links **verses 32-42** is the tight association between Jesus, his people and their mission.

1. *If we welcome Jesus, Jesus will welcome us (**v 32-39**).* There's a chain in **verse 32**: welcome Christ → welcomed by Christ → welcomed by God. In other words, if we put our faith in Christ, then Christ counts us as one of his people, and being connected to Christ in this way means God will accept us eternally. The chain works in the opposite direction in **verse 33**: disown Christ → disowned by Christ → disowned by God. Life-giving faith is more than merely going forward at an **evangelistic** event. Jesus adds the words "before others" in both these verses. The context is persecution, and the words "before others" imply a public **confession** of faith, even when this involves some kind of threat. This is a profession of faith that counts the cost and accepts Jesus as Lord as well as Saviour.

   Verses 34-36 give us a flavour of what welcoming Jesus might involve. "Do not suppose that I have come to bring peace to the earth," says Jesus (**v 34**). Of course, in one sense bringing peace was exactly what Jesus came to do, but the peace he created is between God and humanity (Colossians 1:19-20). Meanwhile, on earth he often brings division. There's no neutrality with Jesus: you're either for him or against him; you either accept him as Lord or reject him as Lord. That inevitably means conflict between Christians and non-Christians, even within families (Matthew **10:35-36**, quoting Micah 7:6). Today, converts from secular families may be estranged from family members while converts from other religions may experience violence and even death. Families' loyalties can prevent people choosing Jesus, but Jesus has a sword that frees people from these bonds (Matthew **10:34**).

   Christians are to do their best to honour their families and live at peace with people. After all, Jesus himself says, "Blessed are the peacemakers" (5:9) and tells us to be at peace with homes that welcome us (**10:13**). "If it is possible, as far as it depends on you," says Romans 12:18, "live at peace with everyone". But sometimes it's not possible. Christians now have a different allegiance with different priorities, and that's going to lead to clashes. We try to avoid them. We flex to fit round family members. But when push comes to shove, "we must obey God rather than human beings!" (Acts 5:29). Jesus puts it like this: "Anyone who loves their father or mother more than me is not worthy of me; anyone who loves their son or daughter more than me is not worthy of me" (Matthew **10:37**). Much of the time we're not forced to choose between Jesus and our families, but when we are, we must choose Jesus. We can feel guilty when relationships with unbelieving children or parents become strained. But **verses 34-37** suggest some level of estrangement is inevitable. We experience this as loss because it is a loss, but it's a loss we bear for Christ's sake.

To follow a crucified King is to embrace a cross-shaped life (**v 38**). This is the first reference to the cross in Matthew's Gospel, and it's a reference to the cross we bear. This call comes with a warning and a promise. Jesus says, "Whoever finds their life [in the sense of getting on in life even when that means putting ourselves or our family before Jesus] will lose it, and whoever loses their life for my sake [in the sense of losing out because of our commitment to Jesus] will find it" (**v 39**).

2. *We welcome Jesus by welcoming his people (**v 40-42**).* Jesus set out a chain of connections in **verse 32**: welcome Christ —> welcomed by Christ —> welcomed by God. But how do we welcome Jesus, especially now he's no longer around on earth? The answer is by welcoming his people: "Anyone who welcomes you welcomes me" (**v 40**). In **verse 42** our attitude to Christ's people is a litmus test of our attitude to Christ himself. If we welcome God's people, especially when they're in need, then Christ will reward us by welcoming us into his eternal kingdom.

We also welcome Jesus by welcoming the *message* of his people. Jesus speaks of welcoming a prophet—someone who speaks on God's behalf (**v 41**). In this sense, every time Christians speak of Christ to unbelievers, they fulfil a prophetic role. The point is we accept Christ by accepting the message of Christ spoken by the people of Christ. "A prophet's reward" and "a righteous person's reward" could be the reward they receive (which those who welcome them share) or the reward they bestow (which those who welcome them receive). Either way, the reward is the same: Christ himself, and the righteousness that is found in him. Even though we're in the wrong, God declares us to be in the right when we accept the message of Jesus. That's because Jesus is the "Righteous One" who "suffered once for sins, the righteous for the unrighteous" (Acts 3:14; 1 Peter 3:18). So now the chain has been extended: we welcome Christ's people and their message → we welcome Christ → we're welcomed by Christ → we're welcomed by God.

Matthew 10 began with Jesus commissioning his disciples to do the task he himself has been doing (9:35; **10:1**), and it ends with Jesus declaring "anyone who welcomes you welcomes me" (**v 40**). Our mission is Christ's mission. When you share your faith or care for those in need, Christ is speaking and acting through you to reach a lost and needy world.

Questions for reflection

How has this section reshaped…

1. your view of what mission is and is like?
2. your view of your own place in Jesus' mission?
3. your approach to who you spend time with and how you speak to them?

PART TWO

In Matthew 10 Jesus prepared his disciples for opposition and rejection (10:16-31). But the opposition the disciples will experience reflects a deeper rejection of Jesus himself. "*On my account* you will be brought before governors and kings," he said in **verse 18**—"You will be hated by everyone *because of me*" (**v 22**, emphasis added). The followers of Jesus need not be surprised at this rejection because Jesus himself has been rejected (**v 24-25**). Speaking at this point in time, Jesus points back to the accusation in 9:34: that he's one with the prince of demons (another term for Satan). But the rejection of Jesus comes to its terrible climax at the cross. Those who follow a crucified King can expect to live cross-shaped lives. As the 4th-century **Church Father** Hilary of Poitiers put it:

> "Knowledge of things to come is very edifying for acquiring tolerance, especially if our own will to endure has been moulded by another's example. Our Lord, who is eternal light and the leader of all believers and the founder of immortality, sent consolations in advance to his disciples for the sufferings they would endure. This was so that no disciple would think himself above his teacher or above the Lord, when in reality he is a servant." (*On Matthew*, 10.15; cited in Simonetti, *Matthew 1 – 13, Ancient Commentary on Scriptures*, p. 203)

So it is that in chapters 11 – 12 we begin to see the rejection of Jesus stepping up a level. Chapter 11 marks the beginning of a new section—**11:1** contains one of the phrases Matthew uses to end a section of teaching and begin a new section of stories: "After Jesus had finished instructing his twelve disciples..." We've seen the authority of Jesus in chapters 8 – 9. We've seen that authority passed on to his disciples in chapter 10. Now we begin to see the authority of Jesus being resisted, just as chapter 10 anticipated.

Jesus Is Questioned by John the Baptist

John the Baptist was the last of the Old Testament prophets (**11:13**). And, like other Old Testament prophets, he saw the coming of God's kingdom as one event involving the redemption of God's people and the judgment of God's enemies. "The axe has been laid to the root of the trees, and every tree that does not produce good fruit will be cut down and thrown into the fire," he had said (3:10). In other words, judgment was about to fall. But judgment hasn't fallen (**11:2**). In fact, it must have felt as though the only person being judged was John himself, because he had been thrown into prison by **Herod Antipas.** John is the new Elijah (**v 14**) and, like the old Elijah in 1 Kings 19, he's demoralised. So he sends a delegation to ask Jesus straight: "Are you the one who is to come?" (Matthew **11:3**). The implication is clear: *This is not what I expected the kingdom of God to be like. Where's the axe? Where's the fire? Where's the justice and judgment?*

Jesus replies by pointing to his miracles as signs of his divine authority and providing an exhortation to keep trusting him (**v 4-6**). It's a strong argument. But there's something missing; a puzzle remains. Jesus' answer alludes to two passages from Isaiah:

> "Strengthen the feeble hands,
> steady the knees that give way;
> say to those with fearful hearts,
> 'Be strong, do not fear;
> your God will come,
> he will come with vengeance;
> with divine retribution
> he will come to save you.'
> Then will the eyes of the blind be opened
> and the ears of the deaf unstopped.
> Then will the lame leap like a deer,
> and the mute tongue shout for joy." (Isaiah 35:3-6)

> "The Spirit of the Sovereign LORD is on me,
> because the LORD has anointed me

to proclaim good news to the poor.
He has sent me to bind up the broken-hearted,
to proclaim freedom for the captives
and release from darkness for the prisoners,
to proclaim the year of the LORD favour
and the day of vengeance of our God." (Isaiah 61:1-2)

Jesus says, "The blind receive sight, the lame walk, those who have leprosy are cleansed, the deaf hear, the dead are raised, and the good news is proclaimed to the poor" (Matthew **11:5**). The echoes of Isaiah 35 and 61 are clear. But notice what Jesus has left out; Jesus is fulfilling so much that Isaiah promised, but something is missing. God has not come in "divine retribution" and "vengeance" as Isaiah promised. We're left asking: what's happened to God's judgment?

It's a question that Jesus will answer when we reach Matthew 13. For now we have another beatitude: "Blessed is anyone who does not stumble on account of me" (**11:6**). It's a call to John to continue trusting in Jesus—even though John languishes in prison. But it's also a call to the readers of Matthew's Gospel to continue trusting in Jesus—even though we may face rejection.

Jesus Is Rejected Along with John the Baptist

Jesus takes the opportunity to speak to the crowd about John the Baptist. John was clearly a prophet for he declared God's word boldly. He wasn't swayed by public opinion like "a reed swayed by the wind" (**v 7**), nor did he kowtow to vested interests or speak for personal gain (**v 8**). No, he was the real deal (**v 9**). It's worth asking ourselves whether we ever adjust what we say in evangelism to avoid confrontation with our culture. Are we like a reed swayed by the wind?

But John wasn't simply a prophet; he was the final prophet (**v 11-13**). He was the one who would prepare for the coming of the Lord (as we saw in 3:1-6). John is the voice in the wilderness promised in Isaiah 40:3 and Malachi 3:1 (Matthew **11:9-10**), and the new Elijah promised in Malachi 4:5 (Matthew **11:14**).

John really is the forerunner, and therefore the kingdom of God really is coming—despite John's doubts. This means that, although John is the greatest prophet, the least in the kingdom is greater than John, because the least in the kingdom has the privilege of seeing the fulfilment of the prophetic promises in Jesus (**v 11**).

Verse 12 could be translated as saying that the kingdom of heaven "has been subjected to violence" (NIV; ESV) or "has been forcefully advancing" (NIV footnote). It's probably saying that, from the ministry of John into the present ministry of Jesus, the kingdom has been coming in power (as the miracles of Jesus demonstrate), but violent people oppose it. We've seen the kingdom advancing in power in chapters 8 – 9, and we're about to see it being forcefully resisted in chapters 11 – 12.

Attitudes towards both John and Jesus are evidence of this opposition to God's kingdom, albeit in contrasting ways. Jesus likens his generation to children who find a dance tune too jolly and a dirge too sad (**11:16-17**). They're looking for reasons to find fault with whatever tune they hear. In a similar way, the people are criticising John for being too austere and then criticising Jesus for being too indulgent (**v 18-19**). They will not recognise the coming of God's kingdom because that calls for repentance, and so they find any fault they can with those who proclaim its coming. "But wisdom is proved right by her deeds," says Jesus (**v 19**): who is right about the kingdom will be seen in what people do and how that is judged by God. Or perhaps Jesus himself is Wisdom **personified**, and his deeds will vindicate his claims.

Jesus then gives us a preview of divine judgment. He name-checks the towns which have seen his miracles (**v 20**). Not only will be they be judged, but they will be judged severely—even more severely than some of the most notorious cities in history (**v 21-24**; **verse 23** alludes to Isaiah 14:13-15). We're not told what the different degrees of judgment will involve, but it's an indication that the final judgment will take into account what people have known of the gospel message.

These towns have no excuse for rejecting the kingdom of God, and nor do we if we've heard these same miracle stories. That's because the miracles of Jesus show us who Jesus is, just as they did for those who first witnessed them.

Jesus Reveals God to "Little Children"

Matthew **11:25-30** is a little interlude amid all the opposition as, in the context of prayer, Jesus reflects on what's happening. It provides a little commentary on the contrasting responses to Christ and his message—then and now. The kingdom of God has come. Some people are welcoming it, and some are rejecting it. What makes the difference? Is it a person's wisdom or learning? Is it the clever people who are recognising Jesus? Quite the opposite. God is hiding the truth from such people (Matthew **11:25**; 1 Corinthians 1:18-20). No one in heaven will be able to say, "I'm here because I was smart enough to figure God out" or "I'm here because I was good enough to merit my place in heaven". It's all down to God's grace, and in his grace God reveals himself to "little children" (Matthew **11:25**). It's a way of describing Christians (as we'll see in Matthew 18). Children here are a picture of helplessness. No human being can figure out God. Only the Son knows the Father—but the Son delights to share his relationship with the Father by making us children of God (**v 27**). The 19th-century Anglican bishop J.C. Ryle commented:

> "Let us watch against pride in every shape—pride of intellect, pride of wealth, pride in our own goodness, pride in our own **deserts**. Nothing is so likely to keep a man out of heaven, and prevent him seeing Christ, as pride. So long as we think we are something, we shall never be saved. Let us pray for and cultivate humility; let us seek to know ourselves aright, and to find out our place in the sight of a holy God. The beginning of the way to heaven is to feel that we are in the way to hell, and to be willing to be taught of the Spirit."
>
> (*Expository Thoughts on the Gospels: Matthew*, p. 116-117)

> Jesus doesn't simply expect our obedience; he also empowers our obedience.

Jesus then gives a lovely invitation to come and find rest in him (**v 28-30**, echoing the Lord's declaration in Exodus 33:14). The religious leaders placed the **yoke** of the law on people, and it was too much to bear (Acts 15:10). On a good day it left you "weary and burdened"; on a bad day it crushed you. Jesus, too, has a yoke. But Jesus is a gentle master, and his yoke is light. There are two reasons for the lightness of his yoke:

1. Jesus doesn't simply expect obedience from his people; he also empowers our obedience. "His yoke is no more a burden than the feathers are to a bird" (Ryle, *Expository Thoughts on the Gospels: Matthew*, p. 120).

2. We're not serving to win acceptance with Jesus or avoid his punishment. Instead, our acceptance is gifted to us in love. It's out of this acceptance that our obedience then flows.

We don't need to live in fear or work like slaves, because we've already been accepted as "little children" through the revelation of God (Matthew **11:25**).

This is an invitation to unbelievers to leave behind their **self-justification** and come as little children to find rest in God. But it continues to be an invitation to Christians. We can become weary all over again, first if we serve Jesus in our own strength, or second if we serve Jesus to prove ourselves. Then service becomes a burden, and we're robbed of our joy. We need to "learn from" Jesus (**v 29**) that we don't need to work hard to win God's approval, because we already have it in Christ and we don't need to work hard to secure our future, because our lives are safe in God's care.

Questions for reflection

1. Do you ever find that the difficulties of living as a Christian and facing rejection causes you to doubt whether Jesus is who he says he is? How can his response to John the Baptist help you when you feel that way?
1. Do you think of yourself as a "little child" in your relationship with Jesus? How does doing so both humble you and give you peace and confidence?
2. "Jesus doesn't simply expect obedience from his people; he also empowers it" (p. 102). How will this shape your thinking about obeying him today?

7. THE AUTHORITY OF THE MESSIAH REJECTED

The story so far: Jesus has come to renew God's people and establish God's kingdom. We've seen his authority over both the physical and spiritual worlds. All seems to be going well. However, there have been a few hints that opposition is possible (5:10-12; 9:3, 34; 10:16-39)—and in chapter 11, that opposition becomes a reality. Then in chapter 12, it continues to intensify.

The Subject of Tricks and Plots

The theme of rest from 11:28-30 continues into chapter 12 with two stories of conflict over the Sabbath. But the wider theme of opposition also remains. The Pharisees question Jesus in **12:2**; look for reasons to charge him in **verse 10**; and plot his death in **verse 14**.

The Pharisees challenge Jesus because his disciples pick ears of corn on the Sabbath (**v 1-2**). They're not bringing in the harvest, but just picking a few grains to eat as they walk along (much as people in the UK might pick blackberries on a Sunday afternoon walk).

Jesus reminds them of a story from the life of David (**v 3-4**). The he bread of the Presence was placed in the **tabernacle** as a picture of God's invitation to fellowship. When David was on the run, he entered the tabernacle (which only priests could do) and took this bread that had been consecrated for God's use (1 Samuel 21:1-6). Yet the Scriptures do not condemn him for this. (Perhaps Jesus and his disciples also parallel David and his men, both groups growing hungry as they fight to liberate Israel, while the Pharisees are like those who opposed David.) Jesus also reminds the Pharisees that the priests break the law by "working" on the Sabbath as they serve in the temple (Matthew **12:5**; Numbers 28:9-10), like pastors today working on a Sunday. He may particularly have in mind the renewal of the bread of the Presence on the Sabbath, since he's just mentioned this in Matthew **12:4** (see Leviticus 24:8).

In both cases, someone breaks the letter of the law to keep the spirit of the law. The Law of Moses spelt out for the Israelites what it meant to love God and people in a host of different situations. But the Pharisees made these stipulations an end in themselves rather than seeing how they shaped love for others. This is why in Matthew **12:7** Jesus again quotes Hosea 6:6 (as he did in 9:13): "I desire mercy, not sacrifice". God wants people to pursue the goal of the law (which is love) rather than simply tick religious boxes. Richard Hays says that "mercy" stands for "a form of **piety** that focuses on God's compassion toward human needs", while "sacrifice" represents "a form of piety that focuses on ritual observances" (Hays, *Echoes of Scripture in the Gospels*, p. 126). The Sabbath was a gift to people oppressed by overwork (former Egyptian slaves in the first instance), but the Pharisees had made it another burden. In contrast, Jesus offers true rest to the overburdened (Matthew 11:28).

God wants people to pursue the goal of the law (which is love) rather than simply tick religious boxes.

Something else is going on here. Jesus says, "I tell you that something greater than the temple is here ... For the Son of Man is Lord of the Sabbath" (**12:6, 8**). That "something greater" is Jesus himself. Jesus is the true temple: the "place" in whom we meet God and come to be cleansed. Jesus can interpret the law because he is the law-giver. He is the one who spoke to Moses at Mount Sinai, and he is the one who has given a new law to a new people on a new mount in Matthew 5 – 7. Jesus himself is the true Sabbath, in whom we find rest (11:28).

In **12:9-14** it happens all over again. On the Sabbath Jesus is presented with a man with a shrivelled hand (**v 9-10**). The Pharisees ask, "Is it lawful to heal on the Sabbath?" Matthew tells us they are "looking for a reason to bring charges against Jesus" (**v 10**). They clearly think it would be wrong for Jesus to heal the man because this would constitute working on the Sabbath. But Jesus highlights their hypocrisy—they would rescue a sheep on the Sabbath (giving a kind of Sabbath rest to a distressed animal), yet a person is worth far more than a sheep (**v 11-12**). They can flex the law when it suits them but won't show the love commended by the law. So Jesus heals the man (**v 13**). Matthew saves this for the end of the story to contrast it with what the Pharisees then do on the Sabbath: plot to kill Jesus (**v 14**). The Pharisees work towards death on the Sabbath because Jesus has worked life on the Sabbath. The Lord of the Sabbath keeps the Sabbath in a richer, deeper way.

Does the way you use your Sunday bring rest or is it a burden? For you? For others?

The Suffering Servant

Jesus evades their plots by withdrawing, but a large crowd follows him, and he heals those who were ill (**v 15**). Again he warns people not to tell others about him (**v 16**; see the comments on 9:30). Matthew adds an editorial comment. He says "this" fulfils the promise of a servant of the Lord in Isaiah 42:1-4. It's not exactly clear what "this" is. But the context suggests a cluster of ideas. First, Isaiah says that the servant will be empowered by the Spirit to bring justice, and Jesus is doing this through his Spirit-empowered miracles. Second, Isaiah says that the servant will nurture the bruised and broken, and Jesus has invited the weary and burdened to come him for rest. Third, Isaiah says that the servant will be "a man of suffering" who is "despised and rejected" (Isaiah 53:3), and in Matthew 11 – 12 we see Jesus being despised and rejected by the people of his day. Matthew uses the Septuagint, the Greek translation of the Scripture, in quoting from Isaiah 42:1-4, which uses "his name" instead of "his teaching" and translates "islands" as "Gentiles". This focuses the quote on Christ (whose name is Immanuel) and makes the scope of his mission more explicit (to all nations).

Accused of Being Satanic

When Jesus heals a demon-possessed man, it amazes the people (Matthew **12:22-23**), but the Pharisees accuse Jesus of using satanic power (**v 24**; 9:34; 10:25). Jesus points out the illogicality of this: why would Satan be casting out the demons who do his work (**12:25-27**)? The more obvious explanation is that the demons are **exorcised** by God's Spirit as a sign that God's kingdom has come (**v 28**). Just as you would need to overpower someone before you could plunder their possessions, so Jesus is overpowering Satan so he can liberate people from Satan's grip (**v 29**). Given this conflict between Jesus and Satan, there can be no neutrality. You must decide whether you are for Jesus or against him (**v 30**).

Jesus says that any blasphemy, even speaking against the Son of Man, will be forgiven if people turn to God in faith and repentance. What cannot be forgiven is blasphemy against the Spirit (**v 30-32**). Various explanations of this apparently unforgivable sin have been suggested, some of which have caused unnecessary fear among God's people. So let's be clear: Jesus will *never* turn away a repentant sinner. It's important to read these verses in context, and in context the unforgivable sin involves attributing the miracles of Jesus to Satan rather than to the Spirit (**v 24, 28**). A person can be forgiven their rejection of Jesus when they don't recognise who he is. Those who reject the gospel are still culpable because they "suppress the truth by their wickedness" (Romans 1:18). But they don't realise this is what they're doing, and if they turn to Christ in repentance, then they will be forgiven. But here Jesus is talking about people who *do* recognise who he is—that he's the Son of God empowered by the Spirit of God. The religious leaders had seen Jesus perform miracles through the power of the Spirit, but they had chosen to attribute those miracles to Satan. When your heart has become so hard that you reject what you know to be true, there's no way back. You've recognised Jesus to be God's way of forgiveness but then chosen to look elsewhere, and that's unforgivable because there is nowhere else to look. Such wilful unbelief eventually becomes terminal. This means that, by definition, anyone who is worried about having committed an unforgivable sin has *not* committed an unforgivable sin! R.T. France sums it up helpfully: "This saying is a wake-up call to the arrogant, not a bogey to frighten those of tender conscience" (*The Gospel of Matthew*, p. 482-483).

Just as you can tell the state of a tree by the fruit it produces (Matthew **12:33**), so you can tell the state of a person by the words they say (**v 34-35**). So when Jesus says we'll be judged according to our words, he doesn't mean that God will pick us up on every off-hand comment or ill-considered word. He's saying that if we profess that he is Lord, then we'll be saved (Romans 10:9)—but if we deny Jesus with our words, then we'll be judged by our own denials (Matthew 10:32-33).

Confronting a Wicked Generation

Some Pharisees ask for a sign (**12:38**). It's hard to imagine what else they want, given the miracles Jesus has already performed. Maybe they're after something that looks more like military victory over the Romans—they want Jesus to conform to their misplaced expectations of God's Messiah. The key thing is that they want to test Jesus. Testing God was a characteristic of the generation that came out of Egypt. Moses called them an "evil generation", and Jesus uses the same phrase for his generation (Deuteronomy 1:35; Matthew **12:39, 45**, ESV). Jesus is replaying the history of Israel—called out of Egypt, tempted in the wilderness, passing through the Jordan River, proclaiming God's law from a mountain. As he does so, Jesus remains faithful, getting it right where Israel got it wrong. But Israel is also replaying her history, and getting it wrong—again.

So Jesus sees their request as an indication of culpable scepticism (**v 39**). The only sign they'll receive is "the sign of Jonah" (**v 39-40**). Just as Jonah spent three days in the fish before being restored to life, so Jesus will spend three days in the tomb before rising again; the resurrection is the ultimate proof that Jesus is God's Messiah. Their culpability is spotlighted by two contrasts. The Gentile men of Nineveh repented at Jonah's preaching despite being notoriously wicked, and the queen of Sheba sought Solomon's wisdom despite having to travel from "the ends of the earth" (**v 41-42**). Meanwhile the Pharisees have the Word and Wisdom of God on their doorstep—and still they do not repent.

The story in **verses 43-45** of an impure spirit who leaves a person only to return with seven more spirits amplifies the declaration in **verse 30** that there is no neutrality. Someone who has been exorcised by Jesus can't assume they are safe if they don't commit themselves to Jesus. This person personifies the warning to "this wicked generation" (**v 45**). An encounter with Jesus will leave people worse off if they don't respond with faith. The same principle applies to anyone who enjoys the benefits of the gospel (perhaps through the fruit of Christian social reform or the blessing of a Christian family) without personally trusting in Christ. Moral reform without saving faith is spiritually perilous.

Misunderstood by Family

This section ends poignantly with Jesus being estranged from his family. Though Matthew says nothing about his family's motives (as Mark 3:21 does), the reaction of Jesus suggests they would divert him from his mission. Jesus himself is the first to experience the division he predicted in Matthew 10:34-37. His allegiance now belongs to the family of God (**12:48-50**).

Questions for reflection

1. "Does the way you use your Sunday bring rest or is it a burden? For you? For others?" (p. 107).
2. Can you think of ways in which you are being called to obey the law in a way that prioritises mercy rather than sacrifice (i.e. compassion rather than ritual observance)?
3. "Moral reform without saving faith is spiritually perilous" (p. 110). Does this prompt you to speak gospel truth to someone you know who is morally upstanding but is not trusting Christ?

PART TWO

Jesus began his ministry by proclaiming the arrival of God's kingdom (4:17, 23). For his contemporaries that meant one thing: God's King was about to arrive in a blaze of glory to defeat God's enemies and vindicate his people. Initially things look promising: Jesus is "healing every disease and illness", news about him is spreading, and crowds are gathering (4:23-25; 9:35; **13:2**). Jesus looks like the real deal.

But Jesus isn't mustering an army. True, he's recruited "Simon the Zealot"—the 1st-century equivalent of a terrorist. But he's also signed up "Matthew the tax-collector", a collaborator with the Romans (10:2-4). Instead of slaughtering God's enemies, Jesus prefers to party with them (9:9-13). So whose side is Jesus on? The Jewish leaders—surely his key allies—have taken against him (12:12-14), and meanwhile the Romans are still in power. There's no sign of divine judgment.

Matthew 13 begins, "That same day..." (**v 1**). Matthew ties the teaching of Matthew 13 with what's preceded it: a day of disputes in Matthew 12. Is Jesus God's King establishing God's kingdom? If so, where's the defeat of God's enemies? Jesus responds to these questions by telling a series of parables about the kingdom of heaven.

The parables are part of Jesus' response to the large crowds which threaten to overwhelm him (**13:2-3**). From now on "he did not say anything to them without using a parable" (**v 34-35**). Jesus begins with the parable of the sower in **verses 3-9** and Matthew records Jesus' explanation in **verses 18-23**. But first Jesus explains to the disciples why it is that he speaks to them in parables (**v 10-15**): "Because the knowledge of the secrets of the kingdom of heaven has been given to you, but not to them" (**v 11**).

The Big Secret: The Kingdom Is Coming in Grace and Will Come in Power

These "secrets" are not the coming of the kingdom—every faithful Jew expected that. Instead, the secret of the kingdom is that the kingdom comes secretly. *While the kingdom will come in glory in the future, it's already come in a secret, hidden, gracious way*. The kingdom comes in two stages: first in grace and finally in glory. (Theologians call this "inaugurated eschatology"; eschatology is the **doctrine** of the end times, but the end times have already begun, even though their full consummation is yet to come.)

The parables protect this secret by revealing the truth to some and keeping it concealed from others. They genuinely announce the coming of the kingdom, but they do so in a way that enlightens the soft-hearted while hiding the truth from those hardened in unbelief (**v 12-13**). **Verses 14-15** are a quote from Isaiah's commission in Isaiah 6: "Here I am. Send me!" he cries. This is sometimes used as a rallying cry for mission. But in fact Isaiah is then told that no one is going to listen to his message—his job is to harden hearts. His words will not only *speak* of judgment; they will also *enact* it. It's the same with Jesus. His parables liberate those with ears to hear (**v 9**) but bring judgment on those whose hearts are hard (**v 13-15**). Jesus concludes his address to the crowds by quoting Psalm 78:2: "I will open my mouth in parables…" (Matthew **13:35**), and we find the same pattern in the psalm. The psalmist retells Israel's history as a parable to teach "the next generation" so that they do not become "a stubborn and rebellious generation" like their ancestors (Psalm 78:5-8; see Matthew 12:39).

So the "secrets of the kingdom" are not deep **esoteric** truths that only an elite can appreciate. No, the knowledge of the secrets "has been given" to the disciples (**13:11**). They're still pretty confused by it all, yet Jesus places them among those with eyes to see (**v 16**). Indeed, they see more than the Old Testament prophets saw because they see Jesus himself the Word made flesh (**v 17**). It's not intellectual understanding that counts, but your attitude to Jesus.

All the parables in Matthew 13 reinforce these secrets of the kingdom:

1. The kingdom *will come* in power as expected: there will be a day of judgment.
2. The kingdom *has already come* in a hidden way: as a gracious invitation to receive forgiveness before it's too late.

So Jesus is making two points in the parables of the kingdom:

1. The kingdom *is coming* now in grace, even though it hasn't yet come in power.
2. The kingdom *will come* in power even though it's already come in grace.

It's all well and good hoping God will come in judgment against his enemies. But the fact is that *we're* God's enemies. We're all rebels against God's rule. During the days of the prophet Malachi, people asked, "Where is the God of justice?" Malachi replied, "The LORD you are seeking will come ... But who can endure the day of his coming?" (Malachi 2:17 – 3:2). You want God to sort out injustice, but that means he'll sort you out. God's victory will be our defeat.

So God's kingdom comes first not in judgment but in grace. It comes not in a blaze of glory but through the proclamation of the word. At the first coming of Jesus, judgment didn't fall. Or rather, it did fall—at the cross, on the King himself. Jesus could have come in power, but that would have meant judgment for his people. So first Jesus came to be judged in our place. This was the way—the only way—that the restoration of God's kingdom can be good news for rebels like us.

The Sower

The parable of the sower teaches this secret: that the kingdom is now coming in grace and will come in power. The "seed" represents "the message about the kingdom" (Matthew **13:19**). Jesus himself is the sower (see **v 37**). But his disciples have also begun to "sow" the message (10:5) as do we today in our evangelism. The kingdom expands whenever people hear its message and submit to the authority of the King in repentance. The kingdom *is coming* largely unseen as the seed is sown through the proclamation of the gospel, and the kingdom *will come* in the form of a great harvest (a common image in the Bible for the final judgment). The word of the kingdom may be rejected, neglected and opposed, but it's also growing and producing fruit.

The parable of the sower is a parable about parables!

But the focus of the parable of the sower is on the mixed response to the message. It illustrates the reason why Jesus speaks in parables—to both reveal and conceal the good news. So the parable of the sower is a parable about parables!

The path = an immediate rejection. Some people immediately dismiss the message (**13:19**), either through hostility or apathy. Jesus attributes this to the work of Satan. Such people may come to church out of habit or with their family. They should beware. The more they hear, the less impact it has (**v 13**). They're in danger of becoming impervious to the voice of God.

The rocky soil = a superficial response. These people respond enthusiastically. They like what they hear. Perhaps they are moved by the eloquence or passion of the speaker. But any profession of faith is merely an emotional response. They haven't counted the cost. So, "when trouble or persecution comes because of the word, they quickly fall away" (**v 20-21**). In contrast, true faith "perseveres under trial" (James 1:12). In our evangelism we mustn't portray being a Christian as a bed of roses. Our call must echo Christ's call to take up the cross (Matthew 16:24).

The thorns = a divided heart. These people may show some initial interest, but they're soon distracted by worldly cares and attractions

(**13:22**). "No one can serve two masters" and these people will not give up serving Money or whatever else has captured their heart (6:24).

The good soil = a fruitful transformation. The kingdom may not be advanced by force in the sense of coercion, but the preaching of the kingdom has the power to change and transform. It's not merely an ideology that inspires; it's a word that brings life and bears fruit.

*This parable is spoken to the crowds (**13:2**).* Its message to them is: "Whoever has ears, let them hear" (**v 9**). At that moment they're enthusiastic, receiving the word "with joy" (**v 20**). But hearing is not enough; coming to church is not enough; having Christian parents is not enough. What counts is persevering faith that produces fruit.

*The explanation of the parable is spoken to the disciples (**v 18**).* To disciples the parable is an encouragement, especially when our message is rejected (2 Corinthians 2:15-16). We shouldn't be surprised or disheartened—rejection is normal. Some Christians assume the problem is with the seed; they think the gospel message needs to be updated for a contemporary audience. But there's nothing wrong with the seed in the parable; the problem is with the soil. So what do we do? We keep on sowing. This parable is a call to persevere. The story doesn't end with barren land; the story ends with a harvest.

The Mustard Seed and the Yeast

Both these parables involve something small—"the smallest of all seeds" and hidden yeast. (In Matthew **13:33**, "mixed" is literally "hid" in the flour, ESV.) But in both cases, they become something big—"the largest of garden plants" and something working "all through the dough" (**v 31-33**). These are another way of expressing the secrets of the kingdom.

1. The kingdom *is coming* now in grace, even though at the moment it looks very small. Don't be misled by that smallness; God is doing a new thing in history (**v 35**).

2. The kingdom *will come* in power. The birds perching in its branches is a picture of people from all nations finding refuge under Christ's rule (**v 32**). The true church usually seems weak and insignificant. Yet somehow the gospel has spread across the globe! You may feel you have little to offer. Perhaps you're right! But look at what God can do with a little!

The Weeds and the Net

Jesus tells the parable of a field in which an enemy sows weeds among the wheat. Rather than risk pulling up wheat plants, the owner tells his servants to wait and divide the wheat and weeds at harvest time (**v 24-30**). The parable of the net makes the same point, using good and bad fish in a net (**v 47-50**). Jesus gives a full explanation of the parable of the weeds (**v 36-43**):

- the owner = the Son of Man (Jesus himself)
- the enemy = the devil
- the field = the world
- the good seed = the people of the kingdom
- the bad seed = the people of the devil
- the harvest = the final judgment
- the harvesters = the angels

Again these parables teach the secrets of the kingdom:

1. The kingdom *is coming* now, even though judgment (the division of wheat and weeds and the division of bad and good fish) has been delayed. It's coming in grace as the word is proclaimed. But don't be fooled: just because the kingdom comes now in grace doesn't mean judgment has been permanently cancelled.
2. The kingdom *will come* in power. There will be a harvest at the end of the age (**v 40-41**).

At the moment, believers and unbelievers live side by side. God doesn't intervene in judgment because he's giving people an opportunity to repent (2 Peter 3:3-9). But we shouldn't misinterpret God's patience as complacent indulgence. There will be a final day of judgment when God's enemies (those who reject Christ) will be judged (Matthew **13:42**) and God's people (those who accept Christ) will "shine like the sun" (**v 43**).

The Treasure and the Pearl

The final pair of parables also teach the secrets of the kingdom, with their contrast between present loss and future gain. But their emphasis is on the worth of the kingdom. With the kingdom's coming in power delayed, being part of Christ's kingdom can be hard. But it's worth it. Both people in these parables sell all they own to gain a treasure—and both gain something they consider far more valuable. These parables are beautiful pictures of the way that those who lose their life for Christ's sake actually find it (10:38-39; 16:24-27) and those who reject treasure on earth gain treasure in heaven (6:19-20). Notice, too, how the first man sold all he had "in his joy" (**13:44**). This future hope—that God's kingdom will come in glory—enables us to rejoice even when we're making sacrifices or when serving Jesus is hard going.

New Treasures As Well As Old

The disciples claim to have understood what Jesus is saying (**v 51**). It's true that they understand more than the crowds, since they've been given the secrets of the kingdom (**v 11**). But they still have a long way to go in their understanding of who Jesus is and what he's come to do (as 15:16 indicates).

13:53 is an example of the formula Matthew uses to wrap a teaching section in his Gospel. So this teaching section ends with Jesus saying, "Therefore every teacher of the law who has become a disciple in the kingdom of heaven is like the owner of a house who brings out of his storeroom new treasures as well as old" (**v 52**). Jesus is talking about teachers of the law who have become Christians and so understand the secrets of the kingdom. That enables them to teach the Bible in a far more enriching way for their hearers. Their teaching is not all new (as if the Old Testament doesn't matter anymore); neither is it all old (as if the kingdom hasn't come). Instead, good Bible teachers show how the Old Testament has been fulfilled in Jesus. It perfectly describes what Matthew is doing in his Gospel.

Rejected at Home

Verses 54-58 begin a new section which runs all the way to 18:35. It focuses on the identity of Jesus, and it centres on Peter's statement that Jesus is the Messiah (16:16). Before we get there, though, we see the identity of Jesus being misunderstood. While most people are more warmly received at home than away, it's common for those who do well in life to be viewed as "putting on airs". So it is that here the people in his home town can't see beyond Jesus' humble human origins (**13:54-57**). Perhaps Matthew is explaining why the Jewish people rejected one of their own, or perhaps he's warning us not to let the humanity of Jesus (Jesus being one-of-us) cause us to reject the divinity of Jesus (Jesus being God-with-us).

"And he did not do many miracles there because of their lack of faith" (**v 58**). This doesn't mean Jesus' power was somehow constrained by their lack of faith. The verse says "did not" (because he chose not to) rather than "could not" (as if he were unable). We must avoid any suggestion that our faith "releases" God's power or that God can only act if we have enough faith. Jesus had the ability to perform miracles, but chose not to because he knew further miracles would only harden people's hearts still further (**v 14-15**).

Questions for reflection

1. How have you seen the truth of the parable of the sower in yourself or in those around you? Why is it encouraging that Jesus foresaw this?
2. What do you make of the idea that the kingdom has come with grace and will come with power? In what way does this make you more grateful to be a part of it?
3. What is it about the kingdom of God which means that it is worth giving everything for, and means that we can give everything for it *joyfully*?

8. THE IDENTITY OF THE MESSIAH REVEALED

Spoiler alert: this section of Matthew's Gospel climaxes with Jesus being acclaimed as "the Messiah, the Son of the living God" (16:16).

As we move towards that moment, we see examples of faith and unbelief. This began at the end of Matthew 13 with Jesus being rejected in his home town (13:53-58). That unbelief extends to the centres of power in **14:1-12**. In **14:13-36** the disciples waver, while **15:1-39** provides two unexpected and contrasting examples: deep antagonism from religious leaders and persevering faith from a pagan woman. Then the focus switches back to the disciples as Jesus feeds a large crowd for a second time because the disciples still haven't grasped the truth (15:29 – 16:12). Then the disciples finally recognise Jesus as the Messiah in 16:13-20. Even at this point, though, they are only halfway to a proper understanding of Jesus, and so Jesus must begin to explain what being the Messiah actually involves (16:21-28). Therefore, the key questions in this section are: who is Jesus? How will you respond to him?

The King Who Reigns with Compassion

Herod suspects Jesus is John the Baptist (**14:1-2**). This conclusion spooks Herod because John is dead and it was Herod who killed him! In **verses 3-12** Matthew inserts a flashback to explain how John was executed for challenging Herod (**v 4**; see Leviticus 20:21). This explains Herod's response in Matthew **14:1-2**, but it also acts as a **foil** to the feeding of the 5,000 in **verses 13-21**. We're presented with contrasting two kings: Herod and Jesus.

Herod	Jesus
Herod is intent on death (**v 3-5**)	Jesus heals those who are ill (**v 14**)
Herod looks with lust (**v 6**)	Jesus looks with compassion (**v 14**)
Herod hosts a feast for the elite (**v 6**)	Jesus hosts a meal for needy people (**v 16-20**)
Herod is governed by public opinion (**v 5-9**)	Jesus governs with authority (**v 15-19**)
Herod's reign leads to death (**v 10-12**)	Jesus' reign leads to satisfaction (**v 20**)

Herod wears a crown, but his authority is limited. His actions are determined by the crowds in **verse 5**, his wife and step-daughter in **verses 6-8** and his guests in **verse 9**. Ultimately, his rule is deadly. In contrast, Jesus has no crown, but his authority is complete, and his rule is life-giving.

Back in 2:1-6, Matthew quoted Micah 5:2 but also added a line from 2 Samuel 5:1-3: "You shall shepherd my people Israel". The tribes of Israel said this as they pledged allegiance to David instead of the house of Saul (Israel's previous king). In chapter 2 Matthew promises a similar transfer of power from the kings of this world to the King of heaven. Now, in chapter 14, Jesus the Son of David stands among us, and we see power slipping away from Herod (the latest version of King Saul) and passing to Jesus (the true King David). This transfer is still taking place. Human rule continues to prevail on earth, but it's limited, and it's deadly. Meanwhile, Jesus is calling people to embrace his compassionate, life-giving rule.

In Matthew's Gospel the fate of John foreshadows the fate of Jesus:

- John is arrested and bound (Matthew **14:3**), and so is Jesus (26:50; 27:2).
- Herod fears the crowds because the crowds believe John is a prophet (**14:5**), and the religious leaders fear the crowds because the crowds believe Jesus is a prophet (21:46).
- Herod is asked by another to execute John and is distressed to do so (**14:6-11**), and Pilate is asked by others to execute Jesus and is reluctant to do so (27:21-26).
- John is buried by disciples (**14:12**), as is Jesus (27:57-61). (Adapted from Davies, *Matthew: A Shorter Commentary,* p. 235).

John was the new Elijah (11:14), contending with Herod and Herodias just as Elijah contended with **Ahab and Jezebel**. Elijah's mantle passed to Elisha, who once fed 100 people with just 20 loaves (2 Kings 4:42-44). If John is the new Elijah, Jesus must be the new Elisha. So... will Jesus feed 100 people with 20 loaves?

Feeding 5,000: Satisfying Our Needs

The crowds have followed Jesus, and he's had compassion on them and healed those who were sick (Matthew **14:13-14**). But the disciples are worried: if Jesus doesn't disperse the crowd soon, everyone will be walking home without having eaten (**v 15**). "You give them something to eat," says Jesus (**v 16**). It's clearly an impossible demand (**v 17**), but it's what we might call "a possible invitation": an invitation to put faith in Jesus as God's life-giving King. As it turns out, the disciples *do* feed the people, but only by passing on what they've first received from Jesus (**v 19**). It's a pattern reflected in all true Christian ministry.

In the meantime, the disciples point to the paucity of what they have: five loaves and two fish (**v 17**). What they don't see are the riches of Jesus. But recognising our inability is the first step towards faith. We can't provide for our needs or safeguard our future; still less can we meet our biggest needs: forgiveness, reconciliation with God and eternal life. So who can meet our needs? The answer in **verses 19-20**

> We can't provide for our needs or safeguard our future. Jesus can.

is King Jesus. Jesus produces bread where there was no bread, and as a result, "they all ate and were satisfied" (**v 20-21**). Indeed, as if to underline the point, the disciples each end up with a basketful of leftovers (**v 20**). The twelve baskets also suggest Jesus can provide for the twelve tribes of Israel: that is, for all God's people.

In the way he tells this story, Matthew alludes to the provision of manna in the wilderness (an allusion Jesus makes explicit in John 6). Back in Exodus 16, the people were without food in a remote place—just as they are in Matthew 14. Back then, God miraculously provided bread where there was no bread—just as Jesus does here. Back then, everyone "gathered just as much as they needed" (Exodus 16:18)—just as in Matthew **14:20** "they all ate and were satisfied". Jesus is the new Moses, who meets the needs of the people of God.

But Matthew goes further. He tells us that Jesus "told the people to sit down *on the grass*" (**v 19**). Why add "on the grass"? It's an allusion to Psalm 23:1-2: "The LORD is my shepherd, I lack nothing. He makes me lie down in green pastures." Now Jesus shepherds God's people, directing them to green pastures.

There's also a glimpse forward in the story. "Taking the five loaves ... [Jesus] gave thanks and broke the loaves. Then he gave them to the disciples" (Matthew **14:19**). Compare this to Matthew's description of the first Lord's Supper: "Jesus took bread, and when he had given thanks, he broke it and gave it to his disciples" (26:26). Both descriptions involve taking, thanking, breaking and giving—in that order. The feast of Matthew 14, in which "all ate and were satisfied", is replicated every time we celebrate the Lord's Supper. We, too, eat and are satisfied (John 6:35, 54-55). This is why we come to the Supper expecting to have our spiritual needs satisfied as the Holy Spirit applies the victory of Jesus afresh to our hearts.

Walking on the Water: God with Us

The disciples are in the middle of a storm when Jesus walks on the water towards them (Matthew **14:22-25**). They assume he's a ghost, but his words reassure them (**v 26-27**). Jesus climbs into the boat, and the storm dies down (**v 32**).

Matthew adds two details to Mark's version of this story which spotlight his message. First, Matthew concludes the story with "Then those who were in the boat worshipped him, saying, 'Truly you are the Son of God'" (**v 33**). When Jesus calmed the storm in 8:23-27, the disciples asked, "What kind of *man* is this?" (v 27). Now, as Jesus again calms a storm, they answer their own question: "Truly you are the Son of God" (**14:33**). In Job 9:8 God treads on the waves, and in Isaiah 43:1-2 the LORD says:

> "Do not fear, for I have redeemed you;
> I have summoned you by name; you are mine.
> When you pass through the waters,
> I will be with you."

Water in the Bible is often a picture of judgment (see the comments on Matthew 3:16). But just as in Isaiah God says, "Do not fear", so here Jesus says, "Don't be afraid" (**14:27**). In Isaiah God promises, "I will be with you"—and Jesus is Immanuel, coming through the storm to his people. Three times in Isaiah 43 the Lord says, "I am he" (Isaiah 43:10, 13, 25). It's an echo of God's covenant name. At the burning bush Moses asked, *What is your name?* and God replied, "I AM WHO I AM" (Exodus 3:14). Now, as Jesus comes to his disciples, he says, "It is I" (literally "I am"). It's the same wording as "I am he" in the Greek translation of Isaiah 43. Isaiah promised a new exodus, and Jesus fulfils that promise by redeeming his people from sin and death. At Mount Sinai "I AM" came to his people. But a barrier was placed round the mountain, and God was hidden in cloud because God and humanity couldn't safely live together. But now Immanuel steps down from the mountain (Matthew **14:23**) and comes to meet us in the storms of life (**v 25**). You and Jesus are in the same boat.

Second, Matthew adds the story of Peter walking on the water (**v 28-29**). It's a great step of faith (literally). But when Peter sees the wind, he begins to sink, and so Jesus has to grab hold of him (**v 30-31**). What does Matthew want us to learn from this?

1. As we build up to the confession of 16:16, Peter illustrates the current state of the disciples: wavering between belief and unbelief. This is why Jesus responds, "You of little faith ... why did you doubt?" (**14:31**).

2. The story models faith for God's people in any age. Peter walked on water when he trusted the word of Jesus (**v 29**); he began to sink "when he saw the wind" (**v 30**). Likewise, we're to walk through the storms of life by faith and not by sight, by fixing our attention on the word of Jesus rather than looking at the threats and seductions of this world.

3. Beneath our faith is a greater faith. Our faith may fail as Peter's does, but Jesus remains faithful. Jesus will catch hold of us when we fall (**v 31**). Here Peter prefigures his fall in 26:69-75—a fall from which Jesus will ultimately lift him.

This section ends with a reiteration of the scope of Jesus' ministry (**14:34-36**). Even in this Gentile-dominated region, touching his cloak is enough to bring healing—just as it was in Jewish territory (9:20-22).

Arguing About Cleanliness

The religious leaders ask Jesus why his disciples don't wash their hands before they eat (**15:1-2**). It's not a question about personal hygiene. In the name of "the tradition of the elders", the Pharisees had extended the ceremonial washing required in the temple to all of life. They wanted to create pockets of purity in a land polluted by Gentile occupation. So the issue is: how can people be clean?

In response, Jesus says that it's the religious leaders who are unclean. Far from making them clean, their traditions reveal their inner filth (**v 3**). Their traditions may not directly contradict Scripture, but by *adding* to Scripture they "nullify" the intention of Scripture. Bible plus = Bible minus. If, today, we treat our traditions as law (rather than at best as wisdom), then those traditions will undermine the grace of the gospel.

Jesus gives an example. The law clearly required people to honour their parents. But the religious leaders evaded this responsibility by declaring as "devoted to God" what they might otherwise have used to care for their parents (**v 4-6**). It's likely this commitment would only be paid at death, so in the meantime people could go on enjoying their possessions. In our terms, it might be something like buying a holiday home rather than supporting a needy parent and justifying this by saying you'll give it to a Christian charity in your will.

The religious leaders' pious claims are empty words because their hearts are far from God (**v 7-8**, quoting Isaiah 29:13). Religious people often look impressive; they appear to take holiness seriously (Colossians 2:23). But they're trusting in their own righteousness, and that's shaky ground. Indeed, they can only keep up appearances by bending the rules. Worse still, they reject God by rejecting the righteousness he offers.

Religious people can only keep up appearances by bending the rules.

In Matthew **15:12**, the conversation switches to the disciples. They are shocked by Jesus' condemnation of the Pharisees because they still assume the Pharisees are the good guys—the people who "do" righteousness to the max. Not so, says Jesus: the Pharisees are plants destined to be burned in the fire (**v 13**; 3:9-10; 13:36-42; Isaiah 5:1-7). They're blind to the grace of God, and to follow them is to share their blindness (Matthew **15:14**).

Jesus then explains what he meant in **verses 10-11**. First, "what goes into someone's mouth does not defile them" (**v 11, 16-17**).

We're not cleansed by ceremonial washing or eating kosher foods. These are external acts that can't change our inner filth.

Second, "what comes out of their mouth, that is what defiles" (**v 11, 18-20**). We'll be judged according to our words and actions, and these flow from our hearts (12:33-37). So an outside-in approach can't work. We can't become righteous people by doing more righteous things. We need inside-out change: we need our hearts to be made new. Matthew 15 only states the problem, but perhaps we're meant to recall the promise of John the Baptist: "I baptise you with water for repentance. But after me comes one who is more powerful than I ... He will baptise you with the Holy Spirit and fire" (3:11, fulfilling Ezekiel 36:25-27). Jesus is the one who cleanses our hearts through the Holy Spirit.

We're meant to respond by giving up on establishing or maintaining our own righteousness and instead coming to Jesus, asking him to renew our hearts through his Holy Spirit. But the disciples are not there yet. "Are you still so dull?" asks Jesus (Matthew **15:16**). It is a sobering moment. But better is to come, for in contrast to the persistent unbelief of the Pharisees and the faltering faith of the disciples, Matthew is about to present a model of persistent faith...

Questions for reflection

1. How has this section made you appreciate having Jesus as the King of your life?
2. How are you being called to live by faith and not by sight at the moment? What will it look like for you to do that?
3. As you seek to live by faith, what difference does it make to know that what matters most is not your faithfulness to Jesus but his constant faithfulness to you?

PART TWO

The stories in Matthew 15 – 16 all revolve round the issue of faith, as we move towards Peter's confession that Jesus is the Messiah in **16:16**.

A Surprising Model of Faith

With the disciples reeling from the news that religious leaders can't be trusted (15:14), they then meet someone who, they know for sure, can't be trusted: a Canaanite woman. Moreover, alert readers still have in mind John's defeat at the hands of Herodias, a new Jezebel. Jezebel was a princess from Sidon (1 Kings 16:31)—and here we meet another woman from Sidon. It doesn't bode well. But in fact we're in for a big surprise, for this Canaanite woman confesses that Jesus is "the Son of David" (Matthew **15:22**). This pagan woman acknowledges Jesus as the promised Davidic Messiah before the disciples. In 12:23 the crowd asked, "Could this be the Son of David?", but the only other people to acknowledge Jesus as the Son of David have been two blind men (9:27; see also 20:30-31). The irony is that it's the blind who recognise Jesus and Gentiles who acknowledge him as Israel's King.

Consider the sequence of events in the story of the Canaanite woman:

- She comes: she "came to him, crying out" (**15:22**).
- She's rebuffed: Jesus ignores her (**v 23**).
- She comes: "she keeps crying out" (**v 23**).
- She's rebuffed: Jesus has other priorities (**v 24**).
- She comes: she "came and knelt before him" (**v 25**).
- She's rebuffed: Jesus says she has no right to come (**v 26**).
- She comes: she accepts she has no rights but pleads for mercy (**v 27**).

Three times she's rebuffed, and three times she persists. *If I'm a dog, then at least give me the crumbs due a dog*, she effectively says in **verse 27**. In the end, Jesus declares, "Woman, you have great faith" (**v 28**). At first, his attitude seems harsh and uncaring. But, as France puts it, "cold print does not allow us to detect a quizzical eyebrow or a tongue in the cheek, and it may be that Jesus' demeanour already hinted that his discouraging reply was not to be his last word on the subject" (*The Gospel of Matthew*, p. 591). Certainly in hindsight it's clear that Jesus was pushing her with a view to revealing the depth of her faith. Jesus ignored her so he might commend her. He rebuffed her so she might become a model of persistent faith. Her "great faith" contrasts with the disciples' "little faith" (14:31; **15:28**).

Jesus says his priority is "the lost sheep of Israel" (**15:24**). It's an echo of 10:6, where the disciples were sent only to "the lost sheep of Israel" (see also 9:36; 12:11-12). But Matthew has already seen beyond this early priority to the gathering of people from every nation. In **15:25** we're told that the woman "knelt" or "worshipped" before Jesus. It's the word Matthew uses to describe the homage of the pagan Magi (2:2, 11) and the worship received by the risen Christ (28:9, 17). As Jesus is about to be proclaimed as Israel's Messiah, Matthew reminds us that he's also the world's King.

The Slow Path to Faith

There's a big sense of déjà vu as we again read of Jesus feeding a large crowd with a few loaves and fish (**15:29-39**; compare with 14:13-21). The parallels are almost painful:

- Crowds come to Jesus (14:13; **15:30**).
- Jesus is said to have compassion on them (14:14; **15:32**).
- Jesus asks his disciples to feed them (14:16; **15:32**).
- The disciples have only a few loaves and fish (14:17; **15:34**).
- Jesus tells the crowd to sit down (14:19; **15:35**).

- Jesus takes, thanks, breaks and gives, in that order (14:19; **15:36**).
- The disciples are given bread to give to the people (14:19; **15:36**).
- "They all ate and were satisfied" (14:20; **15:37**).
- The disciples collect several basketfuls of leftovers (14:20; **15:37**).
- Matthew the book-keeper ends each story with a tally of "the number of those who ate" (14:21; **15:38**).

So why bother including this story when we've seen it all before? The answer is that that's the point! Jesus has revealed himself as the Lord shepherding his people, the new Moses providing bread in the wilderness, the Messiah ruling with compassion. But the disciples don't get it—not yet. So Jesus does it all over again.

The one addition—both to the feeding of the 5,000 in chapter 14 and Mark's version of the feeding of the 4,000 in Mark 8:1-10—is in Matthew **15:30-31**. Here people are amazed because Jesus heals "the lame, the blind, the crippled, the mute and many others". But this is also a repeat of 11:2-6—of Jesus' reply when John the Baptist questions whether he's the Messiah. John's doubts are answered by the miracles of Jesus, and so should the disciples' doubts be.

Another difference between the feedings of the 5,000 and 4,000 is that the latter probably took place in Gentile territory. This is why people are said to praise "the God of Israel" in **15:31** (Jews would have just praised God). The messianic feast of Isaiah 25 is being extended to the nations (Matthew 8:11). In the previous story, the nations get crumbs (**15:27**); now they get more than they can eat!

The Dangerous Influence of Unbelief

The Pharisees and Sadducees (normally enemies but now united by their hostility to Jesus) ask for a sign, even though Jesus has already performed many miraculous signs (**16:1**; 12:38). Matthew tells us that they "tested him". Jesus has just fed people with bread (**15:36-37**), like God feeding people with manna in the wilderness in Exodus 16.

Now the religious leaders "test" Jesus, like faithless Israel testing God in the wilderness in Exodus 17:1-7.

In response Jesus says they can read weather signs but "cannot interpret the signs of the times" (Matthew **16:3**). In other words, it should be clear what's happening: God is restoring his kingdom through his King. But the religious elite stubbornly refuse to recognise this. So the only sign they'll receive will be the sign of Jonah (**v 4**): a reference to the resurrection (as 12:40 makes clear). Jonah was also a prophet who preached to Gentiles—something Jesus has just been doing.

> Like yeast, unbelief has a habit of spreading.

Twice Jesus warns the disciples, "Be on your guard against the yeast of the Pharisees and Sadducees" (**16:6, 11-12**). In other words, don't be influenced by unbelief because, like yeast, unbelief has a habit of spreading throughout the dough. Spending time with sceptics or watching ungodly media or failing to filter advertising may erode our personal faith, while tolerating **heresy** or legalism will erode our communal witness. In Bible times, yeast didn't come in a tin. Instead, you retained a batch of the previous day's dough to leaven that day's bread. So when Israel celebrated the Passover with unleavened bread, it represented a decisive break with Egypt. Israel was leaving its old life behind, not even retaining a batch of the previous day's dough. In the same way, Jesus is about to enact a new exodus, and his redeemed people must leave behind the sinful influences of their old life (1 Corinthians 5:6-8).

But the point of this story is that the disciples miss the point! They think Jesus is telling them off for not having spare bread (Matthew **16:5-7**). *How can you think I'm worried about bread,* Jesus effectively responds, *when I fed 5,000 men with five loaves and 4,000 men with seven loaves?* To drill home the point, he gets them to recollect the amount of leftovers they collected each time (**v 9-10**). "You of little faith," is Jesus' verdict (**v 8** ; 6:30; 8:26).

But that is about to change...

Peter's Confession: Foundational Faith

Jesus asks the disciples who people think he is (**16:13-14**). Some (like Herod, see 14:2) think he's John the Baptist. Some think he's Elijah, since Elijah was expected to return in the last days. But Jesus has already said that John the Baptist is the fulfilment of this hope (11:14). A third option is that Jesus is a prophet. We've seen how Matthew portrays Jesus as a new Moses and Elisha. So this option has some truth to it, but it's very far from being the whole truth.

Jesus then puts the same question to the disciples, and Peter replies, "You are the Messiah, the Son of the living God" (**16:15-16**). This is a central moment in Matthew's story because this is his core message. Jesus is God's King, come to rescue God's people from judgment and restore God's life-giving rule. Indeed, Jesus is God himself, Immanuel, God with us.

So what has changed between **verses 8-9**, where Jesus was complaining about the disciples' misunderstanding, and this moment of insight? In Mark's Gospel this movement is juxtaposed with the healing of a blind man; the disciples are cured of spiritual blindness just as the man is cured of physical blindness (Mark 8:14-29). Matthew strips out that story and instead goes straight to the point: "Blessed are you, Simon [Peter] son of Jonah, for this was not revealed to you by flesh and blood, but by my Father in heaven" (Matthew **16:17**). None of us are Christians because we were clever enough to work it out. Faith is always a gift from God, given through the **regenerating** work of the Holy Spirit (John 3:3-6; Ephesians 2:8).

Jesus changes Peter's name from Simon to Peter, which means "rock". It's a name-change with a promise attached: "On this rock I will build my church, and the gates of **Hades** will not overcome it"

(Matthew **16:18**). Since the **Reformation**, Roman Catholics have said that the rock is Peter and his successors (thus justifying the authority of the papacy, for according to church tradition, Peter was the first bishop of Rome). In contrast, **Protestants** have sometimes said the rock is Peter's confession. It's more likely that Peter himself is the rock. First, Peter speaks on behalf of the other apostles, whose collective testimony will be the foundation of the church (Ephesians 2:20; Revelation 21:14). Second, Peter speaks on behalf of all believers; he's the first disciple to confess Jesus and therefore a model for future disciples (without any implication of papal succession). This fits Matthew **16:19**, where "the keys of the kingdom" refer to the preaching of the gospel, which opens the door of heaven to those who respond with faith while confirming the judgment of those who reject it (see Carson, *The Expositor's Bible Commentary*, Volume 8, p. 370-373).

We mustn't let this dispute distract us from the key promise. There are times when we can feel gloomy about the future of the church. But despite all the external hostility the church faces and all the internal disputes that divide her, Christ has promised to build his church, and for 2,000 years he has kept that promise. Jesus is acclaimed as the Messiah in Caesarea Philippi, a city honouring the Roman emperor, whose rule he is quietly usurping.

Faith in a Crucified Messiah

Jesus orders his disciples not to tell anyone he's the Messiah (**v 20**). That's because they don't yet understand what it means for him to be the Messiah. "From that time on" in **verse 21** marks a new stage in Jesus' ministry. Jesus began the first phase of his ministry by announcing the kingdom (4:17). Here we're told he began the second phase by explaining the cross. Now that the disciples have recognised him as the Messiah, he moves on to Lesson 2: what does it mean to be the Messiah? The Jews expected the Messiah to judge God's enemies (as we saw in Matthew 13), and Jesus confirms this expectation in **16:27**. But first the Messiah must die a violent death (**v 21**). It's Jesus who's going to be judged—not for his own rebellion but for ours. He "must" be killed if we're to be saved (**v 21**)—otherwise his coming in judgment would mean our condemnation.

Defeat and death are not on Peter's agenda, however, and so he rebukes Jesus (**v 22**). Jesus interprets this as a temptation from Satan to avoid the agonies of the cross (**v 23**; 4:8-9). A moment ago Peter was a foundation stone; now he's "a stumbling block".

> A moment ago Peter was a foundation stone; now he's a stumbling block.

Indeed, not only must Jesus accept death; so must his disciples. If **16:16** summarises who Jesus is, **verse 24** summarises what it means to follow him: "Whoever wants to be my disciple must deny themselves and take up their cross and follow me." We're to show the same submission to God, willingness to serve and sacrificial love that Jesus displayed at the cross. For some this may mean martyrdom; for all it means dying to our proud, selfish self: what W.D. Davies calls "the displacement of ego from the centre of its universe" (*Matthew: A Shorter Commentary*, p. 275). There's no point accumulating earthly status or wealth if you lose your eternal soul (**v 25-26**; 6:19-20).

To deny ourselves (**16:24**) doesn't mean we should always default to saying "No" to what we want. I've often ended up (falsely) thinking that the right option must be my worst option, since this involves the most self-denial. The only other time the word "denial" is used in Matthew's Gospel is to describe Peter's denial of Jesus (26:34-35, 75—disown is the same word in the Greek). For Peter, denying Jesus meant not being identified by his allegiance to Jesus. So denying self is to not find our identity in our accomplishments and instead find our identity in Jesus, putting our allegiance to him first. That doesn't necessarily mean saying "No" to what we want, though it may do.

Jesus concludes, "Truly I tell you, some who are standing here will not taste death before they see the Son of Man coming in his kingdom" (**16:28**). Jesus didn't mistakenly think history would end in the 1st century AD. The point is that the victory of Jesus has a number of major anticipatory events coming up, which some of his hearers will witness:

- The transfiguration of Jesus, when Peter, James and John are given a glimpse of his future glory (17:1-8).
- The resurrection of Jesus, when he rises in triumph (28:2-4).
- The ascension of Jesus, when he comes before God to receive all authority (Daniel 7:13-14).
- The fall of Jerusalem in AD 70, when Jesus is vindicated (as we'll see in 24:1-35).
- The expansion of the kingdom of Jesus to all nations through the mission of the church (28:18-20).

Jesus is calling us to deny ourselves and display the kind of sacrificial love he displayed at the cross (**16:24**). That's a big demand. Is it worth it? Yes, because those who lose their life for Jesus will find it (**v 25**); they will be rewarded when Jesus returns (**v 27**). But how can we be sure? We can be sure Jesus will conquer because his transfiguration, resurrection, ascension, and the spread of the gospel are indications that Jesus has *already* conquered. We're on the winning side!

Questions for reflection

1. What does the yeast of the Pharisees and Sadducees look like in your particular context?
2. When did you last give thanks to God for working in you by his Spirit to show you who Jesus is?
3. What will denying yourself in order to follow Jesus involve for you today?

9. THE COMMUNITY OF LITTLE ONES

The stories told in Matthew 14 – 16 have led us to Peter's confession that Jesus is the Messiah and the Son of God. In Matthew 17 we continue the theme of Jesus' identity as we see his divine glory revealed and are reminded of his divine sonship. In Matthew 18 Jesus teaches that to follow the Son, we must live as a community of little sons and daughters.

Transfigured: The Glory of the Son

Matthew begins chapter 17 with a rare indicator of time: "After six days" (**17:1**). It's six days after Peter's confession and six days after Jesus has predicted that some standing with him will see a foretaste of the heavenly glory of the Son of Man (Daniel 7:13-14). As if that wasn't **propitious** enough, Jesus takes Peter, James and John up a mountain. In the Exodus story, a mountain was the place where the Lord revealed his glory to Israel (Exodus 19). In Matthew's story it was where Jesus, as the new Moses, gave a new law (Matthew 5:1-2).

Matthew calls the transfiguration a "vision" (**17:9**, ESV). That doesn't mean it was some kind of dream or hallucination. Referring to the transfiguration, Peter would later say, "We were eye-witnesses of his majesty" (2 Peter 1:16). So this was a real event in human history.

Looking backwards, Moses and Elijah appear to confirm Jesus as the fulfilment of the Old Testament promises. Looking forwards, the transfiguration is a window onto the future glory of Jesus (as Matthew 16:28 indicates). More than this, the transfiguration gives a glimpse of the divine glory of the God-man. It parallels and fulfils Moses' encounter with God on Mount Sinai in Exodus 33 – 34. There, Moses asks to see God's glory, so God hides Moses in a cave, passes by and declares his Name (Exodus 33:18 – 34:7). When Moses comes down the mountain, his face is radiant (34:29-30). But God also says, "You cannot see my face, for no one may see me and live" (33:20).

Here in Matthew 17 is another mountain encounter, another voice from a cloud and another radiant face that evokes fear. But this time, Moses does get to see God's glory, in the face of Jesus Christ. And this radiant glory is not second-hand, as it was for Moses; rather, it radiates from Christ's own person. At his incarnation, Jesus hid his divine glory in human flesh, but for a brief moment at the transfiguration, that glory was seen on earth. The 6th-century **presbyter** Leontius said, "[Jesus] briefly opened the door of his Incarnation for them, and showed them clearly what great glory was concealed within him" (see ed. Brian Daley, *Light on the Mountain*, p. 126).

Jesus is the glory of God, dwelling with his people, wrapped up in human flesh.

"No one may see me and live," God had said to Moses, but now the disciples are seeing divine glory. Peter's solution is to put up three shelters, or tents (Matthew **17:4**). It's not as crazy as it first sounds. God's encounter with Moses in Exodus 33 – 34 came in the middle of the construction of the tabernacle: the temporary way for God to dwell among his people, protecting sinful people from the consuming purity of his holiness. Peter wants to replicate that—the word "shelter" in Matthew **17:4** is the word "tabernacle". But it's Jesus himself who is the tabernacle: John 1:14 is literally, "The Word became flesh and *tabernacled* among us". Jesus is the glory of God, dwelling with his people, wrapped up in human flesh.

In Matthew **17:5** a voice speaks from the cloud (just as a voice spoke from the cloud at Mount Sinai). God the Father repeats what he said at Jesus' baptism in 3:17 with one addition: "Listen to him!" Given what's happening at the time, we might have expected God to say, *Gaze upon him*. But the Father calls on the disciples to listen to Jesus—because they've just refused to listen to Jesus. The previous event in Matthew's story was Jesus speaking of his death and being rebuked by Peter (16:21-23). Now the Father confirms that the cross is part of an eternal plan of salvation. Even as we see the divine glory of Jesus, we're pointed to the centrality of the cross.

There are two distinctive features of Matthew account of the transfiguration. First, Matthew says, "His face shone like the sun" (**17:2**). It's a phrase Jesus has already used in 13:43: "the righteous will shine like the sun in the kingdom of their Father". We're not just seeing Jesus' future glory in the transfiguration; we're also seeing our future glory as children of God! The word translated "transfigured" in the Gospels is the same word translated elsewhere as "transformed" (Romans 12:2; 2 Corinthians 3:18). In the present, our conduct is being transfigured by the gospel so that we shine like stars (Philippians 2:15). Indeed, it's by contemplating the glory of Christ—a glory we see in the gospel—that we're transformed (2 Corinthians 3:18; 4:4-6). And in the future, our whole selves will be transfigured. The medieval theologian Anselm wrote that, at the transfiguration, Jesus "gave a preview of his own glory and of the glory of his own" (see Donald Macleod, *The Person of Christ*, p. 107).

Second, only in Matthew's account of this event does Jesus speak: "Get up ... Don't be afraid" (Matthew **17:6-8**). The fear of the disciples repeats the fear of Israel at Sinai when the voice of God spoke from a cloud (Exodus 20:18-20; Deuteronomy 5:22-27). The word translated "get up" is related to the word for resurrection. The disciples fall "to the ground" like dead men. This is an enactment of the gospel message. Humanity must fall before God's glory. But at the cross, Jesus falls to a grave in the ground, and then three days later he rises. As the firstborn from among the dead, he raises us with him

(Matthew **17:7**; 28:10). So we no longer need to fear judgment or death. We no longer fear the voice of God, for now the voice says, *Come.*

Jesus tells the disciples not to tell anyone about the transfiguration until after the resurrection (**17:9**). That's because (as we saw in 9:30 and 16:20) to see only his glory is to misunderstand what Jesus has come to do, for Jesus has come to die in shame to save his people. We cannot preach Jesus without preaching the cross.

The disciples then ask about Elijah (**17:10**). As we saw in 3:4 and 11:14, the Jews expected Elijah to return as the forerunner of the coming of the Lord. In the transfiguration, the disciples have seen something that looks a lot like the coming of the Lord, including a cameo role from Elijah. But Elijah's appearance was only brief. So is Elijah coming or not? *Yes, he is*, says Jesus (**17:11**). But it was never going to be a literal return. Malachi 4:5-6 looked forward to an Elijah-like prophet, and that person was John the Baptist (Matthew **17:13**). At this point, Jesus brings their conversation back to the main point he wants to make. Look at what happened to John: they executed him. And "in the same way the Son of Man is going to suffer at their hands" (**v 12**).

Affliction: The Absence of the Son

The story comes down to earth with a bump. We descend from the heights of the transfiguration to suffering and failure. Jesus is confronted by a man whose son is afflicted with demonic seizures (**v 14-15**). There is nothing new in that (4:23-24), but Matthew highlights the failure of the disciples (including himself) to heal the boy (**17:16**). The remaining disciples are not doing well in Jesus' absence. Perhaps Matthew is addressing his readers, living as we do after the ascension, without the physical presence of Christ on earth.

Publicly, Jesus rebukes the disciples for being "unbelieving and perverse" before he then heals the boy (**v 17-18**). Privately, Jesus repeats the charge: "You have so little faith" (**v 19-20**). "Little faith" is best understood as "perverse unbelief" or "poor faith" (Carson, *The Expositor's Bible Commentary*, Volume 8, p. 391). The next statement makes it clear that the quantity of faith is not the issue, for Jesus says faith as small as a mustard seed can move mountains—a proverb for overcoming huge problems (**v 20**).

In 10:1 Jesus had given the disciples authority to cast out demons. But perhaps, in his absence, they were trying to do this in their own strength. Their faith was misplaced and getting nowhere. The message is clear: to be fruitful in ministry we must continually feel our dependence on Jesus and look to him by faith to accomplish what he wants to accomplish.

Prediction: The Death of the Son

17:22-23 contains the second of three explicit predictions of his death by Jesus. (The other two are in 16:21 and 20:17-19.) They punctuate this section like the toll of a death knell or the beat of the executioner's drum. Each one represents another step towards the cross. This colours all the teaching that lies in between. The disciples (whether they yet realise it or not) are learning what it means to follow a crucified Lord.

Temple Tax: The Family of the Son

This strange story is unique to Matthew but serves his purpose well. The stories told in Matthew 14 – 17 have focused on the identity of Jesus as the Messiah and Son of God. The teaching of Matthew 18 is going to focus on the identity of *the people* who belong to the Son. In this story, those two themes mesh together.

Peter is asked whether Jesus pays the temple tax, and Peter confirms that he does (**17:24-25**). This was not a civil tax imposed by the Romans but a religious tax paid by Jewish men for the upkeep of the temple (Exodus 30:11-16). Later Jesus invites Peter to reflect on this exchange. "From whom do the kings of the earth collect duty and taxes—from their own children or from others?" (Matthew **17:25**) Obviously, as Peter says, the answer is "From others". "Then the children are exempt," comments Jesus (**v 26**). The meaning is clear: Jesus is under no obligation to pay the temple tax because he is God's Son and therefore exempt. But to avoid causing offence, Jesus pays the tax. He gets Peter to catch a fish in whose mouth, miraculously, there is a four-drachma coin (**v 27**). That would be remarkable enough, but the story reaches its climax when Jesus says, "Take it and give it to them for my tax and yours". I like to imagine Jesus pausing after the words "my tax" before delivering the punchline: *"and yours"*. Jesus is paying the tax even though he doesn't need to, and it's the same for Peter. Peter no longer needs to pay because Peter's become a son of God through his connection to Jesus. Just as one day Christians will share the radiance of Jesus (**v 2**; 13:43), so they already share the sonship of Jesus.

Questions for reflection

1. Which aspect of the transfiguration most thrills you today?
2. How does seeing Jesus in this way enable you to keep denying yourself in order to follow him and live under his rule?
3. How does it encourage you to know that as a Christian you already share the sonship of Jesus and will one day share the radiance of Jesus?

PART TWO

Living as Christ's Little Ones

Chapters 14 – 17 have invited us to consider how we're going to respond to Jesus as he's revealed to be the Son of God. The teaching of chapter 18 explores how we're to treat the people who belong to Jesus—people who share his sonship. Jesus alone is the Son of God by nature, sharing one divine being with the Father and the Spirit. But his people become children of God through their connection to the Son (a move Paul describes as "adoption to sonship" in Galatians 4:4-6).

18:1-5 sets the framework for this. The disciples ask who the greatest in the kingdom is. It's a reasonable question if you're thinking of earthly political structures. Who's going to be the finance minister, the justice secretary, the secretary of state? But this is "the kingdom of heaven": a kingdom of grace in which earthly hierarchies become irrelevant. Jesus doesn't even begin with who the greatest is; he begins with who gets in. Having placed a child in their midst to reinforce his point (**v 2**), he declares, "Truly I tell you, unless you change and become like little children, you will never enter the kingdom of heaven" (**v 3**). It's not that children are models of innocence or trust. It's not about human virtue at all. The point is that children are powerless and therefore models of dependence. You have to humble yourself to enter the kingdom, admitting your need and coming to Jesus in faith.

This humble, humbling, grace-filled entrance into the kingdom then shapes the life of the kingdom. "Therefore, whoever takes the lowly position of this child is the greatest in the kingdom of heaven" (**v 4**). Greatness comes by continuing to be lowly. It's not that lowliness is a tactic to achieve greatness but that all thoughts of achieving greatness fade in the upside-down kingdom of Jesus. That shapes our attitude to ourselves: we see ourselves as needy, lowly people who have been welcomed in grace. And it shapes our attitude to others: "Whoever welcomes one such child in my name welcomes me" (**v 5**).

We don't revere the successful—big names, platform speakers, celebrity converts, missionary heroes. The people we value are the "little" ones. In different contexts that might include children, the poor, the long-term sick, ethnic minorities, people with disabilities, the elderly, the mentally ill, the poorly educated and so on. We do this primarily because they're valued by Jesus. But they also remind us of who *we* are: needy people who have found mercy in Jesus. They're signs—**sacraments**, we might say—of the kingdom of grace. In 25:40 Jesus will say, "Whatever you did for one of the least of these brothers and sisters of mine, you did for me".

Don't Cause Little Ones to Stumble

18:3 introduced us to the "little children" who populate Christ's kingdom. The rest of the chapter elaborates what it means to care for these "little ones"—a phrase repeated in **verses 6, 10 and 14**.

Verses 6-9 first state this negatively: don't cause a Christian to stumble by making it harder for them to follow Jesus. A premature death would be better than the eternal consequences of despising one of Christ's little ones or leading them astray (**v 6**). The phrase "cause people to stumble" can include leading them into sin, damaging discouragement, a lack of pastoral care or a failure to forgive (see France, *The Gospel of Matthew*, p. 682). It's a salutary warning, especially for Christian pastors. Our aim cannot be to make a name for ourselves or stir up controversy or impress with our ingenuity. Our aim must always be to serve Christ's flock through faithful dependence on Christ and faithful adherence to his word. Challenges will come to people's faith, but we're to ensure that we're not the means through which they come (**v 7**).

Verses 8-9 repeat the teaching of 5:29-30, but in the context of Matthew 18 these words take on an added meaning. In Matthew 5 cutting off limbs and gouging out eyes was a picture of taking whatever steps are necessary to avoid sin. Here this expands to include taking whatever steps are necessary to avoid causing *others* to sin.

Do Restore Little Ones who Stray

18:10-20 states our care for little ones *positively*: we're to restore those who go astray.

It can be all too easy to divide people into those who we think contribute to church life and those who are a bit of a drag. If the latter stop coming, then it doesn't really matter. It might even make life a bit easier. But Jesus tells us not to "despise one of these little ones" (**v 10**).

This verse is sometimes used to justify a belief that each child has a guardian angel. But the "little ones" are members (young and old) of Christ's kingdom. Carson suggests that the angels here are the future spirits of departed Christians, who will perpetually be in the Father's presence when they come to heaven (22:30). On this reading, Jesus is saying that we should treat Christians as those who will one day be glorified (see Carson, *The Expositor's Bible Commentary,* Volume 8, p. 401). But given the echoes between **18:12-14** and Luke 15:1-7, it is just as likely that Jesus is referring to the joy experienced in heaven when little ones are restored.

In Matthew **18:12-13**, we're told to be like a shepherd who leaves the majority of his flock to focus on restoring one lost sheep. Elsewhere this picture is used to describe Jesus (Luke 15:1-7), but here Jesus applies it to us. We're to show the same care of others that Jesus showed to us (treating them as Jesus treats us) and to them (treating them as Jesus treats them). Wayward little ones may contribute little to our grandiose schemes, but Jesus warns us not to neglect their needs, for "your Father in heaven is not willing that any of these littles one should perish" (Matthew **18:14**). It prompts us to ask the question: do I need to recalibrate my ministry priorities?

Verses 15-20 are often read as if they are a manual for church government. But in the context of Matthew 18, these verses are about how we restore one of the wandering "little ones" of **verses 10-14**. So this is not a complaints procedure: "to speak of 'grievance' or of 'conflict resolution' here is inappropriate" (France, *The Gospel of Matthew*, p. 692). If someone is fearful of a leader for personal or cultural reasons, for example, they're unlikely to confront them one to one. So these verses shouldn't be used to dismiss concerns simply because people have "skipped a stage":

> "If there is conflict in church life, leaders may become defensive, shut down, panic, or want to ignore the difficulties and become passive. Alternatively, any questions raised can be recategorized as 'complaints' and a disciplinary procedure embarked on when what is needed is an open discussion to resolve a matter."
>
> (Ed. Graham Nicholls, *Challenging Leaders*, p. 39)

Nor do these verses rule out bringing in a third party to help resolve issues, especially when questions have been raised about the leadership or culture of the church (Nicholls, as above, p. 56, 109). Peter Leithart is very helpful here:

> "We are to become like children by assuming a lowly position in relation to others, by becoming their servants. That is what church discipline is about. Those who exercise discipline sometimes assume the position of lords, and they turn church discipline into something heavy-handed and brutal. That is an abuse of Jesus' commandments. Church discipline is not lording it over brothers but serving them."
>
> (*The Gospel of Matthew Through New Eyes: Jesus as Israel*, Volume 2, p. 85)

The focus here is on restoring little ones. You've succeeded only if you've "won them over" (**v 15**). First, you're to talk with them one to one. This is all part of the ongoing process of discipling one another. If someone complains to you about another believer, you should gently invite them to speak with that person. If a one-to-one conversation doesn't lead to repentance, you try again, taking one or two others with you (**v 16**). If that still doesn't work, then you bring the matter to the church (**v 17**). If the wayward brother or sister refuses to listen, then the church is to treat them as if they need to be converted (whether for the first time or all over again is not for us to adjudicate).

"Will be bound/loosed" in **verse 18** can be translated "will have been bound/loosed". Either way, the church doesn't decide what someone's eternal fate will be. Instead, we reflect a person's eternal fate back to them as best we understand it. We do this when we accept people into church membership (however formally or informally a particular church may do this, thereby providing an additional reassurance of their salvation. But we also do this when we **excommunicate** someone. If the evidence of a person's lifestyle suggests they're not submitting to Christ's lordship, then we need to make that reality explicit so that they're confronted with the need to repent:

> The church doesn't decide someone's eternal fate. Instead, we reflect their eternal fate back to them as best we understand it.

> "For Matthew, excommunication, when it comes, will be self-imposed exile. The community, if it is to be true to itself, if it is forbearing, anxious about the welfare of all its members, and animated by a spirit of forgiveness, will give sinners more than a fair chance. If, despite everything, excommunication follows, that can only be because the one excommunicated has finally refused to live within the law of the church."
>
> (Davies, *Matthew: A Shorter Commentary*, p. 311)

This decision should only be undertaken with reluctance. We've just been warned in the strongest terms neither to cause little ones to stumble (**v 6-9**) nor to despise them (**v 10**). Church discipline is not a mechanism for removing awkward people or people who don't share our vision. Though elsewhere Paul says that church discipline protects the flock (1 Corinthians 5:6-8), here the focus is on restoring the wayward. Making that call to excommunicate is never easy. That's why God promises to hear our prayers for these matters, and Jesus promises to be with the church when it gathers for this purpose (Matthew **18:19-20**). What the church does in preaching the gospel, welcoming those who repent and discipling those who refuse to repent, has eternal ramifications. We act with the authority of heaven.

Keep on Forgiving Little Ones

If a wandering "little one" repents, then we are to welcome them back. But what if they wander again? What if they sin against you personally? "Lord, how many times shall I forgive my brother or sister who sins against me?" asks Peter in **verse 21**. Peter puts in an opening bid, one he probably regarded as very generous: "Up to seven times?" But Jesus replies, "I tell you, not seven times, but seventy-seven times" (**v 22**). It's a way of saying we should go on forgiving indefinitely, beyond any number we can reasonably count.

This teaching can be falsely used to claim that abused people should continue to accept their abusers. But repentance and forgiveness go together. God only forgives those who repent (though, in his case, he graciously grants that repentance to his people). In the same way, while we should love and pray for our enemies (5:44), we can only be reconciled to those who genuinely repent. Nor is forgiveness the same as trust. While forgiveness can be given, trust must be earned. So, even when there is forgiveness, a relationship might not go back to the way it was before.

But our focus shouldn't be on what the text doesn't say but on what it does say. Wandering "little ones" who repent should be accepted back again and again and again. Hurtful little ones who repent should be forgiven again and again. But, as Osborne points out…

> "Christ is not saying that forgiveness must be instantaneous. It is a process often demanding a great deal of time and counselling. Still, mercy and forgiveness should at all times be the goal for which we strive." (*Matthew*, p. 998)

The reason why we go on forgiving is that this is how God treats us. This is the point Jesus is making by telling the parable of a servant whose multimillion-dollar debt is forgiven by his king (**18:23-35**). As the servant walks free, he finds a fellow servant who owes him a few cents and violently demands repayment before throwing the second servant into prison (**v 28-30**). News of this outrageous behaviour reaches the king, who has the first servant thrown into prison (**v 31-34**).

The king is Jesus himself, and we're his servants. We can never repay the debt we've accumulated through our sin. But Jesus has paid that debt in full at the cross on our behalf so that we can walk free. Now we're to show the same attitude to those who sin against us. That's the point of the parable (**v 35**). The punishment given to the first servant is to be treated in the same way that he treated the second servant (**v 30, 34**). The appropriateness of this fate is highlighted by the fact that the second servant uses the same words that the first servant used before the king: "Be patient with me" (**v 26, 29**). It's not that we earn mercy from God by being merciful to others. The movement is the other way round: those who have received mercy from God reflect that same mercy in their dealings with other people—as the Lord's Prayer reminds us (6:12, 14).

In Genesis 4:23-24, Lamech (a descendent of **Cain**) boasts, "I have killed a man for wounding me, a young man for injuring me. If Cain is avenged seven times, then Lamech seventy-seven times." Rather than forgiving, Lamech murders a young man (a "little one") as repayment for an injury. When he killed his brother, Cain had begged for God's protection, and so God had graciously declared a sevenfold vengeance on anyone who harmed him (Genesis 4:13-15). But now Lamech arrogantly boasts of his impunity; he'll be avenged "seventy-seven times". Such is life among the descendants of Cain in the kingdom of this world. But in the kingdom of heaven, it's mercy rather than vengeance that flows seventy-seven times.

We *enter* the kingdom as little ones, and we *live* in the kingdom as little ones. Our attitude to Christ's little ones is the mark and measure of authentic ministry. It's easy for the little ones to become the means we employ to fulfil grand plans for saving the world (which are often really grand plans to make us look grand). We lionise visionary or charismatic leaders who can mobilise people to the cause. But, as I've had to learn through my own failures, it's the little ones themselves who are the true "cause".

The church is to be a place where the lost are welcomed and the least are honoured (Matthew **18:1-5**): a place where the vulnerable are safe (**v 6-9**) and where the wayward are pursued in love (**v 10-20**). Yes, it's a community where people let one another down, but it is also one where grudges are not nursed and reconciliation is quickly made. It's a place where the broken, the nobodies and the fragile come together to be the family of God.

Questions for reflection

1. How is Jesus' view of greatness different from the other views you see around you (and possibly within you)? When do you find it easiest to live for a different kind of "greatness"?
2. Is there another Christian whom you need to seek to restore or whom you are being called to forgive?
3. How has the vision of Christian community painted in this section encouraged you to pursue making it a reality in your own church?

10. WELCOMING THE LITTLE ONES

Matthew 19 begins by rounding off the teaching in chapter 18 with Matthew's usual section conclusion (**19:1**). Jesus has twice predicted his death in Jerusalem (16:21; 17:22-23). Now he leaves Galilee and steps closer to Jerusalem, heading towards death rather than running from it (**19:1-2**).

The focus of Matthew 18 was on how we treat "the little ones" who populate the kingdom of Jesus. This theme continues in Matthew 19, where we're presented with three case studies which ask us to consider how we should treat vulnerable women, little children and the economically poor.

Marriage, Divorce and Forgiveness

Some Pharisees ask Jesus about divorce, but Matthew tells us that, in truth, they've come to "test" Jesus (**v 3**). It's important to remember this: what Jesus says here is not his pastoral response to someone in a difficult marriage. John the Baptist had been killed for challenging the legitimacy of Herod's marriage to the divorced wife of his brother (14:1-12)—perhaps the questioners hope Jesus will suffer the same fate. But the Pharisees were themselves divided on the issue of divorce. The traditional position was that divorce was only permitted on the grounds of adultery. Deuteronomy 24:1 speaks of "a cause of indecency" ("something indecent" in the NIV), which everyone interpreted as including adultery. But a new position had emerged which argued that the words "cause" and "indecency" in Deuteronomy 24 describe *two separate grounds* for divorce, with the word "cause" covering virtually any way in which a wife might displease her husband, from bad cooking to diminishing looks. It was known as "any cause" divorce and required no proof in court. It was the original version of "no-fault" divorce, though it was an option only for men. This new view was the popular one—at least with Jewish men. Perhaps his questioners hope Jesus' response will damage his appeal. All this is in the background as they ask Jesus the question in Matthew **19:3**: "Is it lawful for a man to divorce his wife for any and every reason?" In other words, *Do you back the new "any cause" view of divorce?* Jesus is asked to pick a side.

Jesus talks not so much about divorce as about marriage.

It becomes clear that Jesus sides with the traditional position and rejects "any cause" divorce. But he doesn't answer the question directly; instead, he goes backs to basics, talking not so much about divorce as about marriage. And he doesn't go back to Moses, but to creation.

God made two types of people: male and female. Jesus quotes Genesis 1:27 to prove this (Matthew **19:4**). God made male and female to be united with one another in a complementary way. Then, quoting from Genesis 2:24, Jesus reminds us that God's will is that sexual union should take place in the context of a committed marital bond (Matthew **19:5**). Weddings may take different forms in different cultures, but there is to be a public commitment to one another involving covenant commitments. Indeed, marriage is designed to be a picture of the covenant that God has made with his people. When God's Old Testament people broke God's covenant, it was pictured as adultery. So sexual intercourse belongs within marriage, and sex outside of marriage is always wrong.

To the question "Is it lawful for a man to divorce his wife for any and every reason?" comes the answer "What God has joined together, let no one separate" (**v 6**). Every marriage is made in heaven. It's God himself who joins a couple together through the act of sexual intercourse. Every act of intercourse is a supernatural act in which, as I give myself to another, our two selves are fused by God. If I then pull that unity apart, I tear something of my inner self in the process. The way God created the world indicates that a man and woman should be united in marriage for life.

So why then did the law of Moses include provision for divorce? That's the question the Pharisees ask in **verse 7**. They think it's legitimate to divorce your wife for almost any reason because the law of Moses talks about divorce. But Jesus says this law is not a sign of legitimacy but of sin. It indicates hardness of heart—one of the Bible's expressions for rebellion against God (**v 8**). God did not introduce the divorce law because he had changed his mind about divorce (Malachi 2:16), but to limit and regulate the trauma of marital breakdown. It was designed to protect vulnerable women and their children who might otherwise be left without support. "But it was not this way from the beginning," adds Jesus (Matthew **19:8**); human beings were made to flourish within life-long sexual unions.

Notice, too, how Jesus subtly corrects the Pharisees' reading of the law. They speak of Moses *commanding* divorce for adultery while Jesus describes Moses *permitting* divorce for adultery (**v 7-8**). A spouse can choose to forgive a repentant adulterer (though they do not *have* to)—as God himself did when his people were spiritually adulterous (Jeremiah 3:8; Hosea 1 – 3). The preceding passage has commended the repeated forgiveness of repentant sinners (Matthew 18:21-35).

In **19:9** Jesus summarises the logic of his argument: "I tell you that anyone who divorces his wife, except for sexual immorality, and marries another woman commits adultery". Divorce itself doesn't break the marriage bond—that's why Jesus can say remarriage in such circumstances adds up to adultery. But divorce may recognise that the marriage bond has been broken through sexual sin or desertion (including violence and abuse). In such circumstances divorce is not so much sinful as the recognition of sin. Jesus says remarriage after illegitimate divorce is adultery—in my opinion, the implication is that remarriage after legitimate divorce is permissible.

Jesus clearly backs the traditional prohibition of divorce except on very limited grounds. Jesus himself mentions "sexual immorality": a broad term that includes adultery and other sexual sins (see also 5:32). Exodus 21:10-11 suggests desertion is another ground for divorce. Most Christians take desertion to include violence or other forms of abuse. Paul also says that if an unbelieving spouse leaves a marriage, then the Christian spouse should allow this (1 Corinthians 7:12-15). The Christian is then "not bound". This could mean they're not bound to fight the divorce, or it could mean they're free to remarry (since in 1 Corinthians 7:39 being "free" means free to remarry). The **Westminster Confession of Faith** concludes that "nothing but adultery, or such wilful desertion as can no way be remedied by the Church, or civil magistrate, is cause sufficient of dissolving the bond of marriage" (§24.6).

Divorce, then, is either a sin or the result of sin. But it's precisely because we can call it sin that we can speak of forgiveness. This is the good news of the gospel (Matthew 9:9-13). Jesus has died for sin, and he did not die in vain. If someone becomes a Christian and their past relationships are complicated, Paul's rule of thumb is that "each person should remain in the situation they were in when God called them" (1 Corinthians 7:20).

But the concern of Jesus here is not to establish legitimate grounds for divorce (important as that is). His concern is to rule out all the illegitimate grounds. He calls us to work hard at making marriages work well. Matthew places this teaching alongside the call to go on forgiving repentant sinners (Matthew 18:21-35). We're called to love our spouse even when they've let us down seventy-seven times because that's how God has treated his bride (v 22). And we're called to love our spouse by not letting them down because, again, that's how God has treated us.

Divorce is endemic in Western society today, as are sexual unions outside of marriage. The Christian view of marriage has become counter-cultural. But it was counter-cultural in Jesus' day too. The disciples wonder whether marriage is worth the risk, especially if you can't remarry if the marriage sours (**19:10**). Jesus says, "Not everyone can accept this word" (**v 11**), probably referring to the disciples' conclusion that "it is better not to marry". Just as some people (eunuchs) are physically unable to have sex, so others can choose to live without sex in obedience to God (**v 12**). They might do this because they've chosen celibacy to serve Christ better (1 Corinthians 7:32-35) or because their marriage has broken down without legitimate grounds for remarriage (Matthew **19:10-12**).

A person's personal self-fulfilment is what counts in our culture, and if my marriage doesn't provide this, then I'm encouraged to look elsewhere. But Jesus says, "Whoever wants to save their life will lose it, but whoever loses their life for me will find it" (16:25). Jesus himself is heading towards Jerusalem knowing that that means the cross, with all its suffering and betrayal, and he sets the cross as the mark of Christian discipleship, with its model of sacrificial love, self-denial and submission to God (v 24).

Little Children: The Last Will Be First

19:13-15 enacts the teaching of 18:1-5. Jesus had said we must become like children to enter the kingdom, recognising our dependence on God (v 3). He also said we welcome him when we welcome children in his name (v 5). Now the disciples have an opportunity to apply this teaching to a real-life scenario—and they fail. The punchline of chapter 19 is "Many who are first will be last, and many who are last will be first" (**19:30**). The children are a model of the last and least becoming first and foremost in the kingdom of Jesus. In the next story we meet an example of the first and foremost becoming last and lost.

The Rich Young Ruler: The First Will Be Last

"Teacher, what good thing must I do to get eternal life?" This is what the rich young ruler asks Jesus in **verse 16**. "Why do you ask me about what is good?" Jesus replies: "There is only One who is good. If you want to enter life, keep the commandments" (**v 17**). When Jesus says "Why do you ask me... ?" he's responding to the man's description of him as a teacher. *You don't need a teacher,* Jesus is saying in effect. *You don't need more information.* That's because (1) the man already has the commandments; and (2) what he really needs is God. There's only one person who is good (God) and only one way to become good (with God's help).

But the man isn't ready to admit his need. He still thinks eternal life is something we can earn. So he asks Jesus to be more specific (**v 18**). Jesus lists some of the Ten Commandments, plus the summary call to love your neighbour (**v 18-19**; Exodus 20:12-16; Deuteronomy 5:16-21; Leviticus 19:18). They all have to do with external actions, and this gives the man the confidence to claim he's kept them all. In fact, arguably, his words are **blasphemous**, since he's claiming to be good enough to have kept all the law (Matthew **19:20**), when Jesus has just said only God is truly good (**v 17**).

Jesus now moves to expose his heart: "If you want to be perfect, go, sell your possessions and give to the poor" (**v 21**). It's a version of the first and last commandments—"You shall have no other gods before me" and "You shall not covet" (Exodus 20:3, 17)—applied to the specific idols in this man's heart. Jesus isn't saying that every Christian must sell their possessions (there are examples of Christians owning property in the New Testament). But we must be committed to putting God first. For different people the potential rival to God will be different. For this man it was his wealth, and it was a price he was unwilling to pay (Matthew **19:22**). For you it may be career, relationships, sex, pleasure or status. While you might not be called to sell your possessions, for each of us there's a decisive choice to be made to put God first. Peter Leithart links this story back to the message of the Sermon on the Mount:

> "The young man has the righteousness of the scribes, but Jesus requires His disciples to live out a righteousness that exceeds the righteousness of the scribes and Pharisees, a righteousness that is not confined to refraining from evil but expresses itself in doing excessive, redeeming good ... Jesus' own righteousness is a redemptive righteousness, and He invites us to share in that righteousness ... The young man might refrain from theft, but Jesus calls him to give his wealth to the poor."
>
> (*The Gospel of Matthew Through New Eyes: Jesus as Israel*, Volume 2, p. 107)

People assumed that the wealthy were nearer to God because they were receiving more of his blessing. But Jesus turns this on its head (**v 23-24**). Rich people are so used to having status and power that they find it hard to admit they have nothing before God. It's sometimes said that the eye of a needle was a narrow gate into Jerusalem through which you might just squeeze a camel—but there's no historical evidence for this at all. The point is that it's humanly impossible; and that's how the disciples understand it (**v 25**). But then Jesus adds, "With man this is impossible, but with God all things are possible" (**v 26**).

> Rich people are so used to having status and power that they find it hard to admit they have nothing before God.

"Who then can be saved?" ask the disciples. Matthew 19 provides two complementary answers. First, Jesus says, "The kingdom of heaven belongs to such as these [little children]" (**v 14**). Only by admitting we're dependent like little children can we come to God (18:3). Second, Jesus speaks of "the renewal of all things" in **19:28**. He's speaking about the renewal of creation at the end of time. But the word "renewal" is the word "regeneration", which elsewhere describes the way the Holy Spirit awakens our dead hearts and gives sight to our blind eyes (John 3:3-6; Titus 3:5; see also Matthew 20:29-34). So the renewal of creation is anticipated in our regeneration when we become mini new creations (2 Corinthians 5:17). Human resistance to God—including the resistance of the rich—is overcome by the Spirit's transforming work. We can't lead a consistently disobedient life and expect to enter the kingdom of God, but both obedience and its rewards are God's gift (as 20:15 will confirm).

Then and now, it looks as if the world belongs to the rich. Not so, says Jesus. Those who have left everything to follow Jesus will one day rule the world (**19:27-28**). Those who have sacrificed much will be rewarded in the age to come (**v 29**). The cross-shaped kingdom of Jesus is an upside-down kingdom in which women matter (they can't simply be disposed of), children matter (they find a welcome among God's people), and the poor matter (they're not second-best to the rich).

Questions for reflection

1. What do you make of the explanation of Jesus' teaching on marriage and divorce here? Are there ways in which what Jesus says is as countercultural in your own context as it was 2,000 years ago?
2. What are the differences between the little children and the rich young ruler in terms of their attitude to themselves and to Jesus?
3. "Those who have left everything to follow Jesus will one day rule the world." Does thinking about this truth and your own life comfort you or challenge you, or both?

PART TWO

In Matthew 19 we met a group of children and a rich man. Of those two parties, who's done more for God? Who's spent more time in prayer? Who's given more donations? Who's studied the Scriptures the most? The answer is clearly the rich man. Yet we finished chapter 19 with little children being blessed in God's kingdom (19:15) and the rich man walking away sad (v 22). The chapter ends, "But many who are first will be last, and many who are last will be first," and a similar phrase concludes the next parable: "So the last will be first, and the first will be last" (19:30; **20:16**).

Vineyard Workers: Blessing the First and Last

The parable tells the story of a landowner who hires day-labourers to gather his harvest (**v 1**). Some workers are hired early in the morning, and so they work all day (**v 2**). At different points in the day, other workers are hired who then only work part of the day (**v 3-7**). Yet all end up being paid the same wage (**v 8-10**). The all-day workers grumble at this (**v 11-12**). But they receive their agreed wage (**v 13-14**). "Don't I have the right to do what I want with my own money?" says the landowner. "Or are you envious because I am generous?" (**v 15**).

The workers hired late in the day might represent Gentile converts who join the storyline of God's kingdom long after the Jews, but receive the same blessings. That's a theme in Matthew's Gospel, but not in this context. In the Old Testament the vineyard is a picture of Israel (Isaiah 5:1-7; 27:2-3), with God's people as a whole either viewed as fruitful or unfruitful. So the parable might be about serving God's people. But this idea is not the main focus. The parable begins and ends with the reversal of the first and last (Matthew 19:30; **20:16**)—a fact masked by our chapter divisions. This framing of the parable suggests that it's a commentary on the whole of Matthew 18 – 19, and especially the inclusion of "little ones" and "little children" (18:2-6, 10; 19:13-15) and the self-exclusion of the rich man (v 22).

The point is that no one earns their way into the kingdom of Jesus, and no one gains extra status through their good works. It's those who *become* like dependent children who enter the kingdom and those who *live* like dependent children who are great in the kingdom (18:3-4). So when it comes to receiving blessing from God, we shouldn't be surprised if those blessings don't correlate to the merit of the recipient. God's generous grace doesn't work like that. That's just as well, for if we received what we deserved we'd all be in deep trouble. But God in his love blesses us far above and beyond our merits. "Because I am generous" in **20:15** is literally "because I am good". The "good thing" the young man craves in 19:16 is found in God's generous grace. As Matt Searles puts it:

> "Do we begrudge God's generosity to others? To other Christians, or even other churches that we think of as less faithful? ... If we're looking like this at others, it's because we've a wrong view of ourselves ... We think we've earned what we have from God ... We've also a wrong view of God. The true antidote to entitlement is to understand the character of God: like the vineyard owner he is generous and loves to give good things. He never gives less than anyone deserves, but he delights to give more!"
>
> (*Matthew: One Greater than Solomon*, p. 32)

The Ultimate First and Last

Jesus then predicts his death a third time (16:21; 17:22-23), this time adding that he'll be handed over "to the Gentiles to be mocked and flogged and crucified" (**20:17-19**). This follows Jesus saying, "The last will be first, and the first will be last" (**v 16**). Jesus himself is going to be the supreme model of this. On the cross he will be the ultimate person in last place. But then he'll be raised and exalted to the highest place, and when we see him exalted to the position he held before his incarnation, we'll discover he's also been the ultimate person in first place, who in his mercy became last for our sakes.

Two Brothers Who Don't See

The next three stories are linked by pairs: two brothers (**v 20-28**), two blind men (**v 29-34**) and two disciples who collect the donkey upon which Jesus enters Jerusalem (**21:1-11**). It's Matthew's way of alerting us to the thematic links between these stories.

In the first story, the sons of Zebedee (James and John, see 4:21) ask to sit at the left and right of Jesus' throne. Only Matthew tells us that the request came through their mother (**20:20-21**). It creates a comic touch: James and John want positions of authority, but they need their mum to speak for them.

To understand what's right and wrong about this request we need to remember what's been going on.

In 19:28 Jesus said, "When the Son of Man sits on his glorious throne, you who have followed me will also sit on twelve thrones, judging the twelve tribes of Israel". The disciples will be given "the keys of the kingdom", through which they'll pass judgments that span earth and heaven (16:19; 18:18). Here's what the brothers get right: the disciples will exercise authority in the kingdom of Jesus. What they don't realise is that this authority is exercised through the preaching of the word. This is how the kingdom is advanced, and a person's response to this preaching is what determines their future (whether they're bound or loosed).

Jesus has just said that he's about to be crucified and then raised (**20:17-19**), and back in 16:24 he said that the cross would be the pattern for his followers. But the brothers want to skip the suffering and sacrifice, and instead jump straight to the glory and power. It's still a common desire today. Some people promise health and wealth now if we just have enough faith. They want to bypass the way of the cross and jump straight to the blessings of the new creation.

Exercising the authority of the kingdom through the preaching of the word is going to be a hard task conducted in the face of hostility. This is why Jesus says, "You don't know what you are asking ... Can you drink the cup I am going to drink?" (**20:22**). In other words, *You will get your* *wish and exercise authority, but only through suffering.* Don Carson writes, "To ask to reign with Jesus is to ask to suffer with him" (*The Expositor's Bible Commentary*, Volume 8, p. 431). For James it will mean martyrdom; for John it will mean exile (Acts 12:2; Revelation 1:9). It's the cup of suffering that Jesus drinks. Uniquely for Jesus, this includes drinking the cup of God's **wrath**. But in common with his people, the cup represents suffering for God's glory (Matthew **20:23**).

The other truth that the brothers have missed is that greatness in the kingdom belongs to "whoever takes the lowly position of this child" (18:4). Mrs Zebedee comes on behalf of her children like one of the mothers Jesus welcomes in 19:13-15, but her request is diametrically opposed to the spirit of that passage, where Jesus says the kingdom belongs to little children. The other disciples have missed this as well because they're indignant when they hear about the brothers' request (**20:24**). So Jesus has to repeat the lesson of 18:1-5. This time he makes a slave (rather than a child) his model of upside-down greatness (**20:25-27**), but the ultimate model is Jesus himself: "The Son of Man did not come to be served, but to serve, and to give his life as a ransom for many" (**v 28**).

Jesus contrasts the upside-down leadership in his upside-down kingdom with the way the world works.

This remains an important challenge to us. Jesus contrasts the upside-down leadership in his upside-down kingdom with the way the world works. Worldly leadership is all about gaining authority either for its own sake or for your own sake (**v 25**). "Not so with you," says Jesus (**v 26**). Christians are to use authority (whether in the world, workplace, church or home) for the sake of others—to protect, nurture and bless. Think about the authority you exercise. Do you use your authority to serve yourself or to serve others? Is your leadership modelled on the crucified King?

Two Blind Men Who Do See

At one level, this is a straightforward story of a miraculous healing—but Matthew places it side by side with the request of the two brothers. James and John see Jesus as the Messiah, but they don't see what kind of Messiah he is or what kind of kingdom he's establishing. They have physical sight, but they lack spiritual insight. The two blind men also lack sight: in their case physical sight—they have enough spiritual insight to recognise Jesus as a merciful Messiah (**v 29-31**). But by the end of the story, the blind men have "received their sight" (**v 32-34**). Not only that, but they're following Jesus (**v 34**)—literally following him along the road to the cross and figuratively following the pattern of the cross. So this story is a promise that, in the end, James and John will also receive sight (in the sense of insight). John would go on to write the book of Revelation, the central theme of which is the triumph of suffering witness. In **verse 21** the brothers want to sit on thrones; in Revelation 20:4 John says that those who sit on thrones are the martyrs—who, by that point, include his brother James (Acts 12:2).

Two Disciples Collect a Strange Symbol of Authority

The pattern of two key characters acting together continues in the next story: the triumphal entry into Jerusalem. Jesus sends two disciples to collect two donkeys (mother plus colt) which seem to be available for his use by some prior arrangement (Matthew **21:1-3**).

Once again Matthew is exploring the upside-down authority of Jesus. The donkey is a symbol of messianic authority. As we've seen, Matthew loves to spotlight the fulfilment of Scripture (**v 4-5**). Here he takes us back to Zechariah 9:9-10, which speaks of the coming of a king who will proclaim peace to the nations. So those who knew their Scriptures would realise that, by entering Jerusalem on a donkey, Jesus was claiming to be God's promised King (Matthew **21:6-8**). The crowd seem to catch on, for they cry, "Hosanna to the Son of David" (**v 9**)—though they then only describe Jesus as a prophet in **verses 10-11**.

Donkeys had been royal mounts (see, for instance, 1 Kings 1:32-35), but they were also a sign of peace. In Zechariah they're contrasted to the enemy's "chariots" and "warhorses". Imagine a rider on a donkey tilting into battle against a mighty stallion! But King Jesus is not a normal king. He's not coming to conquer Jerusalem but to bring peace. He's come "to serve, and to give his life as a ransom for many" (Matthew **20:28**). Searles points out that...

> "by riding the donkey, Jesus is clearly identifying himself with the king promised in Zechariah. But he is also showing what sort of king he is. There is no horse, no chariot, no show of power or strength. Jesus is a humble king."
>
> (*Matthew: One Greater than Solomon*, p. 34)

In Matthew **21:9** the crowd quote from Psalm 118:25-26, a psalm which speaks of "the festal procession" (v 27). A few verses earlier the psalmist says, "The stone the builders rejected has become the **cornerstone**" (v 22). It's a verse Jesus himself quotes a day or two later, in Matthew 21:42. Like the donkey, it speaks of his authority; he will be the foundation upon which the kingdom rests. But his kingdom will be established only through his rejection at the cross.

Questions for reflection

1. How can you live as a dependent child today?
2. Are there ways in which you're asking Jesus to give you the new creation while bypassing the way of the cross?
3. If you have any position of leadership in one sphere of life or another, what will it mean for you to exercise that leadership in a Jesus-like way?

11. THE FIRST WILL BE LAST: REJECTING THE PROUD

Back in Matthew 11:7-11 Jesus said John the Baptist was the messenger promised by the prophet Malachi. Here's what Malachi had prophesied:

> "'I will send my messenger, who will prepare the way before me. Then suddenly the Lord you are seeking will come to his temple; the messenger of the covenant, whom you desire, will come,' says the LORD Almighty. But who can endure the day of his coming? Who can stand when he appears? For he will be like a refiner's fire or a launderer's soap." (Malachi 3:1-2)

Jesus uses the opening line as a description of John. But what happens next? The Lord comes to his temple to refine and cleanse, smelting out the dross or washing out the dirt—and this is what happens in Matthew 21 – 25. John has come as Malachi promised, and next Jesus comes as the Lord. In Matthew 21:1-11 Jesus enters Jerusalem as the King coming to offer peace to rebels (as we saw in the previous chapter); in **verses 12-17** Jesus enters the temple courts as the Lord coming to refine and cleanse. This is followed by a sequence of conflicts in the temple courts in which Jesus exposes and condemns his opponents (21:23 – 23:36). Jesus is setting in motion a chain of events that will ultimately lead to the destruction of the temple in AD 70, just as he predicts in **21:18-22**, 23.37-39 and 24.15-21.

Casting Out Money-Changers: The Lord Cleanses His Temple

Malachi said the Lord would refine and cleanse the temple, and this is the first thing Jesus does when he enters it. When someone made a pilgrimage to the temple, they needed an animal to sacrifice and to convert their Roman money into the temple currency in order to pay the temple tax (see 17:24-27; 22:15-21). But it seems that having traders *within* the temple courts was a recent innovation. Jesus condemns this in **21:12-13** because...

1. this market-place crowded out space for prayer—hence Jesus' call for the temple to be "a house of prayer" (quoting Isaiah 56:7).

2. this monopoly led to extortionate prices—hence Jesus' condemnation of the temple as "a den of robbers" (quoting Jeremiah 7:11).

But Jesus doesn't simply expel people from the temple. His ultimate goal is to welcome people into God's presence. So Matthew continues: "The blind and the lame came to him at the temple, and he healed them" (Matthew **21:14**). Ordinarily the temple authorities excluded these people from the temple, but in Jesus they find a welcome and healing. And it's not only the blind and lame who are welcomed—those with ears to hear would remember that the Isaiah passage quoted by Jesus speaks of "a house of prayer *for all nations*" (Isaiah 56:7, emphasis added). A market-place in the **Court of the Gentiles** had left no room for the nations to come to God (as Isaiah had promised they would in Isaiah 2:3).

The temple leaders object to what Matthew calls "wonderful things" (Matthew **21:15**), probably because of their messianic connotations. They want Jesus to silence the praise of the children. But Jesus says this is a sign of God's kingdom (**v 16**; 18:1-5; 19:13-15). It's the religious leaders who are going to be silenced (22:34, 46). Psalm 8 speaks of praising of God, which Jesus applies to himself as Immanuel, God with us.

There's an echo here of the founding story of Jerusalem (2 Samuel 5:6-9). When King David first went to capture the city, its inhabitants claimed, "You will not get in here; even the blind and the lame can ward you off". But David did take the city. And now, as David's successor is "recapturing" Jerusalem, the physically blind are welcomed while the spiritually blind again fail to repel the Davidic king (as Matthew 21 – 23 will demonstrate).

This theme of the self-righteous being excluded and the needy being welcomed continues throughout this section (**21:31-32**, **41, 43; 22:8-10**). Jesus is enacting his declaration that, "the last will be first, and the first will be last" (19:30; 20:16).

The Fig Tree: The Lord Curses His Temple

The following morning Jesus finds a fig tree without fruit. Figs appear shortly after fig trees come into leaf, so normally leaves are a sign of fruit (24:32). Probably this is the first and only tree in leaf, but there's no fruit. So Jesus curses the tree, which immediately withers (**21:18-19**). It's an enacted parable (see Jeremiah 8:13; Micah 7:1). Jesus had every reason to expect spiritual fruit from the temple and the religious system it represented. Indeed, like the leaves on the fig tree, the religious leaders declared their fruitfulness. But when Jesus came as the Lord to his temple, he found it barren (Matthew 3:8-10; 7:16-20; 12:33; **21:33-44**). Their fig leaves are more like Adam's (Genesis 3:7), with their protestations of righteousness failing to hide their sin. So the cursing of the tree is an enacted curse on the temple (Matthew **21:43**; 23:37-39; 24:15-21). Everyone "under their own fig-tree" was a picture of peace during Solomon's reign (1 Kings 4:25), but that peace is about to be shattered.

The disciples are more interested in how than why (Matthew **21:20**). So Jesus makes the link to the temple more explicit. This event takes place as Jesus is "on his way back to the city", so "this mountain" is the one in front of them—the mountain upon which the temple stands (**v 17-21**). Those with faith can do to "this mountain" what Jesus has done to the tree (**v 21**). It's not a call to *displace* mountains; the point is that the disciples will *replace* this particular mountain as the place where the nations come to meet God. Hence the punchline: "If you believe, you will receive whatever you ask for in prayer" (**v 22**). This doesn't mean God will give us anything and everything we ask for in prayer. It is not a promise of health and wealth. God always answers our prayers in his love and wisdom, giving us what is truly for our good. When we feel that we're receiving *less* than we asked for (fewer physical blessings), God may actually be giving us *more* than we asked for (an opportunity for spiritual growth). But what this verse *does* mean is that the church community is going to become "the house of prayer"—the place where prayer is answered. When the temple had first been built, King Solomon had prayed, "Hear the **supplication** of your servant and of your people Israel when they pray towards this place" (1 Kings 8:30). "This place" is about to be destroyed, but Jesus promises that God will hear the supplication of those who pray in faith. Is your church known as "a house of prayer"? And is your private "room" a secret house of prayer (Matthew 6:6)?

Parables of Sons and Tenants: The Lord Reallocates His Temple

Back in the temple courts, the religious establishment question the authority of Jesus (**21:23**). It's a reasonable request, since Jesus is acting as the Lord cleansing his temple. But we already know they're indignant with Jesus (**v 15**), and so we know this is really an accusation rather than a genuine question.

At one level, Jesus side-steps their question to avoid premature confrontation. But his response exposes their unbelief. Jesus says he'll answer their question if they first say whether John's authority was heavenly or human (**v 24-25**). If they say heavenly, then they must accept the authority of Jesus, since John pointed to Jesus. But if they say John's authority was human, then they'll anger the people, since John was regarded as a prophet (**v 26**). The religious leaders therefore refuse to answer (**v 27**). Jesus has reframed the question. It's not simply a question of whether you think it was right to overturn the tables in the temple. The real question is whether you'll accept God's word—even if it overturns your world. The hardened hearts of the religious leaders are exposed. "Though seeing, they do not see" (13:11-15).

> The real question is whether you'll accept God's word, even if it overturns your world.

Matthew includes a parable (which Mark and Luke omit) which Jesus uses to comment on the religious leaders' refusal to answer his question about John (**21:32**). A man asks his two sons to work in his vineyard. One son says he won't serve but does, while the other says he will serve but doesn't. Everyone agrees the first son did what the father wanted (**v 28-31**). Jesus then identifies the first son with tax collectors and prostitutes. At the start of their lives, they looked like people who refused to serve God, but now they're repenting of their sin and entering the kingdom through faith (**v 31**). Jesus himself is the ultimate obedient Son (Hebrews 10:5-7), and believing sinners are counted faithful in him. The religious leaders are like the second son. They proclaimed their obedience but then refused to listen to God's prophet (Matthew **21:32**). The religious leaders saw themselves as custodians of the temple, but the house of prayer is being reassigned to repentant sinners.

We find the same theme in a second vineyard parable. A landowner (God) has entrusted his vineyard (God's kingdom) to tenants (the religious establishment) (**v 33**). But when the landowner sends his servants—the prophets—to collect the fruit, the tenants abuse them and refuse to give what they owe (**v 34-36**). So eventually the landowner sends his son—Jesus (**v 37**). But the tenants kill the son—a prophecy that the religious establishment will kill Jesus (**v 38-39**). In response, the owner takes the vineyard from the tenants by force and gives it to others (**v 40-41**).

Jesus' hearers would have heard both these vineyard parables as pictures of the nation and its temple, because in Isaiah 5:1-7 God had pictured Israel as a fruitless vineyard (like the fig tree in Matthew **21:18-19**). The message is clear: God entrusted his kingdom, his people and his message to the religious leaders of Israel. But they have failed to produce spiritual fruit. They have ignored God's prophets, and now they are going to kill God's Son. So the kingdom will be taken from them and given to others—the blind and the lame, the tax collectors and prostitutes, the nations. This message is clear enough for the religious leaders to realise that Jesus is talking about them (**v 45-46**).

The Cornerstone: The Lord Rebuilds His Temple

Jesus continues with a quote from Psalm 118. This is the psalm the crowd shouted as Jesus entered Jerusalem (Matthew 21:9). Just before the verse quoted by Jesus, the psalmist wrote, "Open for me the gates ... through which the righteous may enter" (Psalm 118:19-20). In fulfilment of this psalm, Jesus is opening the gates of the temple to the blind and the lame, to tax collectors and sinners (Matthew **21:14, 31**).

But Jesus goes further, quoting not these verses but subsequent ones: "The stone the builders rejected has become the cornerstone" (**v 42**; Psalm 118:22-23). It's an image of someone who's been rejected turning out to be central to God's purposes. As Jesus predicts the destruction of the Jerusalem temple, he's pointing to himself as the cornerstone at the centre of a new temple (Matthew 12:6). Christ's new temple will not be a bricks-and-mortar temple but a living one, made up of his people (Ephesians 2:19-22; 1 Peter 2:4-8). Again, Jesus says that God's kingdom will be reallocated *from* those not bearing fruit *to* his people (Matthew **21:43**). Jesus is both the stone at the heart of a new temple *and* a stone that crushes unbelievers (**v 44**; see Isaiah 8:14-15; Daniel 2:34-35, 44-45).

These stories explain how it was that 2,000 years ago the centre of God's purposes moved from the temple in Jerusalem to the church of Jesus. But they also continue to remind us that God requires fruit and offers grace. The religious leaders fell short of providing fruit and so bolstered their position by looking down on others. Jesus turns this upside down. He himself is the fruit-bearing vine in whom we are acceptable to God and the life-giving vine who makes us fruitful (John 15:1-8). These stories are a call to ensure that the lost and least find our churches to be houses of prayer in which they are welcomed and in which they can meet God.

The Wedding Banquet: The Lord Reallocates His Temple (Again)

Matthew likes groups of three, and chapter 22 begins with a third parable that reiterates the themes of chapter 21, albeit with a switch from vineyards to weddings (Matthew **22:1**). It seems that Jesus repeated some of his parables, adapting them to different contexts, and this parable combines elements that in other places are separated out.

A king (God) prepares a wedding banquet for his son (Jesus) (**v 2**; 9:15; 25:1; John 3:29; Ephesians 5:25-32). The king sends his servants (the prophets) to invite the guests (the religious establishment) (Matthew **22:3-4**). But the intended guests either make their excuses (**v 5**) or mistreat the servants (**v 6**). So the king judges these rebels (**v 7**), for this is not just a contravention of social etiquette but a rejection of the king's authority. But now the wedding banquet is ready, and there are no guests (**v 8**), so the servants are sent out again (the mission of the church) to invite "anyone you find", "the bad as well as the good" (**v 9-10**).

The parable has a postscript. The king finds one guest "not wearing wedding clothes" and so has him thrown out "into the darkness" (**v 11-13**) This man heard the invitation to come but didn't respond in an appropriate way. You can imagine the poor of the city doing their best to turn up in a way that befits the occasion. But this man doesn't take the occasion seriously and turns up in his work clothes. Jesus comments that "many are invited, but few are chosen" (**v 14**).

Precisely what the inadequate clothes represent is hard to determine. In Revelation 19:8, the clothing worn by the bride (the church) at the wedding of **the Lamb** represents "the righteous acts of God's holy people". But here in Matthew the invitation has gone to "the bad as well as the good" (Matthew **22:10**). Moreover, in Revelation the fine linen worn by the bride "was given her to wear". So here in Jesus' parable, it seems to represent coming in humility and submission. It's an idea that Paul develops a step further when he speaks of Christians being clothed in the righteousness of Christ (Romans 13:14).

The invitation to God's kingdom goes out to all and sundry through the preaching of the gospel. Our commission as the king's servants is to preach to every kind of person—"bad as well as good", rich and poor, white and black, young and old, male and female, blue collar and white collar. All are welcome in the church of Jesus. But people must respond in the right way: that is, with faith and repentance.

Questions for reflection

1. As you see and hear Jesus in this section, does it need to change your view of what he is like and what he most cares about? If so, how?
2. Can you think of ways in which you have submitted to Jesus' word even when it's overturned something previously stable or precious in your world?
3. In what way can you help to ensure that "the lost and least" find a genuine welcome and a real home in your church?

PART TWO

Chapter 22 appears to jump between unrelated issues: paying taxes, marriage in the afterlife, your favourite commandment, tricky **exegesis**. But they're united by a common pattern: the temple leaders come to "trap" Jesus (Matthew **22:15, 23, 34**), but Jesus silences them (**v 22, 33, 34**). The Lord has come to his temple, and no one can defeat him. He comes to refine, and no one can undermine his authority. So the section ends, "No one could say a word in reply, and from that day on no one dared asked him any more questions" (**v 46**).

Taxes, Marriage, Commandments and Lords: The Lord Silences the Temple's Establishment

*Paying tax to Caesar (**v 15-22**).* The religious leaders are afraid to arrest Jesus because the people think he's a prophet (21:46), so they try to discredit him (**22:15**). They start with tax—always a hot topic, but doubly so in an occupied nation. After a bit of flattery to lure Jesus into an indiscretion (**v 16**), they ask, "Is it right to pay the poll-tax to Caesar or not?" It's a lose-lose alternative: answer "Yes" and Jesus is in trouble with the people; answer "No" and he's in trouble with the Romans. Jesus sees past their flattery (**v 18**) and asks them for a coin (**v 19**). The fact they can produce one shows they're "hypocrites"—they are embedded as much as everyone else in the Roman economic system. Jesus asks whose image is on the coin. The answer is Caesar's. Then Jesus declares, "So give back to Caesar what is Caesar's, and to God what is God's" (**v 21**). Jesus has neatly escaped their trap (**v 15, 18, 22**).

But Jesus' words are more than a clever side-step. The Jews assumed a theocratic state, in which rulers were backed by God. Allegiance to Israel's religion meant allegiance to Israel's politicians. Jews should only pay tax to Gentiles if Gentile rule was a judgment from God (Jeremiah 29:4-14). Christ's response represents "a major development in redemption history" (Carson, *The Expositor's Bible Commentary*, Volume 8, p. 459). Christ's kingdom is not of this world and so doesn't compete with earthly powers (John 18:36). While one day Christ will lay claim to the whole earth, in the meantime he extends his kingdom through the word rather than the sword (as we saw in Matthew 13). His kingdom grows as people respond with faith to the preaching of the gospel. That means Christians can and should honour human leaders (Romans 13:1-7; 1 Peter 2:13-17)—as long as this obedience doesn't clash with their obedience to Christ (Acts 4:19; 5:29). Notice Jesus says "give back" in Matthew **22:21**. The government provides ordered rule, and we "give back" through our taxes. But also what we give God is really a *giving back* of what he's first given us (1 Chronicles 29:14).

Christians should honour human leaders—as long as this doesn't clash with their obedience to Christ.

*Marriage at the resurrection (Matthew **22:23-33**).* Another faction within 1st-century Judaism tries to trap Jesus. While the Pharisees were a kind of pressure group, the Sadducees were the ruling elite, not least because they co-operated with the Romans. They also didn't believe in the resurrection (**v 23**). The Law of Moses required a man to marry his brother's widow so their firstborn could inherit his brother's name and property (Deuteronomy 25:5-6). The Sadducees posit a woman who marries seven brothers, one after another. She can't be married to all of them in the afterlife. Therefore the idea of an afterlife is incoherent.

That apparent problem is easily addressed by Jesus: there won't be marriage at the resurrection (Matthew **22:30**). But again he goes deeper. Their reasoning is distorted by their unbelief: "You are in error because you do not know the Scriptures or the power of God" (**v 29**). In the Scriptures God says, "I *am* the God of Abraham" (emphasis added) rather than "I *was* the God of Abraham", because God's covenant commitment is too strong to be broken by death (**v 31-32**; Romans 4:18-25). The real issue (as it always is when people doubt the resurrection) is not the coherence of eternal life but whether we believe there's a God with power over death.

*The greatest commandment (Matthew **22:34-40**).* The third question is "Which is the greatest commandment?" (**v 36**). It sounds innocuous, but Matthew says it was a test following a plot (**v 34-35**, echoing Psalm 2:1-2). The relative importance of the different aspects of the law was a common debate within 1st-century Judaism. And, like any exercise in ranking, this question seems designed to ensure that Jesus annoys at least some people, because he can't put everyone's favourite commandment at the top. It's like being asked, "Who's your favourite child?"

Again, Jesus avoids the trap by summarising the law as two all-encompassing commands: love for God and love for neighbour (Matthew **22:37-40**; see Deuteronomy 6:5 and Leviticus 19:18). But again Jesus goes deeper. As we've already seen, the Pharisees were twisting the wording of the law to evade the spirit of the law (Matthew 5:20-42; 12:1-14; 15:3-9). Jesus takes us to the real meaning and goal of the law: love.

*David's son and Lord (**22:41-46**).* This time it's Jesus' turn to ask a question: "Whose son is [the Messiah]?" They reply, "The son of David" (**v 41-42**). Then Jesus quotes Psalm 110:1: "The Lord said to my Lord: 'Sit at my right hand…'" (Matthew **22:44**). The first "Lord" in this verse is God (Yahweh). The second "Lord" is the Messiah. But there's a third person involved: David himself as the speaker. David calls the Messiah "my Lord", but in Jewish thought a father was always greater than a son. "If then David calls him 'Lord', how can he be his son?" (**v 45**).

There's a ready solution to this poser: the Messiah is not only the son of David; he's also the pre-existent Son of God. He's lesser than David as David's human descendent, but greater than David as David's Creator. David only gives life to the Messiah because the Messiah first gave life to David. If the religious leaders accept this logic, then they must recognise Jesus as Immanuel, God with us. But they don't want to do that, and so instead they say nothing (**v 46**).

Seven Woes: The Lord Condemns the Temple's Establishment

The call to obey the religious leaders in **23:2-3** appears to contradict the warning against their influence in 16:11-12. Perhaps Jesus is affirming the office of teacher even though he's about to reject the office holders. Davies suggests Jesus is describing the public reading of Scripture (*Matthew: A Shorter Commentary*, p. 387). Carson and France think Jesus is being sarcastic (*The Expositor's Bible Commentary,* Volume 8, p. 473; *The Gospel of Matthew*, p. 860, respectively). What's clear is that the disciples are not to follow the *practice* of the religious leaders (15:3-9). Not only do they fall short of what the law requires; they also *add* to what the law requires (**23:4**). The Pharisees extend the cleanliness required in the temple to ordinary life—a standard that poorer people inevitably find impossible to sustain. No one looks good compared to God (19:17), but we can look good compared to notorious failures. So the Pharisees need "sinners" to feel good about themselves, and therefore it suits their interests to do nothing to help (**23:4**). In contrast, the yoke of Jesus is easy, and his burden is light (11:28-30).

Jesus reveals the real motive of the religious leadership: "Everything they do is done for people to see" (**23:5-7**). They pursue the praise of people at the expense of the praise of God (6:1-18). The prohibition of titles in **23:8-10** is probably **hyperbole** since the New Testament does use titles, at least as descriptors of roles (1 Corinthians 4:15; Ephesians 4:11-12). But we're not to be ambitious for such titles, nor flatter people with honours, because we're only servants and glory belongs to God alone (Matthew **23:11**). This doesn't mean we despise human instruction: Jesus adds, "and you are all brothers" in **verse 8** to emphasise our need of one another within the family of God. But, though God may use human agency, it's ultimately God who teaches us, fathers us and instructs us (**v 8-10**). **Verses 11-12** reprise 19:30, 20:16 and 20:26-28, applying them to the teaching ministry of the church.

Chapters 21 – 22 have played out like a court case. The religious leaders have put their case, and Jesus has defended himself. In the end, the religious leaders have been silenced (**22:34, 46**). Now Jesus proclaims the verdict: seven woes. These woes correspond to the Beatitudes of Matthew 5, and together they parallel the blessings and curses of Deuteronomy 27 – 28.

What Jesus said about the religious leaders of his day is true of religious people in any age. As we explore the seven woes, you might want to consider whether this religious hypocrisy partly infects your attitudes or the culture of your church. Nevertheless the primary orientation of these woes is towards enemies of the true church.

- *Woe #1 (Matthew **23:13**).* By adding unnecessary requirements, religious people make it hard for others to enter the kingdom. Other people feel they're not good enough, even though God extends grace to sinners. But religious people are hypocrites because at heart they're no better than those on whom they look down. Plus the religious leaders have repeatedly tried to dissuade people from trusting Jesus (9:33-34; 11:19; 12:23-24).

- *Woe #2 (**23:15**).* Religious people try to "convert" others to their point of view, but a false message produces false disciples. Their legalism produces legalists ("a child of hell").

- *Woe #3 (**v 16-22**).* Religious people create systems to evade the implications of God's word and make it more achievable through human effort. So Jesus reprises what he said in 5:33-37. Carson writes, "Honesty doesn't have gradations: we're to promise what we can deliver and deliver what we promise. All oaths are in some way related to God. All are therefore binding, and thus evasive oaths are disallowed." (Carson, *The Expositor's Bible Commentary*, Volume 8, p. 479). The real problem is that religious people are "blind guides" who allow their own interests to twist their interpretation of God's word (15:14).

- *Woe #4 (**23:23-24**).* Religious people carefully observe the letter of the law (we're to imagine a Pharisee counting out mint leaves) but ignore the spirit of the law. Jesus isn't advocating a relaxed attitude to God's law. ("You should have practised ... the former".) But our law-keeping is meant as a guide as we pursue the real goals of "justice, mercy and faithfulness".

- *Woe #5 (**v 25-26**).* Religious people are hypocrites, who observe external regulations while refusing to repent of their inner greed. Superficially a cup which is clean on the outside but dirty within looks better than a cup that's dirty on the outside but clean within. But from which would you rather drink?! Superficially religious people look impressive, but external regulations cannot change our hearts (7:15-20; Colossians 2:20-23). For heart change we need to come to Christ in repentance and faith.

- *Woe #6 (Matthew **23:27-28**).* It was customary before the Passover to whitewash graves so that visiting pilgrims wouldn't inadvertently step on them and make themselves unclean. But Jesus says that it's religious people who are full of death; they're the graves which should be avoided. Not only does their religion fail to bring life; it whitewashes the problem.

- *Woe #7 (**v 29-32**).* Religious people purport to honour the prophets and **saints** of the past. But their attitude to God's word suggests they're not the children of the prophets but rather of those who persecuted the prophets. In a way they concede this lineage when they (falsely) claim to be different from their ancestors. Perhaps there's a sense too in which human societies honour a visionary only when that person is no longer able to disrupt the status quo. It's easier to admire prophetic figures when your personal interests are no longer on the line. "Go ahead, then, and complete what your ancestors started!" says Jesus in verse 32—

and that's exactly what they will do when they kill the Son a few days later (21:35-39).

Jerusalem, Jerusalem: The Lord Laments the Temple's Destruction

When Jesus calls religious people "snakes" in **23:33**, he's portraying them as the offspring of the serpent in Eden (Genesis 3:15). "I am sending you prophets and sages and teachers," Jesus continues in Matthew **23:34**. It echoes the allusions to the Old Testament prophets in the parables of 21:35-39 and 22:3-6, but it also echoes the commission of the disciples in Matthew 10. The mission of the prophets will be continued in the mission of the church, and the persecution of the prophets by religious people will be continued in hostility towards the true church (5:11-12).

In this way, the religious establishment will bring upon themselves the judgment demanded by the deaths of Abel and Zechariah. Abel was the first person to be murdered (Genesis 4). Zechariah's identity is unclear, but it's probably the prophet Zechariah of 2 Chronicles 24:20-22, who was murdered in the temple courtyard—the spot where Jesus is speaking. (Chronicles and Matthew give him different fathers, but one could be a grandfather.) Chronicles is the last book in the Hebrew **canon**, so Abel and Zechariah are the first and last Old Testament martyrs. Now their blood, and the blood of all those in between, will fall on the generation that rejects the Jesus in whose name they spoke (Matthew **23:35-36**). Human blood continues to cry out for justice, and justice is coming. And we're all in the firing line unless we entrust ourselves to the better word spoken by the blood of Jesus, the ultimate innocent sufferer, who has suffered as the ultimate guilty perpetrator, in our place and for our sake (Hebrews 12:24).

Words on a page cannot convey tone of voice. Someone might say, "That was a good attempt," but how you interpret those words will depend on whether their tone is jocular, sarcastic, encouraging or biting. In the final verses of this section, Matthew gives an insight into Christ's "tone of voice". It's best summarised as *longing*. The condemnations of this section have been spoken with a longing that people might repent (Matthew **23:37**). Jesus has longed to be like a mother hen, protecting her chicks under her wings. But "you were not willing", and so "your house" (the temple) will become "desolate" (**v 37-38**; 24:2). Finally we circle back to where we started (**23:39**). "Blessed is he who comes in the name of the Lord" was proclaimed when Jesus entered Jerusalem in 21:9. The next time Jesus enters Jerusalem (when he returns to earth at the end of history), he'll be coming in triumph as judge of the world.

Questions for reflection

1. In your own life and nation, what will it mean for you to give to Caesar what is Caesar's—not giving more, but also not giving less?
2. As you read the seven woes (p. 177-179), which (if any) might be in danger of infecting your own attitudes? What does that prompt you to pray about?
3. Christians are those who have been gathered under Jesus' wings. Why is that a precious way to think of who we are and who Jesus is for us? Is there a particular sadness or difficulty you are facing at the moment in which this can be a source of comfort?

MATTHEW CHAPTERS 24 AND 25

12. THE END OF THE TEMPLE AND THE END OF HISTORY

In Matthew 21 – 23 Jesus came as the Lord to cleanse his temple. He cursed a fig tree as a sign of the judgment facing the temple establishment (21:18-21); presented himself as the cornerstone of a new temple (v 42-44); and in sorrow declared, "Your house is left to you desolate" (23:38).

The temple authorities have repeatedly challenged Jesus as if he's on trial. But it has become clear that Jesus is the judge, and the religion of the temple is in the dock. Matthew **24:1-2** is the verdict. You can imagine the disciples looking back on the temple as they leave the city and saying, *What a glorious sight that is!* (**v 1**). But Jesus responds, "Not one stone here will be left on another; every one will be thrown down" (**v 2**).

In **verses 3-4** the disciples ask two questions in response to what Jesus has said:

1. "When will this happen?"
2. "What will be the sign of your coming and of the end of the age?

These are two *different* questions about two *different* events. Jesus will talk about...

1. the destruction of the temple by the Romans in AD 70.
2. his return at the end of history.

The difficulty is deciding when Jesus stops talking about the temple's destruction and starts talking about his return. Here are three credible options:

1. Many people assume the transition comes at **verse 26** because **verses 29-30** appear to describe Christ's return. The problem is that **verse 34** says these events (including **verses 29-30**) will happen within a generation.

2. Don Carson (*The Expositor's Bible Commentary,* Volume 8, p. 495) argues that Jesus responds to the disciples' question by saying there will be a delay before his return (**v 4-28**) and that this period of delay will be characterised by persecution and **tribulation**, with the fall of Jerusalem in **verses 15-21** as "one particularly violent display of judgment" during this period. After this period of persecution, Jesus will return (**v 29-31**). The warning in **verses 32-35** then jumps back to the period of tribulation, which will begin within a generation (**v 34**). The problem is that this means Jesus keeps switching between the church age and his return without clearly indicating those switches.

3. I will argue (with France, *The Gospel of Matthew*, from p. 890) that the transition comes at **verse 36**, with **verses 4-35** *all* predicting events that either began, or took place, in the 1st century.

What all three options have in common are that...

- Jesus is predicting the fall of Jerusalem—a prediction fulfilled in AD 70.
- Jesus is predicting his return at the end of history—a prediction yet to be fulfilled.
- the judgment on Jerusalem is a pointer to the judgment on all humanity.
- in between Jesus' first coming and his second, the church will face persecution.

- no one knows when Jesus will return at the end of history.
- it is therefore vitally important to be ready for the return of Jesus.

Signs That Are Not Signs

Verses 4-14 describe signs that are not signs. There will be false messiahs, wars, rumours of war, famines, and earthquakes (**v 5-7**). The church will face persecution, martyrdom, **apostasy**, heresy and **nominalism** (**v 9-12**). Despite this, the gospel will be preached all across the (known/Roman) world (**v 14**).

These are all signs that the last days (the time between Christ's first and **second comings**) have begun. Jesus calls them "the beginning of the birth-pains" (**v 8**). But they're *not* signs that Jesus is about to return. Sometimes Christians say, "When I look at the world today, I can't help thinking Christ's return must be near". There's a good instinct in this: the last days have begun, and Christ could return at any moment. But we need some historical perspective; these things have been going on for 2,000 years. Jesus specifically says such things are *not necessarily* signs that the end is near: "Such things must happen, but the end is still to come" (**v 6**).

Signs That Jerusalem Is About to Fall

Verse 15 describes a much more specific sign. As soon as this sign appears, the Christians in Judea are to flee to the mountains (**v 16**). "The abomination that causes desolation" is a reference to Daniel 9:27, 11:31 and 12:11, which describe a **profanity** in the temple. In 167 BC Antiochus Epiphanes erected an altar to Zeus in the temple and sacrificed pigs (unclean animals under the Old Testament covenant). The Jews of Jesus' day lived in fear of another such "abomination", and indeed this is what took place when the temple was destroyed in AD 70. Luke simplifies this allusion for his Gentile readers: "When you see Jerusalem being surrounded by armies, you know that its desolation is near" (Luke 21:20). When Christians see this taking place, they are to escape as quickly as possible (Matthew **24:16-21**).

So **verses 15-28** describe events *leading up* to the fall of Jerusalem in AD 70. In the Jewish war of 66-70 (when Roman legions fought a widespread Jewish revolt against Roman rule), about one million Jews were killed or died in famine. With Jesus having warned them "in advance" (**v 25**), Christians abandoned the city in 68, two years before its final fall. This was also a period in which a number of people claimed to be the Messiah or to know where he was (**v 23-26**)—but Jesus had warned Christians not to be deceived (**v 4-5**). His return will be unmistakeable and universal (**v 27-28**); if you have to ask whether Jesus has returned, then he hasn't.

The Fall of Jerusalem

Verse 29 begins, "Immediately after the distress of those days…". If **verses 29-31** describe Christ's return, then the implication is that Christ will return after the fall of Jerusalem. If so, 2,000 years later the word "immediately" has become a bit stretched! Instead it is better to read "the distress of those days" as referring back to **verse 21** ("there will be great distress"). So "those days" refers to the days between "the abomination" in **verse 15** and the final fall of Jerusalem in **verse 29**. That means **verses 29-31** must describe what happens "immediately after" that distress (the fall of Jerusalem).

The language of **verse 29** has a number of parallels in the Old Testament. Like this verse, Isaiah 13:10 says, "The rising sun will be darkened and the moon will not give its light". Matthew **24:29** also echoes Isaiah 34:4: "All the stars in the sky will be dissolved and the heavens rolled up like a scroll; all the starry host will fall … like shrivelled figs from the fig-tree". Isaiah 13 is a prophecy predicting the downfall of Babylon, and Isaiah 34 is a prophecy against the nations with a particular focus on Edom. So this language is not being used to describe the end of history; it's describing the downfall of nations. The imagery of stars falling from the sky is not literal; it refers to cataclysmic events in the political realm. We still use this kind of language today when we talk about "an earth-shattering event". What's striking is that this language had previously been used to describe the downfall of Jerusalem's enemies, but now Jesus uses it to describe God's judgment on Israel. Notice, too, that Isaiah 34:4 pictures this cataclysm as the shrivelling of a fig tree—the very picture of the temple's judgment which Jesus himself gave back in Matthew 21:18-19.

If **24:29** describes the fall of one regime, then **verses 30-31** describe the establishment of a new one. They draw on the language of Daniel 7, where Daniel sees great empires pictured as fierce beasts who are ultimately stripped of their power, and instead all authority is given to "one like a son of man" who comes "with the clouds of heaven" before "the Ancient of Days" (Daniel 7:13-14). Daniel is describing the enthronement of Jesus. ("Son of Man" was the phrase Jesus used to describe himself.) Though it's true that Jesus will come "on the clouds" at the end of history (Acts 1:9-11; 1 Thessalonians 4:17), that's not what Daniel is describing. In Daniel 7, the son of man is not coming from heaven to earth but from earth to heaven, and he comes before the throne of God to receive an everlasting kingdom. This is what took place at the ascension, when Jesus passed through the clouds into the presence of God to be acclaimed as King. This is what Jesus is describing in Matthew **24:30-31**. Obviously the ascension (**v 30-31**) took place before the fall of Jerusalem (**v 29**), but Jesus sees them as different aspects of one historical moment in the 1st century, which involves both the end of one era and the beginning of a new one. In 20:16 Jesus had said, "The last will be first, and the first will be last". Here we see this played out on a cosmic

> Jesus sees the ascension and the fall of Jerusalem as the end of one era and the beginning of a new one.

stage; the kingdoms of this world are brought down while the kingdom of the crucified one is exalted.

Jesus says this will be seen by "all the peoples of the earth" (**24:30**). The heavenly enthronement has a visible counterpart on earth. How? First, it is seen in the destruction of the temple, as the temple regime gives way to the messianic regime. Second, it's seen in the worldwide mission of the church. We exercise the heavenly authority of the risen Christ as we call people to bow before their King. This matches 16:28 and 26:64, where Jesus also uses the language of Daniel 7 to say that the people who are then present with him will "see" the Son of Man "coming in his kingdom" or "coming on the clouds".

24:31 speaks of Jesus sending angels to "gather his elect from the four winds" (from the four corners of the earth). The Old Testament speaks of a gathering of scattered Jewish exiles back to Jerusalem in the last times, but it also says this will include a gathering-in of people from all nations (Isaiah 19:23-25). The gap between the first and second coming of Jesus creates a space in which this in-gathering can take place through the mission of the church.

Some people think Jesus is saying that "angels" have some role in the mission of the church. This is possible, but the word translated "angels" in Matthew **24:31** simply means "messengers" (whether human or angelic). Jesus will send his missionary people as his messengers to gather his elect through the proclamation of the gospel—so **verse 31** describes the global mission of the church. In 28:18-19 we are called to go to all nations because Jesus has been given authority over all nations. We might even speak of the enthronement of Jesus partly taking place *through* the mission of the church.

24:30-34 summarises Jesus' answer to the disciples' question back in verse 3: "When will this happen?" Just as the leaves of a fig tree indicate that summer is near, so "when you see all these things, you know that it is near" (**v 32-33**). "It" in **verse 33** is the destruction of the temple and "these things" are the events described in **verses 15-28**. **Verse 34** says this will happen within a generation. That's a problem if you think **verses 29-31** describe the second coming, but it's not a problem if they describe the fall of Jerusalem, because some who heard Jesus would have lived to witness its fall in AD 70.

Jesus concludes, "Heaven and earth will pass away, but my words will never pass away" (**v 35**). Jesus could simply be saying his message is permanent (see Isaiah 40:7-8). But heaven and earth passing away probably alludes back to Matthew **24:29**—the kingdoms of this world pass away, and the kingdom of Jesus will outlast them all.

The Return of Christ

The theologian N.T. Wright argues that **verses 36-51** (and Mark 13:32-37) continue to talk about the destruction of the temple (*Jesus and the Victory of God*, p. 339-368). But there are good reasons to think that Jesus switches his focus in **24:36** from the fall of Jerusalem to his return at the end of history:

1. "But about..." at the beginning of the verse suggests a shift in topic.
2. There's a switch from talking about "those days" (plural) to "that day" (singular).
3. The time references in **verses 5-35** have all been specific. Jesus has told his hearers exactly when they should escape from Jerusalem (**v 15-16**). But the main point of **verses 36-51** is that no one knows when "that day" (the day of Christ's return) will be—not even Jesus himself (**v 36, 42, 44**).
4. The disciples ask both (1) "When will this [i.e. the temple's destruction] happen?" *and* (2) "What will be the sign of your coming and of the end of the age?" Whether or not the disciples see these as one event or two, Jesus sees them as two events and therefore provides two answers. He answers question #1 about the temple's destruction in **verses 4-35**, and he answers question #2 about his return in **verses 36-51**.

5. The word "coming" in **verse 3** is the Greek word *parousia* (literally "presence"), which became one of the terms the church used for the return or "second coming" of Christ. Matthew uses the same word in **verse 27**, when Jesus says his coming at the end of history will be clear for all to see (unlike the alleged comings of false messiahs in the days before the fall of Jerusalem). So when Matthew uses the same word again in **verses 37 and 39**, it's natural meaning is the return of Christ at the end of history. (The word translated "coming" in **verse 30** to describe Christ's coming into heaven at the ascension is a different Greek word, perhaps to avoid confusing **verse 30** with the second coming.)

Jesus reminds us of a previous global judgment: the flood (**v 37-39**). Just as that took people by surprise, so will Christ's return (Genesis 6 – 9; 2 Peter 3:3-10). People will be going about their daily business only to be suddenly taken away (Matthew **24:40-41**).

> We keep watch for Christ's return not by guessing when it will be but by always being ready.

If the coming of "those days" (the fall of Jerusalem) called for watchfulness, how much more does the coming of "that day"—Christ's return (**v 42**). But we don't keep watch by looking for signs or guessing when it's about to happen, because no one knows "on what day your Lord will come" (**v 42, 44**). Instead, we keep watch by *always being ready*, just like a wise homeowner is already ready for a thief (**v 43**; for similar use of this metaphor see 1 Thessalonians 5:2-4; 2 Peter 3:10; Revelation 3:3; 16:15). What does being ready involve? It means going about our master's business (Matthew **24:45-51**). We remain ready for the *future* by serving faithfully in the *present*.

How should those of us who are Gentile Christians read this chapter after the fall of Jerusalem? Certainly not with any ethnic pride or anti-Semitic glee. Instead we should read it with fear and humility. If God could judge his old-covenant people in this way, then he will certainly do the same to godless nations. One reason why it makes sense for Jesus to start talking about his return in **verses 36-51** is that the judgment of the temple *points beyond itself* to the ultimate judgment of all humanity.

The tribulations with which the last days began continue today. We're not to be deceived into thinking Christ's return *will* happen tomorrow, but we are to serve as if it *could* happen tomorrow. "The one who stands firm to the end will be saved" (**v 13**). This chapter also reminds us that Christ is extending his heavenly kingship and gathering his elect through our evangelism.

Questions for reflection

1. Without worrying about what in these verses you *don't* understand(!), what do you find them clearly teaching about the present and the future?
2. Why is it encouraging to know that "if you have to ask whether Jesus has returned, then he hasn't" (p. 184)?
3. What difference would it make if you lived each day as though it could be the day that Jesus returns in glory?

PART TWO

Matthew 24 ended with Jesus calling us to be ready for his return at the end of history: "Therefore keep watch, because you do not know on what day your Lord will come" (v 42). Chapter 25 continues this theme with three parables (Matthew loves groups of three!) which expand what it means to be ready for Christ's return. They all involve being ready for someone whose return is expected but whose time-scale is unknown.

1. The Ten Virgins: Be Ready for Christ's Coming

In Jesus' day, a wedding began with the bridegroom and his entourage travelling in procession to the house of the bride, where various ceremonies would take place. As night fell, he would escort his bride back to his home to be welcomed by her new family. The ten virgins in this parable are waiting for the bridegroom to return with his bride, perhaps to play a role in welcoming her into the family (**25:1**). Since the bridegroom is not expected until after nightfall, everyone needs a lamp; otherwise they may be suspected of being interlopers. So the ten virgins all bring a lamp, but only five are wise enough to bring enough oil (**v 2-4**). The bridegroom is delayed (it seems weddings could drag on back then just as they do today!), and in the meantime the virgins fall asleep (**v 5**). At midnight, the coming of the bridegroom is announced (**v 6**)—but by this point it's too late for the five without oil to buy more, since all the shops are closed. And so they're excluded from the party (**v 7-12**).

Jesus himself tells us the meaning of the parable in **verse 13**: "Therefore keep watch, because you do not know the day or the hour". It's a call to be ready for his return at the end of history (reiterating the message of 24:42-44). To make this main point, the story simply needs to describe an expected event whose time is unknown, but it's surely no coincidence that the story concerns a returning bridegroom, since Jesus has already portrayed himself as the bridegroom of God's people (9:15).

We probably shouldn't read too much into the refusal of the five virgins to share their oil. It's a narrative device to highlight the fact that it's too late to get ready once the bridegroom has arrived. If it has any further significance, it's that saving faith is effective only for those who have personally put their faith in Jesus; we can't believe on behalf of other people.

The parable doesn't define what being ready or keeping watch involve. Its main purpose is to highlight the crucial importance of being ready. But there's a clue in the bridegroom's words in **25:12**: "Truly I tell you, I don't know you". They echo the words of Jesus in 7:21-23. There, false teachers say, "Lord, Lord..." (like the five foolish virgins in **25:11**). Jesus replies, "I never knew you. Away from me, you evildoers!" Being ready means producing "good fruit", because "by their fruit you will recognise them" (7:15-20). In 5:14-16, our "good deeds" are like "a lamp" shining before others to the glory of the Father.

2. The Bags of Gold: Be Ready by Serving Christ Boldly

In the second parable, the expected event due at an unknown time is the return of a master from a long journey (**25:14, 19**). The man has entrusted five bags, two bags and one bag of gold to three different servants (**v 15**). When the master returns, the first two servants have made a 100 percent return on their gold, so the master rewards them with further responsibility (**v 16-23**). But the third man has merely buried his bag in the ground and can therefore offer no return on the money (**v 24-25**)—so his bag is given to another servant, and he is thrown out into darkness (**v 26-30**).

The landowner represents God, and the servants represent you and me. The bags of gold could stand for money, time, health or abilities. Probably it's a bit of all of them. They represent anything God has given us which we can use to serve him. God expects us to use the gifts he's given us to produce a return.

But perhaps the parable seems a bit harsh. After all, the third servant didn't steal his master's money; he was just being cautious. Why is he not only reprimanded but thrown out? The key is the speech of the failed servant: "I knew that you are a hard man ... So I was afraid and went out and hid your gold in the ground" (**v 24-25**). If this is how you view God, then you obviously don't really know him, and it makes sense for you not to risk anything for such a harsh divinity. But in fact God is a loving Father, who cares for his children (6:25-34). As a result, we can "seek first his kingdom" knowing that "all these things [food, clothing and so on] will be given to you as well" (6:33). The first two servants invest their money boldly because they're confident that, whatever happens, they can expect a warm response from a generous master. They're liberated by their master's kindness to take risks in his service. So are we.

We're liberated by our master's kindness to take risks in his service.

The failed servant describes the master (God) as "harvesting where you have not sown and gathering where you have not scattered seed" (**25:24**). This is true, but not in the way the servant sees it. The first two servants sow, but it is God who gives the harvest. The return their gold produces is in his hands. In other words, we do what is before us to do and leave the outcome to God. We don't need to engineer a harvest. In **verses 21 and 23** the good servants are described as "faithful" rather than "fruitful".

The final word to the unfaithful servant is a word of judgment (**v 30**). But the final word to both faithful servants is "Come and share your master's happiness!" (**v 21, 23**). Christ invites us to trust his grace (he will not crush us if we fail) and care (he will not abandon us when we're in need), and therefore serve him boldly. Then one day we will share the mutual joy of the Trinity.

3. The Sheep and the Goats: Be Ready by Serving Christ's People

The final story is not so much a parable as a word-picture of the final judgment. It opens with Jesus coming with his angels to judge the nations (**v 31**, echoing 16:27). Jesus divides people into two groups which are pictured as sheep and goats (**25:32-33**). A shepherd in Jesus' day might well have had a flock of sheep and goats mingled together, but occasionally it would be necessary to separate them out. In the same way, God's people live alongside unbelievers in history, but at the final judgment, humanity will be separated into two groups (13:37-43, 47-50). Notice, too, that Christ's true flock is drawn from "all the nations" (**25:32**).

What distinguishes the two groups is how they have treated Jesus (**v 35-36, 42-43**). No surprise there. Yet neither group is aware of what they have done. Jesus commends the sheep (those who are blessed) for giving him food when he was hungry and so on, and he condemns the goats (those who are cursed) for failing to do so. Both groups are perplexed by this; both are unaware of ever encountering Jesus in need. But the punchline is "Whatever you did for one of the least of these brothers and sisters of mine, you did for me" (**v 40**).

This is not simply a question of how we treat those in need (as important as that is). "The least of these brothers and sisters of mine" is a reference to the church. It's Christians who are Christ's brothers and sisters, and "the least of these" recalls "these little ones" in chapter 18. Back in 10:42 Jesus said, "If anyone gives even a cup of cold water to one of these little ones who is my disciple, truly I tell you, that person will certainly not lose their reward". It's this idea that is being expanded here in chapter 25. In chapter 10 "these little ones" are Christian missionaries. "Anyone who welcomes you welcomes me," says Jesus in 10:40, "and anyone who welcomes me welcomes the one who sent me". We welcome the *messengers* of Christ because we welcome the *message* of Christ. So our attitude to our church family is a good indicator of our attitude to Jesus. Carson summarises the message here like this:

> "The surprise of the righteous makes it impossible to think that works of righteousness win salvation ... The parable therefore presents a test eliminating the possibility of hypocrisy."
>
> (*The Expositor's Bible Commentary,* Volume 8, p. 522)

We must remember that Christ's identification with the poor in this story is set in the context of the final judgment. This is not simply a call to serve Christ by serving the needy. It's also a call to be ready for judgment by accepting the message of Christ.

From medieval times **25:35-36** has formed the basis for the six "corporal works of mercy":

- feeding the hungry
- giving water to the thirsty
- showing hospitality to strangers
- clothing the naked
- caring for the ill
- visiting those in prison

"Corporal" means "bodily" and indicates acts that address physical needs. (A seventh act—burying the dead—was sometimes added.) These verses give a lovely motive for caring for those in need, especially within the church. Feeding the hungry, showing hospitality to strangers, or standing alongside prisoners is rarely glamorous work. It can be tough and demanding—but what we do for others, we do for Jesus. Jesus is Immanuel, God with us (1:23), and he's present with us among the poor (**25:40**; Proverbs 19:17). In John 13 Jesus knelt before his disciples and washed their feet, and then said, "I have set you an example that you should do as I have done for you" (John 13:15). So we follow his example and kneel before the feet of Christ's little ones to wash their feet or care for their needs. But here's the amazing thing: when we look up into their eyes, it is Jesus we see.

As we serve Christ's people, we can remember that one day he'll say to us, "Come, you who are blessed by my Father; take your inheritance, the kingdom prepared for you since the creation of the world" (Matthew **25:34**) – just as the master told his faithful servants, "Come and share your master's happiness" (**v 21, 23**).

The chapter ends, "Then they [those who did not care for the least of these] will go away to eternal punishment, but the righteous to eternal life" (**v 46**). Everyone who hears the story is in one of those two categories. The story divides us, just as surely as Jesus will divide us on the last day. As comforting as it is to think we can meet Christ in the poor, ultimately this parable is designed to unsettle those who claim to be Christians but show little concern for the needs in their church. James echoes this story in James 2:15-17 and provides his own commentary on it: "Suppose a brother or a sister is without clothes and daily food. If one of you says to them, 'Go in peace; keep warm and well fed,' but does nothing about their physical needs, what good is it? In the same way, faith by itself, if it is not accompanied by action, is dead."

Questions for reflection

1. How has Jesus' teaching here shown you what it means to live ready for Jesus' coming? Are there any changes to your priorities or practices that you need to make?
2. How have you been encouraged to start or continue to care for those in need?
3. How does your view of who God is influence how you serve him? What will it look like for you to be "liberated by [your] master's kindness to take risks in his service" (p. 192)?

13. THE FIRST WILL BE LAST: THE PASSION OF THE MESSIAH

Since Jesus has finished teaching his disciples about the fall of the temple and being ready for his future return (**26:1**), the Gospel is now moving towards its climax as we reach the third of five occasions when the Jewish leaders gather to plot against Jesus (12:14; 22:15; **26:3-4**; 27:1; 28:12). It's language that echoes Psalm 2:1-3, where the nations plot against the Lord and his anointed Messiah, except now it's Israel which is conspiring against her own King.

But first Jesus predicts his death (Matthew **26:1-2**). The initiative belongs to Jesus. He is the one who presses "go". The chief priests can only plan once it's clear that this is God's plan.

The Crucified King Is Worth More Than Money

A woman shows her love for Jesus by anointing him with perfume (**v 6-7**). She loves without counting the cost. The disciples crunch the numbers and perhaps lament the loss to their common fund (**v 8-9**). But Jesus says she's done "a beautiful thing" (**v 10**). And Jesus continues to regard our acts of devotion as beautiful. We may no longer be able to care for his physical body, but we can care for his "mystical body", the church (**v 11**; 25:40). "The poor you will always have with you" is an allusion to Deuteronomy 15:11, where it comes with a command to be "open-handed" to those in need. So Jesus is not discouraging care for the poor. Quite the opposite: we show our love for him by caring for those in need.

But this act belongs to a particular moment in time. Jesus interprets it as a preparation for his burial (Matthew **26:12**). Corpses were traditionally perfumed, but not those of criminals. So if Jesus' body is to be anointed, it must be *before* his death. It's another sign that he's choosing to embrace death.

This is the tipping point for Judas, who "then" does a deal to betray Jesus (**v 14-16**). Perhaps he's motivated by money. But perhaps, too, he realises that Jesus' plan involves his death, and a crucified King was not what he signed up for. Perhaps the woman and Judas are the first to realise Jesus is serious about dying, even though they respond in opposite ways. How much is a crucified King worth? Judas settles for 30 pieces of silver—the price of a slave (Exodus 21:32; Zechariah 11:13). The woman anoints Jesus with expensive perfume, and it's her valuation that is honoured wherever the gospel is preached (Matthew **26:13**).

The Crucified King Commits Himself to Us

The Lord's Supper provides an explanation of the crucified King. Matthew begins by drawing our attention to the Passover (**v 17**). God had liberated his people from slavery in Egypt by sending ten plagues to force Pharaoh's hand (Exodus 12). The final plague was the death of every firstborn—God's people were only kept safe by sacrificing a Passover lamb and daubing its blood over their doors. The lamb died in their place. Matthew wants us to realise that Jesus is the ultimate Passover lamb. He dies in our place and we're safe under his blood. As a result, we're liberated from our slavery to sin and death.

In Matthew **26:17** the disciples ask, "Where do you want *us* to make preparations for you to eat the Passover?" (emphasis added). But it immediately becomes clear that it's *Jesus* who's made preparations (**v 18-19**). Jesus then predicts his betrayal (**v 20-25**). It looks as if

Judas has seized the initiative in **verses 14-16**; but, no, it's Jesus who is driving events forwards. Judas acts freely, which is why he is culpable (**v 24**); but his actions are part of God's plan. Again, Matthew is alerting us to the fact that Jesus dies according to a plan that was prepared before the beginning of time. It's a plan that pivots not on what we do for Jesus but on what he does for us. We come to Jesus asking, "What can I do for you?" and first he shows us what he's done for us.

One of the ways Jesus does this is through the Lord's Supper (**v 26-30**). The bread and wine embody the offering of his body and blood for us. "This is my body," he says as he holds the bread (**v 26**). Here is a physical parable of his redeeming work. Then he goes on to say as he holds the cup, "This is my blood of the covenant, which is poured out for many for the forgiveness of sins" (**v 27-28**). This is the new covenant promised in Jeremiah 31:31-34. A covenant is a contract that forms a new relationship. In the covenant of marriage, for example, a man and woman become husband and wife. Here, Jesus enters into a covenant relationship with us. He becomes our husband and we become his bride. He promises to forgive our sins and set us free (Matthew **26:28**; Zechariah 9:11): a promise he delivers as he dies in our place. Because we're sinners whose faith is fragile, it's a promise we need to receive afresh in the Lord's Supper. The bread and wine are like the signature at the bottom of the contract (just as blood ratified the **Mosaic** covenant in Exodus 24:8). We hear his promise in the gospel, and we taste it in bread and wine. It's a commitment that guarantees that will one day we will feast with Jesus in the new creation (Matthew **26:29**; Isaiah 25:6). Only Matthew includes the words "Drink from it, all of you" (Matthew **26:27**). It's an exhortation to believers in all ages.

> We hear Jesus' promise in the gospel, and we taste it in bread and wine.

The Crucified King Represents God's Faithful People

Jesus tells the disciples they'll all desert him—literally they'll "be scandalised" by him, the suffering Messiah (**v 31**; see 11:6). Peter protests, but Jesus says that Peter will disown him three times (**26:33-35**). Jesus frames this with a quote from Zechariah 13:7: "I will strike the shepherd, and the sheep of the flock will be scattered." Zechariah continues:

> "'In the whole land,' declares the LORD,
> 'two-thirds will be struck down and perish;
> yet one-third will be left in it.
> This third I will put into the fire;
> I will refine them like silver
> and test them like gold.
> They will call on my name
> and I will answer them;
> I will say, "They are my people,"
> and they will say, "The LORD is our God. "'" (Zechariah 13:8-9)

Zechariah speaks of God's people deserting God's Messiah. Only a third remain faithful. But now the number of God's faithful people is reduced to just one: Jesus. "You will all fall away" (Matthew **26:31**)—the disciples are about to side with rebellious Israel. This is the human condition. We've all betrayed God. Throughout human history only one person has been consistently faithful to God, and humanity is about to execute him.

But this not the end of the story: "After I have risen, I will go ahead of you into Galilee," says Jesus (**v 32**). The disciples have a future, and so do we. We can be God's faithful people through the faithfulness of Jesus. He will take our unfaithfulness and let us share his faithfulness. We will call on his name, and God will say, "They are my people".

The Crucified King Does God's Will

In Gethsemane Jesus says to Peter, "The spirit is willing, but the flesh is weak" (**v 41**). The "spirit" here is not the Holy Spirit of God, but Peter's own determination. We know Peter's spirit is willing because he's just declared undying loyalty (**v 35**). But Peter hasn't come to terms with his weakness.

In Gethsemane Jesus gives a twofold solution. First, he tells Peter to "watch and pray so that you will not fall into temptation. The spirit is willing, but the flesh is weak" (**v 41**). The *exhortation* is to watch and pray, and the *explanation* is that the flesh is weak.

- To "watch" is to live as those who know the flesh is weak, and so avoid situations when we might be tempted.
- To "pray" is to live as those who know it's God's Spirit who makes our spirits willing, and so cry out for his help.

But Peter doesn't watch and pray—instead, he sleeps (**v 43**). Peter does succumb to temptation (**v 69-75**). So Jesus gives a second solution to our weakness. He not only says to Peter to "watch and pray"; he also says to his Father, "May your will be done" (**v 42**). Like Peter, Jesus is willing. But unlike Peter, Jesus is willing to obey God even when it means draining to the dregs the cup of God's wrath (**v 42**; for the Old Testament background to this image, see Psalm 75:8, Jeremiah 25:15-17; Zechariah 12:2-3; see also Revelation 14:10). Here at last is a human being with human flesh who is faithful to God in the power of the Spirit. In Gethsemane he is pushed to the limit. He looks death and hell and wrath in the face, and he still says "Yes" to God.

We mustn't miss the anguish which Jesus endured to achieve this resolve. The prospect of death under God's wrath was overwhelming (Matthew **26:38**). Every fibre of his humanity shrank from it. Frederick Leahy suggests that Matthew says Jesus "*began* to be sorrowful and troubled" and was "overwhelmed with sorrow" (**v 37-38**, emphasis added) because this was the moment when Jesus first began to be forsaken by the Father (27:46):

> "The cup that was *symbolized* in the Feast (**26:27-28**) was now *actual*: God was placing it in the Saviour's hands and it carried the stench of hell." (*The Cross He Bore*, p. 5)

Jesus is our model because when he faced temptation, he turned to God in prayer—just as he had urged Peter to do. But the good news of the gospel is *not* that we have a model. That's not good news if you can't measure up. The good news is that we have a Saviour! Jesus covers *our past* because we're forgiven in him, and Jesus secures *our future* because we're righteous in him. The cup of God's wrath, which should have been ours, has already been drained by Christ. "If it is possible, may this cup be taken from me," says Jesus (**v 39**). And it was possible. Jesus could have by-passed the cross (as Satan proposed in 4:1-11). But then Jesus would not be "Jesus", the one whose name means "the Lord saves" (1:21). He would have come to glory without a people.

> Jesus could have by-passed the cross, but then he would have come to glory without a people.

The prayer of Gethsemane is answered immediately: "While he was still speaking" people come to arrest him (**26:47**). Judas identifies Jesus with a kiss (**v 47-49**) and Jesus is arrested (**v 50**). But again the emphasis falls on the initiative of Jesus:

- Jesus stops his friends resisting his arrest (**v 51-52**).
- Jesus rejects the option of calling on legions of angels (**v 53**).
- Jesus says that what's happening is a fulfilment of the Scriptures (**v 54-56**).

The man who shrank from death in **verses 38-44** embraces it with conviction in **verses 47-56**. Jesus has wrestled in prayer and concluded, "Your will be done". Jesus is not the helpless victim of injustice; he's the active fulfiller of God's plan (**v 54, 56**).

- Jesus loves his Father and wants to glorify him.
- Jesus loves his people and wants to rescue us.

The Crucified King Offers Hope to Those Who Disown Him

Jesus is brought before the Sanhedrin, the Jewish ruling council (**v 57-58**). The high priest asks him a straight question: "Tell us if you are the Messiah, the Son of God" (**v 63**). Jesus replies, "You have said so ... But I say to all of you: from now on you will see the Son of Man sitting at the right hand of the Mighty One and coming on the clouds of heaven" (**v 64**). It's another allusion to Daniel 7, where Daniel saw the vision of "a son of man" coming on the clouds before the Ancient of Days, before whom "the court was seated, and the books were opened" (Daniel 7:10). It's a description of the ascension of Jesus, when he passes through the clouds into God's presence. The key point is that Jesus comes to the heavenly courtroom to be vindicated by God.

On earth, the Sanhedrin pass judgment on Jesus (Matthew **26:65-66**). They accuse him, though they can produce no real evidence (**v 59-61**). Human judgments on Christ are revealed for what they are: biased and unreliable. It's the human story being acted before us. We pass judgment on God and his Christ, but we get it hopelessly wrong because we're biased. We reject his authority and so we find reasons to dismiss him. But in heaven, Jesus is vindicated and given all authority (Daniel 7:14). The one whom we unjustly condemn turns out to be the Judge of all the earth (Acts 17:30-31).

The rejection of Jesus by the Sanhedrin is followed by the denial of Jesus by Peter (Matthew **26:69-75**). Three times Jesus had invited Peter to pray (**v 38, 40-41, 43-44**), but instead Peter had slept. Now Peter denies his Lord three times. It ends in tears for Peter (**v 75**). Except this is not the end of the story for Peter, and Matthew has embedded some clues that offer hope for people like him. Our sin need not be the final word. While Jesus makes astonishing claims during his trial (**v 64**), Matthew also highlights his silence (**v 62-63**). It's the same before Pilate. Jesus speaks, but at key moments he's silent, to Pilate's great astonishment (27:11-14). Matthew is inserting his version of a hypertext link back to Isaiah. Isaiah had promised a coming Servant of the Lord, who, he said, "was oppressed and afflicted, yet he did not open his mouth" (Isaiah 53:7). The beating and spitting of Matthew **26:67-68** is another allusion to Isaiah's Servant (Isaiah 50:6). This is the Servant who "was pierced for our transgressions" and "crushed for our iniquities" (Isaiah 53:5). Matthew is again pointing to the meaning of the cross. There's hope for Peter because Jesus is about to die in his place, bearing the penalty of sin that he deserves. And there's hope for us in the same way. Matthew's readers knew all about the great apostle Peter ("the Rock"). Perhaps reading about his denial shocked them. Yet it demonstrates that there is a way back for anyone.

Questions for reflection

1. How have these verses prompted you to speak to Jesus in grateful praise?
2. How have Jesus' words helped you appreciate his gift to you of the Lord's Supper?
3. What would Peter have done differently if he had obeyed Jesus' exhortation to "watch and pray"? In what areas of your life do you need to "watch and pray" rather than assuming you can obey in your own strength?

PART TWO

Under Roman occupation, the Jewish leaders had no authority to pass a death sentence. So they send Jesus to the Roman governor (Matthew **27:1-2**). Meanwhile Judas is seized with remorse (**v 3-4**). It may be that Judas' intention wasn't to see Jesus executed but rather to force his hand into leading an armed insurrection or invoking an angelic army—the very things Jesus refused to do (26:52-54). Judas tries to return the money, but it's too late (**27:5**). He has set in train a process that's now out of his control. The chief priests use the money to buy a burial ground for foreigners, thus fulfilling the Scriptures (Zechariah 11:12-13; Jeremiah 19:1-13; 32:6-9).

The account of Judas' death in Matthew **27:5-10** appears to be different from the one in Acts 1:18-19. We can't know for sure how to reconcile them, but we can show that they need not be contradictory. Matthew says the religious leaders bought the field, while Acts says Judas "acquired" the field (ESV). Perhaps the leaders bought the field with Judas' money, which then belonged to Judas in the sense of being his burial place. Matthew says Judas hanged himself, while Acts says his body "burst open" after a fall. One tradition suggests Judas hanged himself from a branch which broke. Alternatively his body may have been thrown in the field so that no one had to defile themselves during the Passover festival by burying him. Carson comments, "We are not so much beset by contradictory accounts as by paucity of information" (*The Expositor's Bible Commentary,* Volume 8, p. 562). It's possible that Judas decided to commit suicide in the field bought with his money since it had been designated as a burial place for "foreigners" to God's covenant, which is how Judas now viewed himself.

Matthew highlights two themes in the story of Judas' death. We've met one already: the **passion** of Christ unfolds according to God's plan revealed in the Scriptures. Matthew **27:1-2** raises the question of who has authority in Jerusalem. For the real answer, we must look beyond Jerusalem and Rome to heaven.

The second theme is the innocence of Jesus. It's implied in the failure of the Jewish court to find any evidence against Jesus (26:59-60), and it's confirmed by the declaration of Judas in **27:4**: "I have betrayed innocent blood". It will be confirmed again when Pilate receives a message from his wife warning him not to get involved with "that innocent man" (**v 19**). In **verse 23** Pilate asks what crime Jesus has committed, and receives no proper answer.

Peter weeps bitterly while Judas is seized with remorse (26:75; **27:3**). They appear to reach the same point. But then their stories diverge. Peter will go on to preach boldly, lead the church and die as a martyr. Judas takes his own life. What matters most in our lives is not whether we sin or not—for everyone sins. What matters is what we do with our sin. We can take it to Jesus in repentance and find forgiveness. Or we can hide our sin, deny our guilt or descend into despair. A "place for foreigners" symbolises Judas' fate (**v 7**); he dies the death of an outsider—not because he commits suicide but because he dies in unbelief. What makes the difference is how we view Jesus: when we recognise the love that chose the cross, we'll run into his arms.

The Innocent One Dies in the Place of the Guilty

Before Pilate, Jesus says nothing (**v 11-14**; see comments on 26:62-63). Pilate finds no reason to condemn him, but Jesus gives him no reason to acquit him either. So Pilate tries another tactic. It was the custom to pardon a prisoner during the Passover, and so Pilate offers a choice between Jesus and Barabbas, "a well-known prisoner" (**27:15-18**). But the crowd cry out for the crucifixion of Jesus, and Pilate caves in to their demands (**v 20-26**). The word "uproar" in **verse 24** is the same word translated "riot" in 26:5. The riot the religious leaders feared is taking place; the irony is that it's directed *against Jesus*.

In these verses an innocent man is condemned and a guilty man walks free. Matthew presents the men as a mirror of one another. Both are called "Jesus" (**27:16-17**). "Barabbas" means "son of a father", so both are identified by their connection to their father (26:63). To all intents and purposes, Barabbas is a dead man; yet he lives because Jesus dies. It looks like a travesty of justice, but Matthew sees it as a picture of the accomplishment of the cross. Jesus, the innocent one, is condemned in the place of guilty sinners like us. That might be an injustice were it not for the fact that Jesus has willingly chosen to die in our place. It would be an injustice if I paid a fine with stolen money or tricked the court into fining someone else; but if a friend gladly chose to pay my fine, then justice would be done and I would receive mercy. It would be my friend who bore the cost. At the cross justice is done, I receive mercy, and Jesus bears the cost.

Barabbas is a dead man, yet he lives because Jesus dies—a picture of the accomplishment of the cross.

"His blood is on us and on our children," the people cry in **27:25**. Tragically, this verse has been used to justify anti-Semitism. It's true that the destruction of the temple in AD 70 brought old-covenant Judaism to an end as the sacrificial system ceased. But it's important to remember that Jesus himself was a Jew, as were most of the early church. Matthew, the author of this account, is also a Jew. It's also important to remember that people from every nation reject Jesus. The faultline is not between Jews and Gentiles but between believers and unbelievers. The Jews are not the church's enemies nor ever have been. Instead, they're the root into which Gentile believers have been grafted (Romans 11:17-21). In fact, Matthew may want us to see hope in the words "His blood is on us". At one level, the people take responsibility for this miscarriage of justice; but the old covenant was sealed when sacrificial blood was sprinkled on the people, and Jesus is initiating a new covenant with blood (Exodus 24:8; Matthew 26:28). Unwittingly, the people are proclaiming their only hope—a hope to which many of them will turn on the day of Pentecost. When judgment comes, the only safe place to be is under the blood of Jesus.

The King Who Saves by Dying

Eight times in his trial and passion Jesus is called "the Messiah" or "the King" (Matthew 26:63, 68; **27:11, 17, 22, 29, 37, 42**). *Every* time it's questioning, ironic or taunting. In the case of the soldiers, it's accompanied by a mock "coronation" (**v 27-31**). Then they nail Jesus to the cross under a sign proclaiming, "This is Jesus, the King of the Jews" (**v 32-37**). What use is a defeated King? Like Joseph in the time of the **patriarchs**, Jesus is stripped of his robe; but, like Joseph, he will go on to be robed with all authority (**v 31**; Genesis 37:23; 41:42). The taunts continue from the crowd and from the religious leaders (Matthew **27:38-44**). Both groups pick up on Jesus' claim to be God. "Come down from the cross, if you are the Son of God" they cry (**v 40, 42-43**). What use is a dead god?

But again Matthew wants us to look deeper. "'He saved others,' they said, 'but he can't save himself!'" (**v 42**). Yet Jesus *does* indeed save others—but he does so by refusing to save himself. *His* forsakenness by God makes possible *our* acceptance by God. *His* death is *our* life. In **verse 39** Matthew deliberately echoes Lamentations 2:15, which speaks of the nations scoffing at Jerusalem. It suggests that Jesus is the embodiment of Jerusalem under judgment. He's not dying on his own account but on behalf of his people. Jesus is the King, but he wears a crown of thorns. He rules through love, ultimately by laying down his life as an **atoning sacrifice** for his people. He releases us from condemnation by enduring our insults. "This is Jesus, the King of the Jews" ceases to be a taunt and becomes his glory and our hope.

Jesus Is Abandoned by God to Unite Us to God

In Matthew **27:45-54**, Matthew describes Jesus' death from three perspectives with three matching consequences.

Jesus is abandoned by God (**v 45-46**)	Jesus unites us to God (**v 51**)
Jesus is misunderstood by humanity (**v 47-49**)	Jesus reveals God to us (**v 54**)
Jesus gives up his life (**v 50**)	Jesus gives life to us (**v 52-53**)

In his last hours, Jesus is betrayed by a friend, abandoned by his followers, condemned by the authorities and insulted by criminals. Now the story moves to another level as Jesus feels forsaken by God (**v 46**). At his baptism and transfiguration, the Father declared: "This is my Son, whom I love; with him I am well pleased" (3:17; 17:5). But at the cross we hear only the silence of God. The Son receives no sign of his Father's pleasure. At his baptism "heaven was opened" (3:16), but now heaven is shut up against Jesus. In every sense this is a moment of utter darkness (**27:45**). The darkness of the land mirrors the darkness of heaven. And yet the cry of abandonment may also be an act of faith, for Jesus quotes Psalm 22:1—a psalm that ends with the psalmist declaring God's name to the people (v 22; see Hebrews 2:11-12).

Darkness is a sign of divine judgment. One of the Exodus plagues was darkness, and God had declared that one day in judgment "I will make the sun go down at noon and darken the earth in broad daylight" (Amos 8:9; see also Psalm 105:26-28). Yet here God is judging God: God the Son being judged by God the Father. God treats his innocent Son as a guilty sinner so Jesus can pay the price of our sin.

As Jesus dies, the temple curtain is torn in two (Matthew **27:51**). The temple invited people to come: the bread of Presence was permanently on a table so that people could eat with God. But as humans approached, all the barriers went up to keep people from the dangerous presence of a holy God. The final barrier was the great curtain, screening off the Most Holy Place. It was symbolically guarded by angels woven into the fabric of the curtain—just as angels had guarded the way back to Eden (Genesis 3:24; Exodus

26:30-33). It was shrouded in smoke from the altar of incense, just as God was hidden in cloud on Mount Sinai. Only the high priest could enter, only once a year, and only through sacrificial blood (Hebrews 9:7). Yet as Jesus dies, the curtain of the temple is torn apart. The God who is inaccessible is now accessible. The way to God is open. The old temple is replaced by Jesus himself as the place where God and humanity meet (Matthew 26:61; John 2:19-21). At the point when Jesus is most alone, he makes us family. As our rebellion reaches its dark, twisted climax, God flings open his arms to embrace us in his love.

Jesus loved us when our hatred plunged as deep as it could go. Perhaps you feel the weight of guilt. Perhaps you doubt whether anyone can love you. But "God demonstrates his own love for us in this: while we were still sinners, Christ died for us" (Romans 5:8). If Jesus loved you as they drove nails into his wrists, then he loves you now.

Jesus Is Misunderstood by Humanity to Reveal God to Us

When Jesus calls out "Eli, Eli", some assume he's calling for Elijah (Matthew **27:47**). It was thought that Elijah might return in the last times (see 3:4; 11:12-14; 17:10-13). So people assume this is a desperate, last-ditch plea of a man whose plans have gone horribly wrong. Still today people look at the cross and miss what's going on. Some people see the tragic end to a heroic life or a romantic gesture that achieves little except perhaps to inspire our love.

Yet in the midst of it all, a centurion declares, "Surely he was the Son of God!" (**27:54**). It's hard to know exactly what this man was thinking, but what's clear is that for Matthew this declaration goes to the heart of what's happening. It looks as if Jesus is another failed messianic pretender: an idealist whose ideals have crumbled in the face of brute force. But Matthew says, *No. That's not what's happening.* This is a revelation of God:

- a God so loving he dies for his people.
- a God so powerful he is not afraid to lay aside his majesty.
- a God so majestic his glory shines bright even under darkened skies.
- a God so wise he conquers through apparent defeat.
- a God so gracious he opens his arms to welcome his enemies.

At the moment at which God is most *absent*—as Jesus cries out, "My God, why have you forsaken me?"—the centurion sees the *presence* of God. The proof that Jesus is God comes not through the fireworks of a mighty miracle but in the self-giving love of the cross. Only God is capable of such love. Jesus proves he is the Son of God by staying on the cross (**v 39-43**). It's not the nails that keep him there; what holds him Jesus on the cross is love—a love so powerful that it could only be the boundless love of God.

It's still possible for us to misunderstand God. Sometimes in our pain, we cry out, "Why me? Why are you letting this happen? My God, why have you forsaken me?" All those cries are echoed by Jesus as he hangs on the tree. Those cries of confusion and pain have become part of the story of Jesus. God himself, in the person of his Son, has experienced what it is to feel forsaken by God (Hebrews 4:15).

Jesus Gives Up His Life to Give Life to Us

Who caused the death of Jesus? The soldiers, Pilate, the crowd, the religious leaders, Judas... all played their part. But in the end it was *Jesus himself*. "He gave up his spirit" (Matthew **27:50**). It was his choice, and he made that choice in love (John 10:18). When things go wrong, we often reflect on how we might have avoided disaster: "If only I'd done that or not said that". Christ Jesus wasn't thinking like that as he hung on the cross. It was always going to end this way. Even before the world was made, the cross was central to God's plan.

As Jesus died, "the earth shook ... and the tombs broke open", and Matthew speaks of dead people coming back to life (Matthew **27:51-53**). Matthew calls them "holy people". These were old-covenant believers. They weren't merely ghosts; their "*bodies* ... were raised to life", and they appeared to people (**v 53**, emphasis added). We don't know what happened to them afterwards—probably they went back to the grave to await the final resurrection. They were simply a foretaste of what is yet to come. While the tombs broke open as Jesus died, the bodies were raised "after Jesus' resurrection" only on the first Easter Sunday (**v 53**). Only once Jesus had conquered death could people escape its clutches (1 Corinthians 15:22-23). So why does Matthew include their resurrection *here* and not in chapter 28 when it actually took place? Matthew **27:51** begins, "At that moment": Jesus gave up his life, and at that moment tombs broke open. Matthew wants us to see cause and effect. Jesus gives up his life, and as a result we receive our life.

Questions for reflection

1. Reread the ways in which the cross reveals God to us that are listed on p. 211, and let them turn your heart and lips to praise.
2. Which aspect of Jesus' work on the cross has particularly struck you as you've read this section?
3. "What matters most in our lives is not whether we sin or not [but] what we do with our sin. We can take it to Jesus in repentance and find forgiveness. Or we can hide our sin, deny our guilt or descend into despair" (p. 206). Is there someone you know (and perhaps it is you) who needs you to point them towards taking their sin to Jesus in repentance and finding the joy of forgiveness?

MATTHEW 27 VERSE 55 TO 28 VERSE 20

14. THE LAST WILL BE FIRST: THE RESURRECTION OF THE MESSIAH

What happened on the first Easter Sunday?

A Real Resurrection (Not a Resuscitation)

Muslims claim Jesus fainted on the cross and revived in the tomb. But Matthew describes the burial of Jesus in some detail (**27:57-61**; Deuteronomy 21:22-23). We get a sense of the care with which Joseph handles the body of Jesus: taking it, wrapping it, placing it. He would have noticed if Jesus was still breathing. More significantly, Jesus didn't "dip" into death. Sometimes people claim near-death experiences in which they see a light beckoning them. Whatever you make of those stories, that's clearly *not* what happened to Jesus. Jesus didn't die momentarily. He was in the tomb for two nights and three days. Whatever happened on Easter Sunday, it wasn't a resuscitation. Jesus was dead and buried.

Matthew highlights the fact that Joseph of Arimathea was "a rich man" (Matthew **27:57**). This is significant because Isaiah had said that the Servant of the Lord would be "assigned a grave ... with the rich in his death" (Isaiah 53:9). Matthew is adding one more spot of glue to fix in our minds the thought that Jesus is the suffering Servant who, Isaiah said, would be "pierced for our transgressions" (v 5). Matthew is also giving us a hint of what's coming, for Isaiah goes on to say the one who has borne our iniquities "will see the light of life" and "will justify many" (v 11).

A Real Resurrection (Not a Stolen Body)

Fearing the disciples might steal the body, the religious leaders persuade Pilate to make the tomb secure (Matthew **27:63-64**). The guards prevent anyone getting in, and the seal prevents anyone getting out. Yet having made theft impossible, this is the explanation of the empty tomb that is then proposed by the religious leaders—even though it's the one explanation they know cannot be true (**28:11-15**). Whatever happened on Easter Sunday, it wasn't body-snatching.

Matthew is writing to Jewish converts, probably in Judea, who may have come across this explanation. So he goes out of his way to disprove the lie. His account of the resurrection is not that long, yet he spends almost two-fifths of it proving that the body couldn't have been stolen. That's because it's vitally important to show that the resurrection of Jesus was a real resurrection. It wasn't a mistake—Jesus really did die. Nor was it a hoax—his body couldn't have been stolen..

It seems astonishing that the chief priests don't pause for a moment to consider that the empty tomb might mean Jesus is who he said he was. In 27:42 the Pharisees promise to believe Jesus if he comes down from the cross. But even when Jesus steps from the tomb, they refuse to believe. That's because the root of unbelief doesn't lie in the intellect but in the heart. The real problem is that if the resurrection is for real, everything changes. It means there's a God whom we should obey, and it means Jesus is his Son. But people don't want to obey God or acknowledge their need of Jesus, so it's more "convenient" not to believe—in this case, by believing that the disciples stole the body.

So what did take place on Easter Sunday? A human being who had died came back to life again: a real death followed by a real resurrection. It's not simply that the ideals of Jesus live on. We sometimes talk of people living on in our memories or their example continuing to inspire, but the resurrection of Jesus was so much more than this. Or some theologians claim the consciousness of Jesus continues in the mind of God. But Matthew—and he was there—is quite clear: Jesus rose again with a real, functioning human body. In **28:7** the angel says, "You will see him". In **verse 9** the women "clasped his feet". There was something substantial to take hold of—real human flesh and blood.

The Beginning of the End

We find the resurrection hard to believe because we've never seen a resurrection. It's not the sort of thing that happens round here! But that's the point—resurrection is not the sort of thing that happens in a world under the dominion of death (Romans 5:12, 17). We're under death's jurisdiction, and so people don't come back from the dead. But the resurrection of Jesus is not part of this world. Yes, it happened in this world, in our history, on a day in the 1st century. It was a real resurrection with an empty grave and a physical body. But the resurrection of Jesus is the beginning of a *new* world.

The message of the resurrection is not "Anything is possible in this world. Even when things seem hopeless, hope might yet emerge." Instead, in the resurrection God is saying, "Behold, I am making all things new" (Revelation 21:5, ESV; see Isaiah 43:19; 65:17). Jesus is "the firstborn from among the dead"—the first person to be birthed out of the grave into a new life in a new world (Colossians 1:18). The tomb becomes a womb—the end of life in one world and the beginning of a new life in a new world. Christ's resurrection is witnessed by two women called Mary, one of whom may be his mother, and his burial is facilitated by a man named Joseph—just as his birth was. It seems that Matthew wants to portray his resurrection as a new birth.

So the number one reason to reject the resurrection turns out to be the number one reason to embrace it: the resurrection doesn't make sense in our world of death, but that's because it's is the promise of a *new* world of life.

The resurrection is an "**apocalyptic**" event. It's not simply a particularly magnificent miracle, like walking on water with added oomph. Instead, in this moment the whole course of life, history and creation shifted. It was like tectonic plates colliding, except more so. For the resurrection of Christ impacted not just continents but galaxies. It was like the fall of Rome or the collapse of the Soviet Bloc, except more so, for the significance of the resurrection goes far beyond human empires. The only events that come close are the creation of time and the end of time. The resurrection is an eternal event that took place in history. The reign of life and grace erupted from the tomb, and the reign of death was served its eviction notice.

At the resurrection, the reign of death was served its eviction notice.

Here, then, is *the beginning of the beginning of the new age*. Matthew doesn't usually give precise indicators of time, but he begins his resurrection account with two: "after the Sabbath" and "at dawn on the first day" (Matthew **28:1**). The old creation took place over seven days, and this is the age in which we currently live. But Easter Sunday takes place "after" the Sabbath day. Easter is the beginning of a new work of creation—a renewed humanity living in a renewed world. And the resurrection takes place "at dawn" because the resurrection is itself a "dawn"—of a new age. The resurrection is just the beginning; but the beginning has begun. The tectonic plates of time and eternity have shifted—already the new age dawns, and already its light illuminates the horizon. Look up and see it: a new day is coming.

This is why the resurrection is accompanied by an angel (**v 2**). The heavenly realm has gate-crashed our earthly existence with an "appearance … like lightning" (**v 3**). It's not that we go to heaven at the end of time but that Jesus will come from heaven to earth with his angels (16:27). The new Jerusalem will come down out of heaven, and the heavenly and earthly realms will be united (Revelation 21:1-5). On Easter

Sunday we had a little preview of this as angels hang around, talking with God's people, mingling earth and heaven (Matthew **28:5-7**).

And here, also, is the beginning of the end of the old age. "There was a violent earthquake" (**v 2**). Tectonic plates are *literally* moving! The prophet Joel had spoken of the coming of "the day of the LORD": "The LORD thunders at the head of his army" and "before them the earth shakes, the heavens tremble" (Joel 2:1, 10-11; see also Isaiah 13:13; 24:18-20; 29:5-6). On Easter Sunday the Lord thunders out from the tomb, and the earth shakes because he's coming to judge the nations (Haggai 2:6-7; Hebrews 12:26-27). The earthquake on Easter Sunday is the beginning of the end for the old age.

This is a moment of life, for life has burst from the tomb. Imagine time-lapse footage of an animal decomposing. Then imagine that in reverse, so that the animal re-composes, moving from decay to life. Except that in the case of Jesus, we mustn't start with a decayed body that comes back to normal, because his body didn't decay in the tomb (Acts 2:31; Psalm 16:10; Acts 13:35-37). So think of time-lapse footage of a body gaining more life and more power, transforming into a "heavenly man" (1 Corinthians 15:47-49). This is life in top gear. The air is fizzing with vitality.

And yet, while all this was happening, the guards "became like dead men" (Matthew **28:4**)! They're the one sign of death in the midst of all this life. For God's people, this is the moment of triumph; but for God's enemies, this is their defeat. For the time being, the battle rages on, and often today in the West it feels like a battle we're losing. But we're not the ones who are "like dead men". This age will pass, for Jesus has risen in triumph.

The End of Fear

The women have two resurrection encounters: with an angel and with Jesus. In both cases, the first words they hear are "Do not be afraid" (**v 5, 10**). This is the message of the resurrection: Jesus has risen to end our fear.

We don't need to fear sin, for the crucified one is risen. The angel could simply have said, "I know you're looking for Jesus. He's not here; he has risen." But he adds, "who was crucified" (**v 5-6**). This is not merely another miracle, like the raising of the synagogue ruler's daughter in 9:18-26. The one who was rejected by humanity has been vindicated by God; the one who was forsaken by God has been raised by God. Jesus died under the judgment of God, and he could only rise if that judgment has been satisfied. And it has! The resurrection is God's declaration that the price is paid. It's not Jesus the good man who rises—that would mean hope only for those as good as Jesus. It's Jesus the God-forsaken man who has risen—and that brings hope for sinners.

Perhaps there's a sin that weighs heavy on your heart. Hear the words of the angel to you today: "Come and see the place where he lay" (**28:6**). Come and see. The tomb is empty. The penalty of the sin that nags your conscience has been paid in full. We don't need to fear sin, for the crucified one is risen.

We don't need to fear people, for the rejected one is risen. The account of the crucifixion ends with the women "watching from a distance" (**27:55-56**). All the way through the passion story, the action has involved men. What do the women do? Nothing. They stand on the periphery with no role and no voice. Matthew says they had "followed Jesus from Galilee" (**v 55**). They had accents that marked them as uneducated, unsophisticated, unimportant. They're from the margins, and they stand at the margins. The "people that matter" are wealthy and powerful men. The same thing happens again at the burial of Jesus (**v 61**). The men act while the women look on.

But not on Easter Sunday! Not in the new day that's dawning. In Matthew's resurrection account, men are notable by their absence. It's women who come to the tomb, witness the earthquake, are spoken to by the angel, first meet the risen Christ and are given a job to do (**28:1-2, 5-10**). Today on Easter Sunday the women are movers and shakers.

The kingdom of Christ turns the priorities and verdicts of this world upside down because the one who was rejected has been exalted. The men of chapter 27 passed their verdict on Christ: they dismissed him as a religious blasphemer and a political rebel. But the resurrection is *God's* verdict. The verdict of humanity is overturned in the heavenly court of appeal. Jesus is the ultimate nobody who turns out to be the ultimate somebody.

Still today women are regularly overlooked and forgotten. Still today the people of Christ—men and women—are mocked and ridiculed, and Christian beliefs and ethics are often marginalised. But the verdict of the world has been overturned in heaven, and one day it will be reversed on earth. "Many who are first will be last, and many who are last will be first" (19:30; 20:16). It's a promise for us as we find ourselves, as it were, at the back of the queue. The cross and resurrection are the supreme embodiment of this promise that the last will be first. The rejected will be exalted. We don't need to fear people, for the rejected one is risen.

Questions for reflection

1. Which aspect of the resurrection discussed in this section has most encouraged or inspired you?
2. How are you most tempted to fear sin or fear people, and what difference will the resurrection make to that?
3. With whom could you share the hope of the resurrection?

PART TWO

In **28:7** the angel says to the women, "Go quickly and tell his disciples: 'He has risen from the dead and is going ahead of you into Galilee.'" In **verse 10** Jesus himself says to the women, "Go and tell my brothers to go to Galilee; there they will see me". Then in **verse 16** we read, "The eleven disciples went to Galilee, to the mountain where Jesus had told them to go". We know from the other Gospels that Jesus appeared to the disciples in Jerusalem—on Easter Sunday and then again a week later (John 20:19, 26). But Matthew leaves all this out so that the focus falls entirely on the encounter in Galilee (Matthew **28:10**). The first time anyone sees the risen Christ, he's setting up another meeting (**v 10**). When he had predicted their desertion, Jesus told the disciples, "But after I have risen, I will go ahead of you into Galilee" (26:32). All the action of Easter Sunday points forward to this meeting on the mountain in Galilee.

In 4:12-17 Jesus "withdrew to Galilee" to fulfil Isaiah's prophecy of light dawning in "Galilee of the Gentiles" (Isaiah 9:1-7). As we saw, Galilee was to the north of Israel, and so it was on Galilee that darkness had first fallen when the Assyrian army had invaded from the north, just as Isaiah had warned in the 8th century BC. But Isaiah had promised that it would be on Galilee that *the light* of God's salvation would first dawn. In chapter 4 Matthew said this promise was being fulfilled in the coming of Jesus. The miracles and preaching of Jesus were the first ray of light on the horizon. Now, at the end of his Gospel, Matthew again leads us to Galilee of the Gentiles. That's because now the light of God's salvation is about to radiate out from Galilee to all nations. It starts in Galilee (to fulfil Isaiah's prophecy), but from Galilee light will spread across the world.

Not only does Matthew lead us to Galilee; he also leads us "to the mountain" (Matthew **28:16**). In 5:1-2 Jesus had given a new law for his new people on a mountain, just as Moses had received the old covenant law on Mount Sinai. In 17:1-2 Peter, James and John had seen the glory of Jesus on the Mount of Transfiguration, just as Moses had glimpsed the glory of the Lord on Mount Sinai. It was at Mount Sinai that Israel received its commission to be "a kingdom of priests and a holy nation", making God known to the nations through the distinctive character of its shared life (Exodus 19:3-6; Matthew 5:14-16). Now, here on a mountain, Christ's new-covenant people receive their commission to make him known to the nations.

Matthew spotlights these two locations to amplify his message: *the fulfilment of the resurrection is the worship of the nations.*

The Risen Christ Deserves Our Worship

There are only two resurrection encounters in Matthew's Gospel, and both involve people worshipping Jesus (**28:9, 17**). No one tells anyone to do this. Instead, people instinctively recognise that the risen one is worthy of their allegiance. The disciples had spent three years with this man. They'd witnessed his humanity up close and personal, smelling his sweat and hearing him snore. Yet on the mountain they worship him, the man who is God.

Matthew leaves us with two options: worship or doubt. **Verse 17** says, "When they saw him, they worshipped him; but some doubted". Matthew is asking us to place ourselves in one of these two camps: will we worship Jesus, or will we doubt him? There's no neutrality. If Christ is risen, then Christ must be worshipped, with our lips and lives.

The Risen Christ Receives All Authority

As God, Jesus has always had complete authority. But as a man, Jesus came as the son of David to claim David's throne. He came as the Messiah to re-establish God's kingdom on earth. He came with royal authority to heal the sick, feed the hungry, liberate the possessed and preach good news. But his royal authority was resisted and rejected. In the end we crucified our King.

But now Jesus has risen and is about to ascend into heaven. Jesus will pass through the clouds to receive the authority of God and the praise of heaven (26:64; Daniel 7:13-14). Matthew gives us a little preview of all this. Jesus is about to ascend into heaven to be worshipped by angels, and in Matthew **28:16-17**, Jesus ascends a mountain to be worshipped by disciples. He's about to crowned in heaven as God's King, and in **verse 18** he declares, "All authority in heaven and on earth has been given to me". King Charles III became king when Elizabeth II died, even though he hadn't then been crowned. Jesus' coronation is about to take place at his ascension, but he's already King as he speaks with the disciples, because he has risen. On the day of Pentecost Peter declares, "God has raised this Jesus to life, and we are all witnesses of it ... Therefore let all Israel be assured of this: God has made this Jesus, whom you crucified, both Lord and Messiah." (Acts 2:32, 36). God makes Jesus King by raising him to life.

And if Jesus is God's King, then we must bow before him. Every area of life is to be governed by his rule. He has, he says, received "*all* authority". He is Lord of your work, your marriage, your wallet, your leisure, your service, your family. The burden of his rule is light, for he's a liberating King who reigns in love (11:30). But nevertheless, he is our King, and he must be obeyed.

So the kingship of Jesus is a challenge, but it's also our comfort. Paul writes, "God placed all things under his feet and appointed him to be head over everything for the church, which is his body" (Ephesians 1:22-23). Christ rules for the sake of the body to which he is intimately joined in love, like a husband to his wife (5:25-33). Jesus exercises his authority to protect you, guide you, keep you and ultimately lead you home to glory. You're safe in the hands of the one who holds the world in his hands.

The Risen Christ Calls All Nations

Now we reach what we call "the great commission". The first time Jesus met the disciples he sent them "to fish for people" (Matthew 4:19). Now, in their final meeting on earth, he sends them "to fish for people" from all nations. **28:19** begins, "Therefore". The *great* *commission* is the logic of the *great enthronement* in **verse 18**. It's because Jesus has received authority over all nations that he sends us to all nations. The logic is there in the word "all" (**v 19**). Jesus is given "*all* authority"; Jesus sends us to "*all* nations"; we are to teach "everything" (literally "*all* the things") Jesus has commanded us. As King, Jesus commands us, and we pass on his commands.

Those who worship the risen Saviour must follow the call of the sending Saviour. In **verses 9-10** the women fall before him and worship him—but they're soon back on their feet, sent to summon the disciples. Now, in **verse 17**, the disciples fall before him and worship him. And guess what? They, too, are soon back on their feet, sent to summon the nations. Literally **verse 19** reads, "Going, make disciples of all nations, baptising them ... teaching them..." So the central command is "to make disciples" with three **participles** that describe *how* this command is to be fulfilled: going, baptising and teaching.

Every time you speak of Christ, you speak with the authority of the risen Lord.

Jesus has authority over every group of people and every aspect of life. Already in heaven he receives the worship of every nation and language. Our role is to extend that worship on earth. That means every time you speak of Christ, you speak with the authority of the risen Lord. We are ambassadors of the King, sent ahead of his coming to call on people to turn to him. He *will* be King over all; he will defeat his enemies; every knee will bow. In the meantime, he offers wonderful, generous peace terms: he offers forgiveness.

The mission to the nations is the climax of the Easter story, but it's also the climax of Matthew's Gospel. All the way through his Gospel, Matthew has pointed us forward to the mission to the Gentiles, or nations. Jesus is the son of Abraham who will bless the nations (1:1; Genesis 12:1-3). At his birth, the Magi bring the worship of the nations (Matthew 2:1-12). John the Baptist declares, "I tell you that out of these stones God can raise up children for Abraham" (3:8-9). God will raise up a new family—not sharing the genes of Abraham (though some will) but sharing his faith. When Jesus sees the faith of a Gentile centurion, he says, "I say to you that many will come from the east and the west, and will take their places at the feast with Abraham, Isaac and Jacob in the kingdom of heaven" (8:11). And so it continues (11:20-24; 24:14). All the way through his Gospel, Matthew has been preparing for the moment when the gospel goes to all nations.

Even the structure of Matthew puts the focus on our mission. As we've seen, Matthew's Gospel is divided into five sections, each of which ends, "When Jesus had finished saying these things" (7:28; 11:1; 13:53; 19:1; 26:1). But what happens when the story reaches its climax with the death and resurrection of Jesus? Instead of more teaching *from* Jesus, we find Jesus commissioning *us*, his church. And what are we to do? *Teach them to obey everything I have commanded you* (**28:19**). Indeed, in the fifth and final summary statement, Matthew adds the word "all": "When Jesus had finished saying *all* these things..." (26:1). It's an indication that Christ's earthly teaching ministry is now complete. Now that ministry passes to us. We're to carry on the teaching of Jesus. Matthew 28 is not the end of the story—Matthew's Gospel is the preface, and the main story is 20 centuries (so far) of global mission. We're still writing it now. You have a pen in your hand, as it were. You can write the next chapter as you proclaim Christ to the nations.

Do you feel the logic of the resurrection?

- Jesus has risen, and therefore he is Lord.
- Jesus is Lord, and therefore he claims the nations.
- Jesus claims the nations, and therefore he sends us to call people to repentance.

Global mission is not a niche interest for Christians. We're *all* called to play our part: all authority, all nations, all things, *all Christians*. What that might mean for you? Praying each day for missionaries you know.

Financially supporting their work. Signing up for prayer news. Or today the risen Christ might be calling you to leave your home and take the good news to another nation.

The Risen Christ Accompanies Our Mission

It's all too easy for us to think of the resurrection simply as an act in the past—a triumph that took place 2,000 years ago. We emphasise the resurrection as an historical fact, and it is! The problem is that that can make it sound like it belongs in the past. But no, the resurrection is a present reality. Or perhaps it would be better to say that the risen Christ is a present reality. Jesus has not just risen: he's alive. He's part of our lives, and he accompanies us on the mission he's given us. So Matthew ends his Gospel with Jesus saying, "And surely I am with you always, to the very end of the age" (**28:20**). It's literally "all the days"—a fourth "all" to add to all authority, all nations, and all things.

Jesus has ascended into heaven, and so he's physically absent. You can't see him in the room with you. But Jesus is with us through the Holy Spirit. He's sent his Spirit to his people, and the Spirit is the Spirit of *Christ*. They share one being, so the presence of the Spirit makes Christ really and truly present—not physically but spiritually (in the sense of "by the Spirit"). Jesus is with you in your home, with all the challenges which that involves. He's with you in the workplace when your faith is being mocked. He's with you when you serve the needy, so much so that in serving them, you serve him (25:34-40).

Right back at the beginning of the story, as the physical human frame of the Son of God was being formed in Mary's womb, Matthew wrote, "All this took place to fulfil what the Lord had said through the prophet: 'The virgin will conceive and give birth to a son, and they will call him Immanuel' (which means 'God with us')" (1:22-23). Jesus is Immanuel, God with us. He was Immanuel when he walked on this earth: God made flesh, sharing our lives. And he is Immanuel *today* as *we* walk this earth: God with us through the

Holy Spirit. I don't know what problems you're facing. But I do know this: Christ is risen. He's alive. And he's with you always, to the very end. He is *your* Immanuel.

Questions for reflection

1. To what extent is your life shaped by the Great Commission? Does anything need to change?
2. Why is the truth of Jesus' kingship good news?
3. What difference will it make to you today to live knowing that the resurrection is not a past event but a present reality—that, right now, Jesus is alive?

GLOSSARY

Abraham: the ancestor of the nation of Israel, and the man God made a binding agreement (covenant) with. God promised to make his family into a great nation, give them a land, and bring blessing to all nations through one of his descendants (see Genesis 12:1-3).

Ahab and Jezebel: a particularly evil and God-rejecting king and queen of Old Testament Israel (see 1 Kings 16 – 22; 2 Kings 9).

Apocalyptic: relating to the apocalypse, a word that means "revealing" and refers to the end times when Jesus will return, as described in most detail in Revelation.

Apostasy: the abandonment of a religious belief or principle. An apostate is someone who once seemed to be a believer but who later totally rejects Christ, turns away from sound teaching, and leaves the church.

Apostles: men appointed directly by the risen Christ to teach about him with authority.

Atoning sacrifice: Christ's death, which provides the means for a person to come back into relationship with God. Atonement is the process by which two people who were not friends are made "at one" with each other.

Ascension: when Jesus left earth to return to heaven, to sit and rule at God the Father's right hand (see Acts 1:6-11; Philippians 2:8-11).

Baptism: a symbolic washing with water, either by sprinkling or total immersion, to reflect someone coming to faith in Christ and having their sin washed clean.

Blasphemous: disrespecting or mocking God, or in some way putting yourself in God's place.

Brethren: brothers.

Cain: the eldest son of Adam and Eve. He murdered their second child, Abel (see Genesis 4).

Calvary: the place on the outskirts of Jerusalem where Jesus was crucified.

Canaanites: of the land or people of Canaan. Canaanites did not worship the God of Israel and were enemies of God's people throughout the Old Testament.

Canon: the collection of texts which are accepted as God's word.

Church discipline: the practice of warning church members when they are perceived to have sinned, in hope that the offender will repent and be reconciled to God and the church. It is also intended to protect other church members from the influence of sin.

Church Father: one of the influential theologians and church leaders in the early church.

Commissions: here, meaning giving a duty, responsibility, task or appointment.

Communion: here, meaning an intimacy and closeness of relationship and connection.

Confession: here, meaning stating what you believe about something or someone.

Cornerstone: a stone that forms the base of a corner of a building, joining two walls.

Court of the Gentiles: the large, outermost area of the temple in Jerusalem which was open to non-Jews (who were not permitted to enter the inner courts).

Deserts: what you deserve or have earned.

Day of Pentecost: a Jewish feast celebrating God giving his people his law on Mount Sinai (Exodus 19 – 31). On the day of this feast, 50 days after Jesus' resurrection, the Holy Spirit came to the first Christians (Acts 2), so "Pentecost" is how Christians tend to refer to this event.

Doctrine: the study of what is true about God; or a statement about an aspect of that truth.

Eden: the flawless garden God gave the first humans in which to live, enjoy his presence, and work for him (Genesis 2:8-17); also the scene of those humans deciding to rebel against God's rule, part of the judgment for which was being shut out of Eden (3:1-13, 23-24).

Ethic: a moral principle.

Esoteric: mysterious, hidden, secret, only accessible to a chosen few.

Evangelism: telling non-Christians the good news about Jesus Christ. An event or initiative that is **evangelistic** is one whose main aim is to tell people about Jesus.

Excommunicate: exclude someone from the church, so that they are no longer recognised as a member of the church.

Exegesis: interpreting and explaining the Bible.

Exodus: literally "way out" or "departure"; the historical period when the people of Israel left slavery in Egypt and began to travel toward the promised land (i.e. the events recounted, unsurprisingly, in the book of Exodus).

Exorcised: the casting out of an evil spirit (or spirits) from a person who is possessed by them.

Foil: here, meaning something that has the effect of contrasting with something else, and therefore highlighting a particular quality or aspect of that other thing.

Genealogy: a list of ancestors.

Genesis: literally "beginning" or "origin"; the first book of the Bible.

Gentile: either refers to everyone who is not a Jew (i.e. not part of Israel); or to everyone who is not a member of God's people (so in the New Testament, it sometimes refers to non-Christians).

Gospel: One of the four historical records of Jesus found in the New Testament—written by Matthew, Mark, Luke, and John.

Grafted: joined onto something else in order to become part of it.

Hades: the realm of the dead in Greek mythology.

Hebrew: the language in which most of the Old Testament was originally written.

Heresy: a belief which directly opposes the biblical gospel.

Herod Antipas: the nephew of Herod the Great. Antipas ruled the regions of Galilee and Perea.

Herod ("the Great"): king of Judea, under Roman authority, when Jesus was born. He was known for his ambition and brutality, as well as for his building projects such as the Jerusalem temple.

Hyperbole: deliberate exaggeration to make a point.

Idolatry: serving and worshipping something other than the true God.

Isaiah: an Old Testament prophet who spoke God's word primarily to the northern kingdom of Israel in the 7th century BC.

Judah: in this context, the southern kingdom in which God's Old Testament people lived, centred on the capital, Jerusalem (there was also a kingdom to the north in which God's people lived, known as Israel).

Judaizers: believers in the early church who taught that non-Jewish (Gentile) Christians needed to adopt Jewish laws and customs, such as circumcision, in order to be truly saved or fully accepted by God.

Judean: belonging to the land of Judea. Judea was the name of the Roman province in which Jesus was born and lived, which covered roughly the same area as the Old Testament kingdom of **Judah**.

Justify: to make it so that someone can be declared not guilty, not condemned, completely innocent.

Kingdom of heaven: life under Jesus Christ's perfect rule. We enter the kingdom when we turn to God's Son, Jesus, in repentance and faith; we will enjoy the kingdom fully when Jesus returns to this world and establishes his kingdom over the whole earth.

Lamb, the: a name of Jesus, because he is the one whose sacrifice rescues us from judgment, just as the sacrifice of lambs did at the first Passover (see Exodus 12 – 13) and in the Old Testament sacrificial system (see Leviticus 16).

Legalists/legalism: living by following rules in the belief that keeping these requirements will earn blessing or salvation.

Liberals: professing Christians who do not view Scripture as without error.

Lord's Supper: communion; sharing bread and wine together to remember the body and blood of Jesus.

Messiah: Christ, the anointed one. In the Old Testament, God promised that the Messiah would come to rescue and rule his people and to bring God's promises to fulfilment.

Mosaic: to do with Moses, the leader of God's people in the books of Exodus, Leviticus, Numbers and Deuteronomy

New birth: a phrase meaning to become a Christian by placing your faith in Jesus as Lord and Saviour and therefore being given eternal life. It comes from Jesus' conversation with Nicodemus in John 3.

Nominalism: a belief or view held in name only. A nominal Manchester United fan would be one whose actions and emotions are rarely, if ever, shaped by the team's results, and who never accepts a cost or makes a sacrificial commitment to support the team.

Pagans: people who don't know and worship the true God.

Participles: words formed from a verb but used as an adjective or noun, e.g. reading, walking, climbing or cooked, typed, written.

Passion: here, meaning the story of the cross. This word comes from the Latin "passio", which means "suffering".

Patriarchs: the "first fathers" of Israel, to whom God gave his promises—Abraham, Isaac and Jacob.

Paul: a persecutor of the church who was converted when he met the risen Jesus on the Damascus Road (see Acts 9) and was appointed an **apostle** by the Lord. He spent the rest of his life sharing the gospel and starting churches around the eastern Mediterranean, particularly among non-Jews. He wrote a significant proportion of the New Testament.

Personified: a concept represented as, or that has become, a person.

Piety: religious good deeds.

Prerogative: privilege or right.

Presbyter: a church minister or elder.

Prodigals: in this context, meaning someone who has turned their back on Christianity, lived in a very sinful way, and then come back to Jesus in repentant faith. See Jesus' story in Luke 15:11-32.

Profanity: obscene, blasphemous speech or event.

Propitious: favourable, indicating a positive outcome.

Protestants: the name given to people and churches who follow the teachings of the **Reformation**.

Purge: remove people from a wider group or place, in an abrupt way.

Rabbinic: coming from a rabbi or group of rabbis. Rabbis were Jewish religious teachers.

Reformation: a process in parts of Europe in the 16th century in which biblical teaching on how people are saved and what the church is (among other **doctrines**) was rediscovered. (See **Reformer**.)

Reformer: one of the first two generations of people in the 16th century who preached the gospel of justification by faith, and opposed the Pope and the Roman church. They were known as **Protestants**.

Regenerating: the action of making someone spiritually alive through bringing them to put their faith in Jesus as their Lord and Saviour. It is a work that the Holy Spirit does in a person.

Remnant: a small remaining quantity of something. In the Bible, it refers to the small number of Jews who returned to Jerusalem and the rest of their land from the exile in Babylon.

Sacrament: a ceremony which symbolises a spiritual reality. In the Protestant church, the Lord's Supper (communion) and baptism are considered sacraments. Other denominations hold that there are more, and other, "sacraments" (e.g. Roman Catholic "mass").

Saints: a biblical term for all people who trust in the God of the Bible.

Second coming: a term used to describe the return of the Lord Jesus to judge the world, to save his people and to bring the new creation (see, for instance, Revelation 21 – 22).

Secular: attitudes or activities that have no religious connections.

Self-justification: in this context, the attempt to do enough or perform well enough to be in right relationship with God based on your own efforts.

Sinai: a mountain in the desert between Egypt and the promised land (which came to be called Israel). Here, God revealed himself to Moses, established his covenant with Israel, and gave his people his law (see Exodus 19). Mount Sinai is also called Mount Horeb.

Spoil: here, meaning possessions and valuables taken from someone by force or theft.

Supplication: earnest prayer of request.

Tabernacle: a large, tented area where the Israelites worshipped God from the time of Moses until the rule of Solomon. This was where his presence symbolically dwelled (see Exodus 26; 40).

Tribulation: a time of great suffering or difficulty.

Westminster Confession of Faith: a statement of faith and doctrine drawn up by English and Scottish theologians in 1646.

Wrath: God's settled, deserved hatred of and anger at sin.

Yoke: a heavy piece of wood fastened over the necks of animals and attached to a plough or cart that they are to pull.

BIBLIOGRAPHY

I've not had space to defend the historical reliability of Matthew's Gospel, nor to explain all the apparent discrepancies between the Gospel accounts. For these issues I commend the commentaries below by Carson and France. Books marked with an asterisk are particularly recommended.

- Augustine, "Sermons on New Testament Lessons, Sermon 2.1" in *The Nicene and Post-Nicene Fathers: First Series*, Volume 6, ed. Philip Schaff (Hendrickson, 1994)
- Craig L. Blomberg, *Matthew*, New American Commentary (Holman, 1992)
- Craig L. Blomberg, "Matthew," in *Commentary on the New Testament Use of the Old Testament*, eds. G.K. Beale and D.A. Carson (Apollos, 2007)
- Dietrich Bonhoeffer, *The Cost of Discipleship* (Macmillan, 1963)
- * D.A. Carson, "Matthew," in *The Expositor's Bible Commentary,* Volume 8 (Zondervan, 1984). Also available in a two-volume paperback edition (Zondervan, 1995)
- Tim Chester, *Life with Jesus* (The Good Book Company, 2024)
- Ed. Brian Daley, *Light on the Mountain* (SVS Press, 2013)
- W.D. Davies and Dale C. Allison, *Matthew: A Shorter Commentary* (T&T Clark, 2004)
- Daniel M. Doriani, "Matthew," in *ESV Expository Commentary Volume VIII: Matthew-Luke*, eds. Iain M. Duguid, James M. Hamilton Jr. and Jay Sklar (Crossway, 2021)
- Sinclair Ferguson, *The Sermon on the Mount* (Banner of Truth, 1987)

- * R.T. France, *The Gospel of Matthew*, New International Commentary on the New Testament (Eerdmans, 2007)
- John D. Hannah, *Matthew*, Focus on the Bible (Christian Focus, 2024)
- Richard B. Hays, *Echoes of Scripture in the Gospels* (Baylor University Press, 2016)
- David Jackman and William Philip, *Teaching Matthew: Unlocking the Gospel of Matthew for the Bible Teacher* (Christian Focus, 2nd. Ed., 2009)
- Mark Jones, *Knowing Jesus* (Banner of Truth, 2015)
- Craig S. Keener, *Matthew*, IVP New Testament Commentary Series (IVP, 1997)
- Reggie M. Kidd, "Matthew," in *A Biblical-Theological Introduction to the New Testament*, ed. Michael J. Kruger (Crossway, 2016)
- Frederick Leahy, *The Cross He Bore* (Banner of Truth, 1996)
- * Peter J. Leithart, *The Gospel of Matthew Through New Eyes: Jesus as Israel* (Athanasius Press, 2017)
- Martyn Lloyd-Jones, *Studies in the Sermon on the Mount* (Eerdmans, Volume 1, 1959 and Volume 2, 1960)
- Donald Macleod, *The Person of Christ* (IVP, 1998)
- Leon Morris, *The Gospel According to Matthew*, Pillar New Testament Commentary (Apollos, 1992)
- Ed. Graham Nicholls, *Challenging Leaders* (Christian Focus, 2023)
- Grant R. Osborne, *Matthew*, Zondervan Exegetical Commentary on the New Testament (Zondervan, 2010)
- * Jonathan T. Pennington, *The Sermon on the Mount and Human Flourishing* (Baker, 2017)

- John Piper, *Let the Nations Be Glad! The Supremacy of God in Missions* (Baker, 2003)
- David Platt, *Exalting Jesus in Matthew* (B&H, 2013)
- J.C. Ryle, *Expository Thoughts on the Gospels: Matthew* (William Hunt, 1856)
- Matt Searles, *Matthew: One Greater Than Solomon* (10Publishing, 2018)
- Ed. Manlio Simonetti, *Matthew 1-13, Ancient Christian Commentary on Scriptures: New Testament Volume 1a* (InterVarsity Press, 2001)
- Charles H. Spurgeon, *The Treasury of the Bible: The New Testament* (Marshall, Morgan and Scott, 1962)
- * Glen. H. Stassen, *Living the Sermon on the Mount* (Jossey-Bass, 2006)
- Glen. H. Stassen and David P. Gushee, *Kingdom Ethics: Following Jesus in Contemporary Context* (Eerdmans, 2nd. Ed., 2016)
- * John Stott, *The Message of the Sermon on the Mount: Christian Counter-Culture*, Bible Speaks Today (IVP, 1978)
- N.T. Wright, *Jesus and the Victory of God* (SPCK, 1996)
- N.T. Wright and Michael F. Bird, *The New Testament in Its World* (SPCK, 2019)

God's Word For You

Accessible Commentaries That Everyone Can Enjoy

Old Testament, including:

New Testament, including:

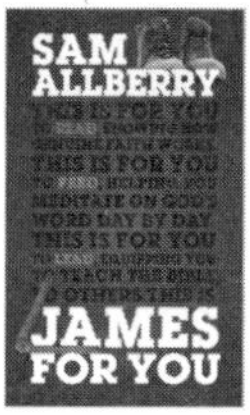

Less academic than a traditional commentary, these expository guides take you verse by verse through books of the Bible in an accessible, applied way. These flexible resources can enrich your personal devotions, help you lead small-group studies, or aid your sermon preparations.

Use with accompanying Good Book Guides to study these books of the Bible in small groups.

thegoodbook.com/for-you
thegoodbook.co.uk/for-you
thegoodbook.com.au/for-you